D0095923

NICE GIRLS
JUST DON'T
GET IT

ALSO BY LOIS P. FRANKEL, PhD

Nice Girls Don't Get the Corner Office

Nice Girls Don't Get Rich

See Jane Lead

Stop Sabotaging Your Career

Women, Anger, and Depression

ALSO BY CAROL FROHLINGER, JD

Her Place at the Table (coauthored with
Deborah Kolb, PhD, and Judith Williams, PhD)

NICE GIRLS JUST DON'T GET IT

99 WAYS TO
WIN THE RESPECT YOU DESERVE,
THE SUCCESS YOU'VE EARNED,
AND THE LIFE YOU WANT

LOIS P. FRANKEL, PHD
CAROL M. FROHLINGER, JD

WOMEN'S
BUSINESS
PRESS

Copyright© 2018 by Lois P. Frankel, PhD and Carol M. Frohlinger, JD

This book was written for information purposes only. It contains general information and, because everyone's situation is unique, readers are encouraged to consult with appropriate professionals to obtain advice specific to them. The authors disclaim any responsibility for actions taken by readers as a result of the general information contained herein.

All rights reserved.

Published in the United States by Women's Business Press.

ISBN-13: 978-1985859982

ISBN-10: 198585998X

Jacket design by Lisa Graves

First Edition Published by Crown Publishers

Second Edition Published by Women's Business Press

PRAISE FOR NICE GIRLS JUST DON'T GET IT

"This book is a treasure! It's filled with down-to-earth strategies for building a fulfilling life."
Anne Fisher, Ask Annie columnist, CNNmoney.com

"Frankel and Frohlinger break down why so many women go through life harboring resentment and frustration: It's about respect and no one is going to hand it to us."
Carolyn Kepcher, former Trump executive vice president and bestselling author.

"You don't have to be a drop dead diva to love this book. Every women can win the life she wants by following its sage advice."
Josh Berman, creator of Drop Dead Diva.

"I've read all the Nice Girls books and now a gem in the series appears – this one is the crown jewel!"
Hamida Belkadi, CEO of De Beers, North America.

"Frankel and Frohlinger have done it again! Nice Girls Just Don't Get It is easy to read, practical, and crammed with great advice for all women. It's a gentle wake-up call and powerful resource for everyone from teenagers to top executives. Brilliant!"
Liz Cornish, author of Hit the Ground Running: A Woman's Guide to Success for the First Hundred Days on the Job.

"Stop stifling yourself! That's the message delivered with a velvet-covered mallet in Nice Girls Just Don't Get It. This books wants you to think of yourself as an asset because you are!"
Valerie Coleman Morris, author of Mind Over Money Matters and former CNN business anchor.

WHAT READERS ARE SAYING

"If you struggle with issues like negotiation and boundary setting, "Nice Girls Just Don't Get It" is a must-read. It's a guide to achieving large and small goals in every aspect of life, ranging from dealing with your boss to dealing with your mother-in-law. Highly recommend." Lindsey P.

"These authors really know what they are talking about. I felt that they were talking directly to me at some points in this book. I liked that there were a lot of helpful points to incorporate into everyday life. I would definitely recommend this book." Beth S.

"I wish that I'd had this book to refer to while growing up! It really is an awesome reference tool and gives very practical advice about how to handle potentially uncomfortable situations!" TF

"This book really opened my eyes to the mistakes I'm making professionally. For a long time I believed being assertive, as a woman in business, gave colleagues and managers the impression that I was being difficult, or to be frank, a bitch. The authors equip you with the knowledge to approach that pink line without crossing it. Well done, ladies." Shelbi R.

"The best parts of the book were when Frankel and Frohlinger used realistic case studies. For example, they discussed situations where you may be in a relationship that is not ideal, whether it's with a boss, a colleague, an in-law, or a significant other. Their advice wasn't just "leave," which often is not an option. Instead, it was on how to manage the situation/relationship. Other helpful tools include examples of tough conversations and a thought-provoking self-assessment quiz at the beginning." Diane D.

"Nice Girls Just Don't Get It is like finding a pot of gold at the end of a rainbow. I love how the book is broken down into seven different strategies with each strategy having multiple tactics to help you to implement those strategies. The self-assessment, at the beginning of the book, is a great tool to help you identify the behaviors that may be holding you back from getting the things you want in life. The book is a must read for women of all ages at all stages in their lives." Linda S.

CONTENTS

STRATEGY II
BUILD RELATIONSHIPS
THAT WORK FOR YOU

STRATEGY III

MANAGE EXPECTATIONS

INTRODUCTION

ALL ABOUT *NICE GIRLS*

If you often feel invisible, taken advantage of, treated less than respectfully, or at a loss for how to get the things you most want in life—join the club. The *nice girls* club, that is. *Nice girls* are women who hold themselves back in life by conforming to the stereotypical behaviors they've been socialized to believe are necessary for survival. These are women who unwittingly sabotage relationships—in their romantic lives, with family members, at work, or with just about anyone else—and, as a result, fail to get the things they want most out of life. As women, we're bombarded throughout our lives with messages that try to convince us that being "nice" is more important than getting the things we want. Even if no one has ever said this to you explicitly, we're guessing you've most likely absorbed the message that putting your needs first will land you on the "bitch list."

Here's an example of how messages from childhood can hurt you in the present. Cheryl is a manager in a large aerospace firm. She's well respected at the office, but she's still treated like a child by her parents. As a single woman, at holiday get-togethers with family, she's expected to sit at the children's table because there isn't enough room at the dining room table for all the adults. Needless to say, it's something that bothers her greatly, but she doesn't know what to do about it. When she suggested that it was time for her to be seated at the adult table, she was told that she was being overly sensitive. So now she holds her tongue and goes along for the sake of getting along, not wanting to ruin family gatherings.

Reluctance to make waves has impacted her at work as well as at home. She's known as an affable and easygoing woman, but is not considered "high potential" because she won't express opposing opinions—even ones that could help the company to grow. Being a nice girl has gotten her to where she is—but it won't get her to where she wants to go. The messages she received in childhood and now carries into the present are getting in the way of her ability to accomplish her adult goals.

Childhood behaviors, whether learned from implicit parental expectations or explicit demands, pervade every aspect of our experiences as women. From being unable to leave an abusive relationship, to being immobilized in a career, to being reluctant to question a physician about a prescribed course of treatment, *nice girls* are more concerned with how others may react, or what others may think of them, than they are with their own well-being.

Don't get us wrong. Being nice is important, but niceness alone will not get you what you want out of life. Being kind, considerate, and generous is an ingredient for success in every endeavor or interaction, but it's simply not sufficient. We know, from years of personal and professional experience, that you *can* reach your personal and professional goals and do it nicely. It's not an either-or proposition.

Winning women are women who have learned how to win the respect they deserve, the success they've earned, and the life they want without being labeled a "bitch." By "things" we don't mean only tangibles such as a new home, a good deal on a car, or a better job. We mean creating situations where your voice is heard, your needs are met, and, regardless of the outcome, you feel good about how you handled yourself. Being a winning woman doesn't mean you'll always get everything you want, but it does mean you'll go after your goals in ways that are authentic, intentional, skillful, and mature. Consider these differences between nice girls and winning women:

NICE GIRLS	WINNING WOMEN
Put their needs last	Factor their needs in with those of others
Rarely ask for what's important to them	Clarify their needs without equivocation

NICE GIRLS	WINNING WOMEN
Tolerate inappropriate behavior	Confront those who treat them disrespectfully
Are reluctant to communicate in assertive ways	Deliver concise and direct messages
Fail to leverage relationships	Understand and capitalize on the relationships in their lives
Have an inordinate fear of offending others	Do everything possible to maintain healthy, mutually beneficial relationships with appropriate boundaries

How This Book Will Help You Become a Winning Woman

In *Nice Girls Don't Get the Corner Office* and *Her Place at the Table*, we focused on how to overcome the nice girl behaviors that can prevent you from achieving your career goals. From what we've heard from many of you who read these books, acting on our advice made a difference! Some women wrote to tell us they got promotions they wanted, others got raises, and yet others had the courage to walk away from toxic or unhealthy employment situations. To you, we tip our hats. Now we want to provide a broader set of skills you can use with *anyone, anywhere*: your landlord, mother-in-law, clients, neighbors, children—you name it. The truth is that many of the same skills, with only minor variations, apply across situations and relationships. And it all starts with *you*. To what degree do you understand why you act as you do (or don't)? How willing are you to make changes?

If you are the quintessential nice girl, one who acts in ways she was socialized to behave, others in your life don't have much interest or investment in helping you change. Why should they? By putting your needs last, you are meeting *their* needs. But it's not about *them,* it's about *you.* In this book we'll help you resist this external pressure to stay the same and at the same time identify your true supporters—the ones who have your best interests at heart. These are people who act as role models, mentors, and cheerleaders for you. You're going to need their support to build your winning woman muscle.

The other thing that is important to recognize at the outset is that the messages nice girls internalize about how to behave are deeply culturally ingrained. They are constantly reflected and reinforced by our traditional family structures, social norms, and established business practices. We are hopeful that societal pressure will eventually force reevaluation and redesign, but shifts of this type and magnitude take time. We make this point not to discourage you but to suggest that, in the meantime, you must create your own opportunities to move from *nice girl* to *winning woman.* That's exactly what this book is designed to help you do.

Nice girls don't live the lives they want for one of two reasons: either they are unaware that their own behaviors are holding them back, or they don't know what to do about it. *Nice Girls Just Don't Get It* provides the antidote to both. Whether you are a stay-at-home mom, a CEO, a student, an entrepreneur, or anyone in between, you most likely have your own Achilles' heel when it comes to getting the things you want and have earned. We believe that understanding and strengthening the weakest link in your chain is the only way to transition from nice girl to winning woman. Here, we'll arm you with the skills, beliefs, and knowledge needed to jump-start this transition and overcome the challenges that prevent you from getting the things you most want out of life. To that end, we've identified seven critical strategies and ninety-nine supporting tactics that countless winning women we've worked with have used successfully to achieve their personal and professional goals.

Like many readers of our previous books, in these pages you may just find the secrets to getting what you deserve, need, and want.

STRATEGIES VERSUS TACTICS

One of the reasons we distinguish between strategies and tactics is to help you think about achieving your goals in new ways. As the winning woman graphic on the next page shows, getting from where you are to where you want to be involves a complex interaction of factors. So we've decided to outline a set of strategies, the overarching behaviors in which you must engage if you are to get what you want. You'll use not just one strategy, but rather a combination of strategies to make the changes you want. For example, if you have a friend who you feel takes advantage of your good nature, you should use all of the following: evaluate the past to identify the reasons why you tolerate her inappropriate behavior; manage expectations; communicate more clearly; and prepare for resistance. Strategies, in short, help you to see the big picture.

But identifying strategies isn't enough. You probably already know *what* you should be doing. This is where the tactics come in. Tactics are the *how*—the specific things you must do to implement the strategies. Each of the ninety-nine tactics provided can be used in a variety of situations. Think of the strategies as toolboxes and the tactics as tools that you can draw on as needed. And just as certain behavioral changes will require the use of several strategies, particular situations will benefit from multiple tactics. Since similar actions can be helpful in approaching different situations from different perspectives, you will find some overlap in tactics. For example, when framing desired outcomes (Tactic 41), we suggest that doing your homework is essential. This is also an important component of Tactic 44: Use Facts, Not Feelings.

To illustrate how these strategies and tactics can be used, we've included scenarios and examples drawn from our coaching and consulting work. Although we've changed the names to maintain confidentiality, these are stories of real women, sometimes from our own personal experiences.

Consider the situation a woman we'll call Barbara presented to us.

Her entire life she's been known for her ability to go with the flow and get along with almost anyone. She learned this behavior in childhood from a mother who constantly reinforced the message that it was important to please others and act selflessly. In fact, she remembers one Christmas when she told her mother that she was about to divorce her husband, and her mother told her not to mention it so as not to spoil everyone's holiday!

As a result of these ingrained messages, in group situations Barbara was almost always willing to do what the majority of her friends wanted—at the expense of what *she* wanted—rarely suggesting

alternatives to the plan decided by the more vocal members of the group. Then Barbara had a serious car accident in which she almost lost her life. It was a wake-up call. She decided life was too short to always give in to what *others* wanted. She wanted to do more of what *she* wanted. The strategies she needed to work on included building relationships with people who considered her needs along with their own, managing people's expectations about what she was and wasn't willing to do, communicating more effectively about what she wanted, and living her values. Yet she still had to figure out how to change a lifetime of nice girl behavior. So she started small.

If a friend suggested going to a particular restaurant that she had just been to, for example, she employed Tactic 43 (If You Have to Say No, Support It with a Legitimate Rationale and Alternatives) to make her wishes known. Instead of just going along with her friend's suggestion, she now said, "I love that restaurant, but I was just there a few days ago. I suggest we try the new Thai place everyone is raving about." When friends wanted her to join them on a trip she couldn't afford, she used Tactic 57 (Practice Contrasting) to let them know her true feelings about not being able to join them: "I don't want you to think I don't want to join you all on that trip, because I do. Given that I've been out of work for a while and also saving to buy a house, I'm going to have to pass on this one, though." Over time, Barbara found her voice, stopped allowing others to dictate how she would spend her time and money, and, in turn, felt more in control of her life.

If you're a nice girl, many of the tactics we're about to describe may feel alien to you. All we ask is that you consider each one individually and not be overwhelmed by having to make huge changes in your behavior all at once. Like Barbara, take it one step at a time. Sometimes simply engaging in just one tactic paves the way to more comfortably engage in others in the future. The more you practice new tactics, the more natural they will become. In fact, there are situations in which you will want to use multiple tactics. Remember, our goal is not to suggest you *change* who you are, but rather, to enable you to *be* who you are—to provide you with the tools you need to live your life more fully, authentically, and with the utmost satisfaction.

SELF-ASSESSMENT: JUST HOW NICE ARE YOU?

Let's begin by identifying your strengths and your areas to work on. Most likely, you're already doing a lot of things right. The self-assessment that follows will help you to pinpoint the nice girl behaviors that are holding you back. This will be useful in figuring out which strategies and supporting tactics you need to focus on most closely and in understanding your behaviors in the context of each. No two people are the same, and completing the self-assessment before reading the book will help you to focus on your unique strengths and areas for growth.

Keep in mind that no "test" can tell you more about yourself than you already know. You may take the self-assessment and find it's not a 100 percent accurate appraisal of where you are in your life. Or, you may find that it's a precise portrayal of you and your gaps. Either way, we believe it will get you thinking about the ways in which you may be holding yourself back and help you to put yourself on the path to change.

Nice Girls Just Don't Get It Self-Assessment

This self-assessment is designed to help you identify the behaviors that may be holding you back from getting the things you most want in life. Without spending too much time thinking about the statement, honestly assess the degree to which each one is descriptive of how you think, feel, or act. Don't answer the questions indicating what you *want* to do, but rather what you *actually* do in the present. Remember to be candid and rate every statement using the following scale.

>   1 = Not at all descriptive of how I think, feel, or act.
>   2 = Not descriptive of how I think, feel, or act most of the time.
>   3 = Descriptive of how I think, feel, or act some of the time.
>   4 = Descriptive of how I think, feel, or act most of the time.

1. _____ I don't allow childhood messages from my family to have undue influence on my current choices and decisions.

2. _____ I seek to build relationships with people who are unlike me because I know I will learn from them.

3. _____ I don't allow others to take advantage of me.

4. _____ Without waiting to be asked, I give my opinion.

5. _____ When others disagree with me, I find new ways to make my case rather than simply let the matter drop.

6. _____ When necessary, I ask friends to make introductions to others who can help me achieve my goals.

7. _____ Without hesitation, I can tell you the three things I value most in life.

8. _____ I am clear about what I do and don't want.

9. _____ When meeting new people, I actively try to make them feel comfortable.

10. _____ I set clear boundaries with others.

11. _____ I express myself clearly and concisely.

12. _____ When making a proposal to a group, I lobby in advance to increase the likelihood of acceptance.

13. _____ I spend time each week building my personal and professional networks.

14. _____ It's hard to make me feel guilty.

15. _____ Negative reactions from others don't impact my decisions.

16. _____ Regardless of what is happening in the moment, I devote my full attention to the person trying to speak with me.

17. _____ When starting a new project or embarking on an adventure, I ensure at the outset that everyone's role is clear.

18. _____ I don't ask permission; I inform others of my decisions.

19. _____ When it's clear a difficult conversation is going nowhere, I'll suggest a time-out, then schedule a time to revisit the issue.

20. _____ When I don't know something, I look for someone in my network who does and ask that person for help.

21. _____ Each week I do something to promote living my values.

22. _____ I have no problem breaking the rules if the situation calls for it.

23. _____ Although I might be nice, I don't *need* people to like me.

24. _____ I say no to unreasonable requests.

25. _____ Others describe me as a great listener.

26. _____ I don't give up after hearing one "no" to a request.

27. _____ I not only join professional associations, I regularly attend their meetings.

28. _____ I know the things that are nonnegotiable for me.

29. _____ I can clearly describe my Achilles' heel.

30. _____ I would rather allow someone to save face than suggest that the other person is wrong.

31. _____ I have no problem engaging in difficult conversations to express my needs.

32. _____ When the message is important, I plan in advance what I'm going to say.

33. _____ I turn differences of opinion into ways to create better outcomes.

34. _____ I volunteer for high-profile opportunities at work, in the community, at church, etc.

35. _____ When my plate is overloaded, I delegate.

36. _____ No one but me controls my future.

37. _____ I leave unhealthy relationships and move on.

38. _____ I enjoy negotiating.

39. _____ I create win-win situations where my needs are met as well as those of others.

40. _____ I vary my approach based on the person I want to influence.

41. _____ I have no problem questioning the opinions of "experts" such as doctors, professors, lawyers, etc.

42. _____ Others describe me as a "take-charge" person.

43. _____ I've been a good steward of my future.

44. _____ I maintain positive relationships with people I don't particularly like.

45. _____ I make my case using facts, not feelings.

46. _____ Before trying to influence others, I try to learn as much as possible about their needs, opinions, or positions.

47. _____ I plant seeds in advance of presenting new ideas or requests.

48. _____ I mentor others.

49. _____ I am living the life I want.

50. _____ I have a clear mental picture of how I want my life to be in the future.

51. _____ I honor the quid pro quo in relationships (rate yourself a 1 if you don't know what *quid pro quo* means).

52. _____ I don't hesitate to ask for help when I need it.

53. _____ When ignored, I continue to make my voice heard rather than simply acquiesce.

54. _____ I choose my battles carefully.

55. _____ I connect people with common interests.

56. _____ I behave consistently with Socrates' statement, "The unexamined life is not worth living."

Self-Assessment

SCORE SHEET

Instructions for Scoring

1. Enter your ratings to each of the statements in the boxes below (the number in each box corresponds to the statement number).

2. Add your ratings *down* in each column to determine the specific areas that require your attention if you are to achieve your life goals. The items you rated as 1 or 2 are those on which you should focus most closely at the current time. You may want to read the section corresponding to your *lowest* column score first.

3. Add the column totals *across* to determine your overall score. An interpretation of your overall score can be found on the next page.

I Evaluate the Past and Envision the Future	II Build Relationships That Work For You	III Manage Expectations	IV Craft Meaningful Messages	V Prepare for Pushback	VI Use and Share Your Connections	VII Live Your Values	
1.	2.	3.	4.	5.	6.	7.	
8.	9.	10.	11.	12.	13.	14.	
15.	16.	17.	18.	19.	20.	21.	
22.	23.	24.	25.	26.	27.	28.	
29.	30.	31.	32.	33.	34.	35.	
36.	37.	38.	39.	40.	41.	42.	
43.	44.	45.	46.	47.	48.	49.	
50.	51.	52.	53.	54.	55.	56.	
Total	Total	Total	Total	Total	Total	Total	Overall Score

Analyzing Your Score

If your total score is **56–96** *or* If your score in any one category is **8–13**	**Your picture is next to the word *nice* in the dictionary!** You are the quintessential "nice girl." Your challenge is to develop a sensible strategy to get more of the things you want, have earned, and deserve. This book was written for *you*.
If your total score is **97–142** *or* If your score in any one category is **14–19**	**Fine-tuning is the name of your game!** You're not unhappy with where you are in your life at the moment, but you do want more in some areas. At times you hesitate to move from nice girl to winning woman. Supplement your existing skill set with the tactics in the book to increase your fulfillment.
If your total score is **143–186** *or* If your score in any one category is **20–28**	**Congratulations!** You've mastered the fine art of getting most of the things you want in life with courage and confidence. You are neither overly confident nor too nice. Focus on those areas where you rated yourself a 1 or 2 to maintain your winning game plan.
If your total score is **187–224** *or* If your score in any one category is **29–32**	**Caution!** Your high score could be an indication that you are, at times, more interested in winning than working toward win-win solutions. If you're wondering why you don't always get the things you've worked hard for, it could be that you're not nice *enough*. The strategies in this book will help you to create a greater balance.

EVALUATE THE PAST AND ENVISION THE FUTURE

THE TACTICS IN STRATEGY I FOCUS ON

- Understanding the genesis of your behaviors, attitudes, and preferences.

- Reflecting on what is (or isn't) working for you now.

- Identifying what you need to change so that you can win the respect you deserve, the success you've earned, and the life you want.

Without a doubt, our past affects our present and our future. We are products of the messages we received not only from parents or other family members or caregivers, but also from teachers, friends, television, magazines, movies, music, the Internet, and so on. Consciously and otherwise, we absorb these messages and they become part of the fabric of who we are, how we choose to be in the world, how we interact with others, and what we think we are entitled to have in our lives. If we're lucky, our parents endow us at a young age with the belief that we can achieve anything we want. But even then, studies show that as we move into adolescence, the rules change.

As girls, we are socialized to focus on relationships, so we seek similarities as a means of bonding with others. This begins when we're very young. In fact, by about the age of thirteen, most girls are already showing behaviors geared to pleasing others and fitting in—often at their own expense. At around this age, girls become less verbal in class, are less likely to state an opinion or preference that might set them apart from others, and conform more to societal expectations for females. Somewhere along the way, many of them lose their sense of self and get stuck in the nice girl trap, setting themselves up for a lifetime of putting other people's needs ahead of their own.

The first strategy for getting more of the things you want from life involves examining how your unique past creates a filter for your present behaviors. It's critical to understand that behavioral change is difficult because our behaviors serve a purpose in our lives. Even when we are not aware of it, we act with intention. For example, if you were always the peacemaker in the family, chances are you don't like conflict and will do *almost anything to keep the peace now. This might explain why you have so much difficulty saying you really don't want to go skiing on vacation and would prefer a week at the beach. Or, perhaps as the oldest child, you were expected to be a role model for the younger family members when it came to achievement in school. It's no wonder, then, that you might be inclined to perfectionism as an adult. Only when we bring the reasons why we behave as we do to the forefront of our consciousness can we make the difficult decision to add new behaviors to our repertoires. We are not suggesting that you have to give up your past to create a better future. We propose that you use this section to identify the old messages that are holding you back and gain clarity about who you are and what's most important to you.*

ILLUMINATE AND OVERCOME CHILDHOOD EXPECTATIONS

Let's face it. There are rules for membership in every family. These are the things you learn early you must do to get attention and affection. These rules aren't posted on the refrigerator, and they're more often implicit than they are explicit. Nevertheless, by the time you're about three years old, you already instinctively know which behaviors will serve you well and which will displease your parents or other caregivers. The rules are different from family to family but, for women in particular, they often include messages such as these: *Children are to be seen and not heard, Be helpful, Take care of your siblings, Don't make noise when Daddy comes home, Be kind, Get good grades in school,* and *Be productive.*

These messages aren't all bad. They can and often do form the foundation of our greatest strengths. For example, we wouldn't argue that being productive is a positive attribute. It becomes problematic only when that behavior becomes extreme, or when you overrely on that behavior to the point where you're unable to make alternative choices when appropriate. This was the case for Jamie, who was always overextended. When she was a child, her parents signed her up for all kinds of activities and classes, instilling in her the message that idleness was bad. As a result, in her adult life, whether at work or home, she was the poster child for the maxim "A woman's work is never done." In addition to holding a full-time job, she was active on the board of her community association, heavily involved with her church, and constantly busy with events planned by her parents and siblings.

This was all well and good until Jamie's husband asked that she spend more time with him in leisure activities. They had both worked hard their entire lives and they were at a point where he wanted them to enjoy the fruits of their labors. Not only was it difficult for Jamie to acknowledge her husband's request, she resented it. Didn't he know that all of the things she was involved in were very important? Did he expect her to just drop them to go off and play?

This is how unexamined childhood expectations can impede your ability to have your needs met in the present. Jamie's husband's request wasn't unreasonable or ill-intentioned. He wasn't demanding that she give up the things that were important to her. He just wanted to spend more quality time with his wife. But the filter through which Jamie viewed the world made it difficult for her to shift priorities even for the sake of having a healthier and happier relationship with her husband. And unexamined assumptions on both of their parts prevented them from communicating clearly with one another. With counseling, she came to understand that she had taken to the extreme her parents' expectations that she always be the productive "nice girl" who had to take on any task or project asked of her. And that, as a result, her personal life had suffered. Eventually she was able to make different choices based on what suited her needs now, not as a child.

MAKE IT WORK FOR YOU

- **Identify the childhood messages that drive your current behavior.** Ask yourself, "What were the rules for membership in my family growing up?" Then think about what happened when you did or didn't engage in those behaviors.

- **Describe the ways these messages contribute to your greatest strengths as well as how they hurt you.** Think about what you do well and how those strengths relate to early parental expectations. How do these same messages impede your ability to see what's on the periphery or act differently when the situation calls for it?

- **Consider the ways in which you take the lessons learned from childhood to the extreme.** Do you always put your needs behind everyone else's? Are you reluctant to question authority? Do you avoid confrontations, even those that would help you to meet your goals? Being nice and well-behaved may have worked for you as a child, but as an adult, these attitudes and behaviors can become detrimental when taken to the extreme.

- **List two or three behaviors you wish had been instilled in you as a child.** What behaviors would complement your existing strengths? Choose ones that you think would help you move from nice girl to winning woman. It might be helpful to examine your responses on the self-assessment—particularly those areas where you rated yourself a 1 or a 2.

EXORCISE YOUR PARENTS

We don't mean that literally, of course. What we mean is that inside the head of every nice girl looms the influence of her parents, and too often their voices influence her interactions with others—particularly those she may view as authority figures. For example, if every older man with whom you come into contact reminds you of Dad, you'll always see yourself through his eyes, as a child, and you're not going to be able to engage with that man as the adult woman you've become. Or, if Mom was a strict disciplinarian, chances are you'll ascribe negative intentions to women even when none are there. In psychological terms this is what's known as transference: *bestowing on people in the present characteristics of people from childhood.*

It's not only negative transference that gets in the way of getting what you want; positive transference can interfere as well. One woman we know had the most loving and supportive father you could ever hope for. He made her feel good about herself and instilled in her a sense of confidence. When she came into contact with men who were not as—shall we say enlightened?—this strong and savvy woman fell to pieces wondering what she was doing wrong.

Although the workplace is rife with opportunities for transference—ascribing attributes of your mother to your boss, for example—it happens in other aspects of our lives as well. Not being able to ask your doctor probing questions because you're afraid you'll insult him by questioning his authority, tolerating less than appropriate behavior from a store clerk because you don't want to "make trouble," and consistently dating the same "wrong" kind of person because they're somehow familiar to you are all examples of how your childhood relationship with your parents impacts your present choices.

Our relationships with our parents change over time, but inside, each of us remains the little girl who remembers them "back when." So you might say that you have a great relationship with your parents

now, but that's the adult speaking. If you have unresolved parental issues from childhood, those voices may still haunt your subconscious,
causing you to miss out on opportunities because you continue to interact with those you perceive as having more power or control than
you as the child you were, rather than the adult you've become.

MAKE IT WORK FOR YOU

- **Dissect unusually strong reactions.** These are typically signs that
  something old is at play. Rather than continue to engage in the interaction, take an emotional break. Ask yourself if the person you're
  having the over-the-top reaction to reminds you of anyone from
  childhood.

- **Rewrite the script.** See your parents and other childhood influ-
  ences for who they really are; then reframe the situation and re-
  engage from a place of adulthood. Give yourself permission to
  communicate adult to adult.

- **Avoid the repetition compulsion.** We often stay in toxic situations
  or tolerate inappropriate behavior longer than we should because
  the other person's behavior is familiar to us. Again, it's the child
  inside who believes this is just how the world is supposed to be,
  and we repeat early experiences. A good example is when a woman
  from an alcoholic home first marries an alcoholic, divorces him,
  then marries a compulsive gambler. She may believe she chose better the second time around, but, in fact, she chose the same kind of
  person once again. Identify the situations where you seem to make
  the same mistakes over and over and determine whether familiar-
  ity is at play. If so, strive to identify the familiar patterns so you can
  make better choices in the future. As Anna Freud said, "Creative
  minds have always been known to survive any kind of bad training."

- **Seek professional help.** Healing old wounds from childhood isn't
  easy, but it's not impossible. A good therapist will help you to remove the filter of the past and make better choices in the present.

The best referral to a therapist usually comes from a trusted friend, physician, or your company's Employee Assistance Program. Be a good consumer when it comes to selecting a mental health provider. Ask questions, expect results over a reasonable period of time, and trust your instincts.

DON'T LET EARLY EXPERIENCES OR EXPECTATIONS DEFINE YOU

Marta is a thirty-two-year-old Latina who grew up in her grandparents' home in the inner city. No one in her family went to college, no one was expected to, and none of the high school classmates with whom she associated were college bound. At fourteen she joined a gang. At eighteen, her grandparents kicked her out of the house as they no longer received federal assistance for her care and therefore no longer "needed" her. She lived out of a decrepit camper on her grandparents' property and used the facilities in the house after they went to work. Based on these experiences, you can see how easy it would have been for her to define herself as disposable or worthless.

Then Michele Ruiz, a Los Angeles journalist and child rights advocate, heard her story. Michele brought Marta into her own home to live with her family. In exchange for this kindness, Marta cooked meals. Pretty soon she took an interest in culinary arts and showed such promise that Michele paid for Marta to go to cooking school. Now, Marta is a successful chef making a good living doing something she loves—a life she could never have envisioned during her traumatic childhood.

Your story may not be quite as dramatic as Marta's, but chances are others had expectations of you that were different from those you had for yourself. Sometimes they're the result of the "role" you have in the family. Maybe you're the "pretty" one who will get married but won't have a career. Or you're the "smart" one who will become a doctor. Lois often tells the story of how her mother was willing to pay for her college education but *only* if she'd become a teacher (her father didn't think she needed a college education at all), when what she really wanted was to be a psychologist. In the end she did meet her mother's expectations, as well as her own, by getting dual degrees— one in education and one in psychology!

It's not only childhood experiences and expectations that define us but also early adult ones. We know countless women who never went to college but started work right after high school (if they finished high school at all). They often begin in jobs such as administrative assistant, waitress, or child care assistant, only to find that even if they later go back and earn a college degree, they still can't advance in their career, despite having gained years of experience *and* a degree. They find themselves stuck at the same level they were when they entered the company. Why? Because either they still see themselves as being the kind of person who belongs on the bottom of the totem pole and they project themselves as such, or other people haven't changed their opinion. In other words, they let early professional status continue to define them, even when circumstances have changed. Remember that regardless of expectations or experiences, *you* control your destiny—no one else.

MAKE IT WORK FOR YOU

- **Draw a picture of yourself five years from now.** You don't have to be an artist to do this exercise. It can even be a stick figure. Surround the picture with either words or graphic depictions of the things you want in your life—a house, a child, peace of mind, financial freedom, a job you love—but have never truly believed yourself capable of achieving. Then post a list of attributes you believe define the type of person who attains these things. We're guessing you'll discover you actually have most of them already. Finally, put this list in a place where you will see it every day. It may sound hokey, but it works, and it's important to have continual reminders of where we're going if we don't want to remain defined by the past.

- **Compare yourself.** There are times when comparing ourselves to other women is a bad idea, but in this case, it can help you to redefine yourself as the person you want to be, rather than the person you think you're expected to be. Who is currently doing what *you* want to be doing? For example, if you've defined yourself as the eternal office assistant, when what you'd really like to be is the manager, talk to someone who has worked her way up from where you are. Be prepared to ask probing questions about what she did to get from where she was to where she is now and solicit advice about challenges you are likely to face on the path you're envisioning. You don't have to know her personally—we speak with plenty of women whom we've never met but who had the courage to ask to speak with us for just fifteen minutes. In short, learn as much as you can about what you want to do from those who have already achieved it.

- **Surround yourself with those who can see beyond the "old" you.** When an addict wants to remain clean, she doesn't go to bars and continue to party with the crowd that contributed to her drug use in the first place. If those with whom you currently associate can only see you as you were, or treat you in ways other than how you now want to be treated, it's going to be tough to redefine yourself. Find groups and individuals with whom you can forge new and different relationships based on your vision for the future.

- **Make a plan and take action.** You'll never overcome past experiences if you continue to wallow in them. Life may have dealt you a difficult hand, but that doesn't define your future. Studies done of concentration camp survivors found that those who had a mental image of what they had yet to do in their lives were more likely to survive than those who didn't. This speaks to the power of taking charge of our lives. Your plan doesn't have to be grand or stretch you beyond your capabilities; it only has to be enough to keep you on the path you want to be on. Lao-tzu was right when he said, "The journey of a thousand miles begins with a single step."

EXAMINE YOUR CHOICES

Nice girls don't proactively make choices for themselves, because they are unduly influenced by the choices that others have made for them. Sometimes, they are so stuck in choices that were made in the past, they don't even recognize they have a choice in the future.

Such was the case with Dory. She came from a family of lawyers. So, when she graduated college, her parents expected that she too would apply to law school, and attend if she was accepted. Without stopping to think, Dory did exactly that. The problem? She hated practicing law. But she felt stuck because by the time she realized she was unhappy, she had invested so much time and money in her training that she was reluctant to walk away. This is a common nice girl mistake. Too often, choices we've made in the past put us on a path we don't really want to be on, but we think it's too late to turn back. Wrong. It's never too late to change course. Trust us, retracing a few steps is much better than getting to the end of the road and realizing you've landed in the wrong place.

Here's another example. Andrea and her boyfriend had been dating for a few months when her lease was about to expire. They decided this was as good a time as any to move in together—they spent most of their time together anyway and there was no sense in paying rent for two places. The problem? Andrea, who was in her thirties, didn't see moving in with her boyfriend so much as a choice she was making, but as a convenience. She assumed things would go a certain way—for example, that he'd let her know when he was planning a night out with the boys, but she never discussed her expectations with him. When things didn't turn out as she thought they would, it caused her a lot of heartache.

Although making choices can be difficult, it's much easier once you keep in mind that your choices don't always have to be limited to yes or no. Picture the ideal solution and then think about ways you might be able to negotiate to make it a reality. Our favorite story from *Her Place at the Table* is about a woman who was offered a wonderful promotion. It was the kind of opportunity that came to people only once in a career at her company. She knew she could succeed at the job but it would require a lot of travel, and because she had two teenage kids, she was reluctant to sign up for a position that would have her frequently on the road. Turning the job down would certainly have been understandable, particularly if she'd been a nice girl. But she wasn't. Instead, she made a counterproposal to restructure the job responsibilities so that two of her colleagues would do most of the travel (she conferred with them first).

Because she didn't see her choice as solely yes or no, she was able to create a win-win-win-win. Her employer won because she was the best person for the job. Her colleagues won because their personal situations were different, and they were delighted with the chance to rack up frequent-flier miles. Her kids won because she was able to be at home—even though as teenagers they may not have appreciated it at the time! And, finally, *she* won because she got the job she wanted without having to make compromises that weren't right for her.

MAKE IT WORK FOR YOU

- **See choices as opportunities to make your life what you want it to be.** Don't put your life on autopilot—actively make your choices. If you can't see the choices available to you, brainstorm with a trusted friend or family member whose vision might not be clouded by past decisions.

- **Don't limit your choices to yes or no.** Seeing things narrowly, or as black-and-white, limits creative problem solving that can help us get what we want. Look for the gray. Invest the time to decide whether there are any choices *between* yes and no.

- **Don't apologize for the choices you make.** As long as your choice isn't illegal or unethical, it requires no defense. Unless you were dishonest with yourself about your needs and goals, however things turn out, you can be secure in the knowledge that you made the best choice you could with the information you had at the time. Given that we know the outcome of a choice only in retrospect (not even winning women can see into the future), apologies and self-blame are not only unnecessary but unproductive.

- **Unless your choice is irrevocable, give yourself permission to change your mind.** If a particular path isn't working as well as you had anticipated, choose another one! Consider each choice as an experiment in your life. With the exception of having children, nothing is the *final* step, just the next step.

IDENTIFY BLOCKS TO "KNOWING"

Many women have a difficult time articulating what they most want. They often know what they *don't* want (a loveless marriage, unsatisfying friendships, less than desirable economic status, difficult familial relationships, etc.), but they aren't sure what they *do* want. You may have clarity about what you want in one aspect of your life, but not another (e.g., you know what you want in a life partner, but perhaps not in a career). Or, like many women, you may not have given much thought at all to what you want. Instead, you go along with the program to keep the peace and not make waves. You go along to get along. Pretty soon, your needs and desires are entirely occluded. The causes of not knowing are varied, but almost always stem from being too focused on others and neglecting oneself. Whatever the reason, if you don't know what you want, how can you expect to get it?

Not knowing what you want can make you feel stuck, depressed, or anxious. It may seem as if it's someone else's life you're living rather than your own. When we don't know what's best for us or what we want, there's often someone else's voice in the back of our head speaking more loudly than our own. It could be a parent saying, "Why would you want to live in that city?" or a spouse asking, "Why would you want to work full-time?" It could also be a less distinct voice, more like an ever-present noise that drowns out our own.

A fellow author who had put a lot of effort into writing her books but never quite made it as a commercial success wanted to be more successful. But when asked what success would look like to her, she couldn't quite answer. When prompted if she wanted to be famous, rich, or invited for more speaking engagements, she still couldn't respond. Then she shared the story of growing up in a home with a mother and aunt who had instilled in her all kinds of fears about the world. As immigrants who couldn't speak English, they lived a sequestered life, never venturing much further than the few square blocks around their home. When she expressed a desire to go to college, they insisted it be one where she could remain living at home. As she related the story, it was as if a light went on for her. She realized these childhood messages that those in authority were the only ones who knew what was best for her were hampering her ability to define success on her own terms.

At one time or another, most of us hear old voices from our past that impact our present behaviors. If we're lucky, they're positive voices that cheer us on, telling us we can do even the things that are most difficult. At other times, they instill hesitance, create apprehension, or drown out our own voices entirely. Identifying your blocks to "knowing" is one of the critical first steps toward winning the game of life. You must come to know—undisputedly—what you want and that you have the right to achieve it.

MAKE IT WORK FOR YOU

- **Identify the overpowering voice(s).** The path to "knowing" begins with identifying the voice or voices and the messages from the past that drown out your own. They're often those of a parent, but can also be those of a sibling, schoolyard bully, spouse, or teacher. Think back to when you received these messages and how they influence current choices and decisions. There's no need to judge them as good or bad; simply understand where they come from and whether or not you agree with them.

- **Create your adult countermessage.** When we don't know what we want, it can be because we're stuck in a childlike state. If "Father knows best," how can I possibly know what I really want? It's the little girl inside you who hesitates to identify and go after what *she* wants. To move from little girl to winning woman, you must consciously develop a countermessage, write it down, and say it silently to yourself, or say it out loud when it feels safe to do so. For example, if your mother always told you how she couldn't wait for you to get married and start a family, but you're at a point in your life where your career comes first, your countermessage might be something like "I'm in charge of my life and no one will ever take better care of me than I will care for myself," or "I will not let anyone tell me what's best for me." Over time, *your* messages, not your mother's, will become those you hear loud and clear.

- **Visualize what you want.** It might sound silly, but visualization exercises can help you tap into those subconscious desires you might not be aware of. Before you go to sleep at night, when all the lights are out and everything is quiet, listen to the rhythm of your breathing. With your eyes closed, picture yourself in a meadow, at the ocean, or anywhere else that brings you comfort and peace. After being in that place for a few minutes, silently ask the question, "What do I really want?" You might have to do this several nights in a row before you get an answer, but eventually something will come up. Trust your instincts and explore whatever comes to mind. Don't be afraid of it or mentally push it away—the answers really are inside you.

- **Recognize and resist manipulation.** Once you recognize what it is you want most or what success means to you, remember that there may be people around who'll try to keep you from it; they may be invested in keeping you in a place where they have more control over you. Sometimes friends will tell you they like the "new you" but then say subtle things to sabotage your efforts at personal growth (like, "Are you *sure* now's really the time to start that business you always dreamed about?"). Expect it, prepare for it, but don't go for the bait.

- **"Knowing" can come from anywhere, at any time.** For some women it takes something dramatic—even a drastic change like the death of a parent who abused them, divorce from a narcissistic partner, or getting fired from a job they hate—to find the quiet space around them and hear their own voice. But at the same time, you don't have to wait for something like this to happen. Just because you don't know what you want today doesn't mean you won't tomorrow or next month or even next year. Insight can come when you least expect it. Keep your countermessage close, consciously observe the ways in which others cause you to doubt yourself, and focus on even the smallest things you choose to do that contribute to fulfillment. Remember, *courage does not always roar; sometimes it is a quiet voice that says, "I'll try again tomorrow."*

BEWARE OF YOUR ACHILLES' HEEL

According to Greek mythology, Achilles was the bravest hero who fought in the Trojan War. When he was born, his mother wanted to make him immortal, so she immersed him in the River Styx, holding him by one heel. Because that heel wasn't submerged, it became the most vulnerable part of an otherwise impenetrable warrior, and an arrow that struck his heel in battle became his ultimate downfall. Today, an Achilles' heel refers to our greatest vulnerability in the midst of our great strengths. And guess what? We *all* have one. Knowing exactly what yours is not only enables you to compensate for it but also helps you to protect yourself from those who might try to use that weakness to their advantage.

An Achilles' heel can be tough to spot. Perhaps you're known for being the life of the party, but your lack of diplomacy causes people to avoid spending one-on-one time with you. Or maybe you're terrific at organizing the details for projects at work, but your failure to think broadly causes you to miss issues on the periphery. Our inability or unwillingness to see our Achilles' heel inevitably impedes success in our undertakings and relationships, and not just in the workplace.

A model called the Johari window (developed by psychologists Joe Luft and Harry Ingham) can help you to pinpoint and understand your Achilles' heel (sometimes referred to as a blind spot, because of our chronic difficulty in seeing it). As you can see in the diagram of this model on the following page, there are four aspects to our public personas:

- Box 1, the *public arena*, is what we allow others to know about us. People know these things because we choose to share information with them and give them glimpses of who we really are and what we really want.

- Box 2 represents our *blind spot* or *Achilles' heel*. It's what others see but we ourselves can't see, or won't acknowledge. Because you can't know what you don't know, decreasing the blind spot and protecting your Achilles' heel requires insight and feedback from others.

- Box 3 is our *façade*. We all have *some* information or aspects of our lives that we keep private. That's completely fine. It's when we try to obscure our private lives by putting up a false image of who we are that we run into trouble. When the façade predominates in our interactions with others and they feel as if they don't really know us, they may not trust us or openly share information with us when we really need it.

- Box 4 is the *unknown* or *unconscious*. But it doesn't have to remain that way. Often the process of receiving feedback, reading books like the one you're holding in your hands, attending self-help workshops, or engaging in therapy helps to diminish the size of this box.

	KNOWN TO YOU	UNKNOWN TO YOU
KNOWN TO OTHERS	Public arena 1	Blind spot or Achilles' heel 2
UNKNOWN TO OTHERS	Façade 3	Unknown or unconscious 4

You'll notice that the interior lines of the windows are dotted. That's because the size of the windows differs depending on the person—how insightful she is, how much information she shares, and the degree to which she is interested in and works toward probing unknown areas of her personality. Ideally, your public arena should be the window that opens the widest, indicating you are both giving and receiving information and feedback on a regular basis, thereby decreasing the size of the other three boxes.

MAKE IT WORK FOR YOU

- **Do an honest inventory of your strengths.** The self-assessment in the introduction is a good place to start understanding where your Achilles' heel may be, but go beyond that. We believe you can't know your weaknesses without first identifying your strengths, so list your greatest assets, then look for what's missing. Think about the skills and behaviors you've neglected to develop because you tend to rely on these strengths. For example, maybe you spend so much of your time being productive, you fail to build relationships that will help you to work smarter rather than harder. Or maybe being an intensely private person has helped you forge an unbreakable bond with your spouse, but holding back information that would enable others to better understand you gets in the way of your other friendships.

- **Pay attention to *subtle* messages given to you by others.** Many times the best feedback is the subtle kind, but because it is so understated, we overlook or minimize the message. If a friend tells you, "What I like about you is that I always know where I stand," could it mean that at times you are brutally honest? Similarly, when your child asks, "When will it be time to play?" she may really be telling you that you're too busy and she's feeling neglected. Honesty and productivity are good attributes, but they become our Achilles' heels when not balanced with the other things that matter most to us.

- **Ask for feedback like you mean it.** No one really likes to hear about their weaknesses. Which is why, all too often, people ask for feedback in ways that, consciously or not, discourage the other person from actually giving it. This is a common nice girl mistake. After all, if confronted with our weaknesses, we might actually have to make a change! So when you solicit feedback, make it clear you really want it. Don't ask vague questions like "What don't you like about me?" and don't ask for simple yes's or no's, such as, "Does it offend you when I do XYZ?" Most people won't give honest answers to those questions, and even if they do, the answer will be so unspecific it will be easy to dismiss. Instead, ask, "Would you tell me one or two things you think I could do more or less of that would help me to achieve my specific goals?" This puts the feedback in behavioral terms that is safe for others to express.

FOCUS ON YOUR UNIQUE
PERSONALITY PREFERENCES

A number of years ago when the Myers Briggs Type Indicator (MBTI®) reached the peak of its popularity, people all of a sudden started asking each other "what's your type?" instead of the age-old "what's your [astrological] sign?" Numerous versions of the test are available today, but they all originate from the work done in the early twentieth century by a mother-daughter team, Katharine Briggs and Isabel Briggs Myers, who used the models of Swiss psychologist Carl Jung to isolate sixteen personality "types"—each with a unique way of seeing and interacting in the world. These ultimately became known as MBTI® "preferences."

An easy way to understand your preferences is to think of them as a filter through which you see the world—kind of like the lenses of your glasses. If you put on someone else's eyeglasses or contact lenses, the world would look fuzzy and out of focus, right? Each of you can see perfectly through your own eyeglasses (or without any, if you're blessed with perfect vision), but when you swap them, they just don't work. Similarly, your personality preferences are uniquely yours, formed through a combination of nature and nurture—both the characteristics with which you were born and those that resulted from how you were raised. And, just like wearing another person's eyeglasses would lead to all kinds of errors in vision, failing to understand and honor these preferences causes us to make errors in judgment. As a result, we wind up feeling frustrated, misunderstood, and unfulfilled. In contrast, knowing our preferences gives us both the self-confidence and the language to describe our needs and feelings and to make decisions that better suit us.

The chart on page 40 will help you to identify and understand your own preferences. There are four scales, each representing a continuum of behaviors. Typically, we aren't all the way at one end of the scale or the other, but we do tend to lean toward one end of the spectrum. Examine each of the four scales and determine where your preferences lie within each one.

Preferences matter in virtually every relationship in our lives. When people with opposite preferences marry, they find themselves confronted with conflicts that are tough to resolve. When children have different preferences than their parents, it creates a tension in the parent-child relationship that often frustrates parents and causes children to feel as if they're doing something "wrong" or are "bad." And when people with different preferences enter into negotiations of any kind, they can find it more difficult to reach agreement.

However, there are ways to reconcile these differences within a relationship. Kristen and Steve are a good example of this. Despite the fact that they loved each other very much, they always seemed to be at odds over certain decisions and ways of doing things. For example, while Kristen enjoyed small gatherings where she knew everyone present, Steve preferred large parties. He liked to be the first to arrive and the last to leave, whereas she would prefer to put in a quick appearance or decline the invitation altogether. Whenever the issue came up, each felt the other was just being difficult.

When Kristen attended an MBTI® workshop through her employer and brought the workbook home to show Steve, it was like a lightbulb went on. Suddenly they realized they had simply been seeing the situation through their unique filters. Once they had a model to understand why they each liked doing things in a specific way, they were able to respect the other person's way of seeing the world and come up with compromises that better suited both their personalities. Although Kristen was never going to be the life of the party, she would understand Steve's need to interact with lots of other people and try not to feel as if this was taking something away from her. And Steve would find ways to satisfy his social appetite by going out with his friends, allowing Kristen quiet time alone at home to recharge her batteries. Amazingly, they learned that their differences with regard to how they liked to spend their time actually complemented each other perfectly.

MBTI® PREFERENCES*

EXTROVERSION ←————————→ INTROVERSION

What Gives Energy to You or Takes Energy Away from You

Extroverts are energized by their interactions with others. They prefer working collaboratively on projects and charge their batteries through leisure activities that include many other people.

Introverts are energized by the opportunity for quiet concentration. They work well independently and prefer to charge their batteries alone or with just one or two other people present.

SENSING ←————————→ INTUITION

What You Like to Pay Attention To

Sensors like to pay attention to what is real, concrete, and tangible. If they can see, hear, smell, touch, or taste it they are more likely to pay attention to it. They value data, facts, and figures. Their motto is often "If it ain't broke don't fix it."

Intuitors prefer to pay attention to ideas, concepts, and theories. They like to see the connections between things. They often live in a world of what could be, rather than what is and seek new and better ways of doing things.

THINKING ←————————→ FEELING

How You Make Decisions

Thinkers make decisions based on logic and fact. Data fuels their decision-making process. It is important to them to be fair and just in their decision making rather than rely on personal values.

Feelers take into account how their decisions will impact others. Their decision-making process often factors in their values and "hunches." It is more important that others see them as compassionate than fair.

JUDGING ←————————→ PERCEIVING

How You Like to Live Your Life

Judgers like to live their lives in an orderly, planned fashion. They like to plan their work and work their plans. They like to put closure on things rather quickly, then move on to the next thing on the list.

Perceivers like considering all of their options and weighing them carefully before taking action. They believe by waiting, more information or insights will come to them that enable them to make better decisions. They are spontaneous.

*Source: Modified and reproduced by special permission of the publisher, CPP, Inc., Mountain View, California 94043, from the *Introduction to Type*, 6th ed., booklet by Isabel Briggs Myers, as revised by Linda K. Kirby and Katharine D. Myers. Copyright 1998 by CPP, Inc. All rights reserved. Further reproduction is prohibited without the publisher's written consent.

MAKE IT WORK FOR YOU

- **Learn more about the MBTI® and preferences.** You can start by going to the website www.keirsey.com and clicking on the tab to take the KTS-II at no cost. Although David Keirsey uses different language to describe types and preferences than those described on the chart just presented, his personality instrument will illuminate a lot about yourself and those around you. To take an actual MBTI® inventory, you must do so through a licensed provider. If you are employed, ask your human resources department for help locating one. The book, *Please Understand Me* by David Keirsey and Marilyn Bates, also contains valuable information to help you understand your own preferences and filters as well as those of others.

- **Honor your preferences.** Perhaps you've always been "different" from the other members of your family or circle of friends. They enjoy rowdy get-togethers and you prefer quiet one-on-one encounters. Or they're always trying to drag you to a nightclub when you'd prefer to be curled up by a fire reading a good book. As a result, you might think there's something "wrong" with you. Often you might even go along with the program so as not to disappoint others, but wind up feeling uncomfortable or out of place. Well, there isn't anything wrong with you, and there's no reason for you to keep doing things you don't enjoy simply to please the group. Knowing your preferences will help you to stand by your decisions for all the right reasons. It may even help you find a whole new circle of people who see the world through a similar filter, and whose company you enjoy more.

- **Honor the preferences of your children.** Children gain self-confidence by being allowed to pursue the activities that best suit their preferences, not the preferences of their parents. If you were a soccer star in college but your child clearly prefers tennis, don't push it. Forcing your own preferences on her will only saddle her with the kinds of messages and expectations you're trying to overcome by reading this book. We heartily recommend reading

Nurture by Nature: How to Raise Happy, Healthy, Responsible Children Through the Insights of Personality Type by Paul Tieger and Barbara Barron-Tieger. It will help you identify your children's preferences and teach you ways to interact with them to promote self-esteem.

- **Use different preferences to your advantage.** If it drives you nuts that your husband can't buy a car without researching every model available, whereas you quickly know what you want and are ready to buy first time out the door, think about how each of your preferences might lead to a better buying decision in the long run. For example, being aware of your insistence on getting the car during those "end-of-year clearances" might just prompt him to get his research done a little earlier than he might otherwise. The result: a carefully chosen car, for a lower price.

STEP ON THE CRACKS

We all know people who are superstitious. Some have lucky numbers; others believe they'll have seven years of bad luck if they break a mirror; still others refuse to walk under ladders, open umbrellas indoors, or step on a crack in the sidewalk (surely you've heard the dire prediction "step on a crack, break your mother's back"). In psychology, the term *superstitious behavior* refers to acting in certain ways because we believe to do otherwise will cause some kind of catastrophe. Going by this definition, we can also recognize less common superstitions that are unique to each of us because they stem from our upbringing and experiences. For example, if when you became angry as a child you were punished and told that boys don't like girls who are angry, chances are you've internalized the notion that if you yell at your spouse, your entire relationship will fall apart. Or, if you were good in sports but were teased about being a tomboy, you might have stopped playing sports forever because you believed no one would ever date you. These would be superstitions. The cause and effect *seem* logical based on the messages you received, but in reality they aren't connected.

Superstitious behaviors like knocking on wood, avoiding the path of a black cat, or carrying a rabbit's foot are usually pretty harmless. It becomes detrimental, however, when, as in the two examples above, they have a negative impact on your decisions, self-perceptions, and actions. In other words, when they turn you into a nice girl. For example, if you superstitiously believe that anytime you voice anger it will be met with disapproval, you'll always be missing an emotion critical to success in relationships. Or if you superstitiously believe that you must always poll people before making a decision, then you'll never learn how to weigh your needs in decision making and come to your own conclusion.

Our very scientific answer to this dilemma is to encourage you to step on the cracks! We *know* it won't break your mother's back. As

Eleanor Roosevelt has said, "We gain courage and confidence from doing the things we think we cannot do." Facing your superstitious beliefs or fears requires you to think rationally, not emotionally, about the behaviors you've been avoiding, and more often than not, you'll realize there was nothing to be afraid of. Psychologist Albert Ellis developed a program called Rational Emotive Behavior Therapy to help people do just this. Here are the ABC's of the process:

A = Activating event: Identify what triggers your fear of acting in a way other than that which would bring you more satisfaction. For example, "Whenever I think about speaking before a group, my heart starts racing, my palms get sweaty, and I begin to perspire."

B = Irrational belief: What is the irrational belief that causes you to become anxious? Using the same example, you may think, "I believe I will become tongue-tied and nothing will come out of my mouth."

C = Consequences: What happens when you have this irrational belief? Perhaps in this instance it would be "I avoid speaking before groups of any size at all costs."

D = Dispute the irrational belief: Ask yourself questions such as "Why wouldn't I be able to speak?" or "Has there *ever* been a time when I was speaking and nothing came out of my mouth? Something *always* comes out of my mouth!"

E = Effective new thinking: Substitute something rational in place of the irrational belief. "If I prepare and practice, there's no reason why speaking before a group will present a problem. I may not like it, but I can make it work."

MAKE IT WORK FOR YOU

- **Identify your unique superstitious behaviors and thoughts.** What are the beliefs that keep you from moving confidently toward your goals? Write them down so that you can actually see them, rather than have them waft through your head. Making them tangible is a first step toward conquering them.

- **Give yourself permission to step on the cracks.** Nice girls can spend their entire lives waiting for someone in "authority" (a parent, sibling, spouse, etc.) to give them permission to act in ways other than how they were taught or expected to act. If you're reading this book, you're an adult woman who has the right to make choices about how she will behave. The only one who can give you permission to confront your fears and superstitious beliefs is you. *Give it.*

- **Have a sense of humor.** The ability to laugh at ourselves and our foibles is part of what makes us uniquely human. Sometimes lightening up and poking fun at our own idiosyncrasies is the best way to overcome the superstitious behaviors holding us emotionally hostage. And really, when you think about it, the idea that stepping on a crack will break anyone's back *is* kind of funny.

- **Employ rational thinking.** Use Ellis's model or your own rational self-talk to move away from irrational beliefs toward more functional, rational ones that work for you rather than against you. If necessary, use a friend as a sounding board to help you identify logical alternatives to your superstitions. Remember, *we can't see what we can't see!*

ASSESS THE MESSENGER

Nice girls can be naïve. Trusting that others always have their best interests at heart, they absorb negative feedback like a sponge. Nice girls don't stop to ask themselves whether the person offering it may have a hidden agenda. Or, for that matter, whether he or she has the credentials or expertise to provide useful evaluative information.

While the word *feedback* has its origins in the 1920s in the field of electrical engineering, today the word is used as a metaphor for providing evaluation, either positive or negative. But when people skip the positive feedback (which is unfortunate, because positive feedback reinforces effective behaviors) to get right to the negative part, that's a red flag. Be alert when those who "only want to help" critique your haircut, your friends, your parenting skills, or your work performance—pointing out what you should do instead of simply criticizing whatever it is you are doing now.

In other words, feedback is subjective—it's an opinion! And, although soliciting developmental feedback and acting on it is indeed critical for personal growth, you shouldn't accept and act on feedback offered without first viewing it through a lens of healthy skepticism.

MAKE IT WORK FOR YOU

- **Consider the circumstances.** Have you invited the feedback? If so, then the person offering it is responding to your request, and the motives are transparent. On the other hand, if someone offers unsolicited feedback, think about what might be beneath the surface. If it comes from your boss as part of your performance evaluation, then clearly there's no mystery. But if negative feedback about your presentation skills is offered by a colleague just before you are scheduled to give an update at the department meeting, it may be that he's trying to unnerve you. And, when feedback of any kind is served up at a holiday dinner paired with wine, be very dubious.

- **Think about the delivery.** Did the person send the feedback via e-mail or text or was it delivered by phone or face-to-face? How did the words strike you? Was the tone respectful? Was your privacy respected? Were specific examples provided of the behavior the person suggested that you change?

- **Determine whether there's a pattern.** Is the person supplying the feedback intent on furnishing it to you alone or does he spread the wealth around? Does he or she consistently share insights about things you should change when certain other people are present?

- **Respect credentials.** Does the person providing the feedback have relevant expertise or experience? If she's recommending that you redecorate your home, is her style consistent with yours? If he's suggesting your business isn't being run well, does his consistently deliver profits?

- **Trust your instincts.** Sometimes the feedback you receive just doesn't "feel" right. In this case, thank the person for the input, think about it, and decide later whether or not it has merit.

BE CLEAR ABOUT WHAT YOU WANT

Nice girls often fail to realize that they've got to know what they want to what they want. Focused on making other people happy at their own expense, they've lost track of what will satisfy *their* interests and needs. Corrie, for example, was working on a project as part of a dysfunctional team. The team leader was in over his head, wasn't pulling his weight, and, as if that wasn't enough, treated people badly. Corrie had a strong relationship with the team leader's manager, Bob, and initiated a conversation to discuss the situation, but nothing changed. Why? Because she wasn't clear about what she wanted Bob to do about it. Reassign her to a different project? Speak to the team leader on her behalf? Corrie provided Bob lots of details about what was going wrong, but because she wasn't clear about what she wanted, he did nothing more than listen empathetically.

In any given situation, identifying a SMART outcome that will satisfy your interests is the first step to take. Borrowed from the business world and adapted for our use, SMART outcomes are

Specific: "I want a better relationship with my father" may be the goal, but it's fuzzy and amorphous. Instead, be more specific about what you want, such as "I want to meet with or talk with my father once a week without having an argument."

Measurable: You won't be able to tell if you were successful if you can't measure the outcomes. That's why specificity is so important. If you set a specific goal, it will be easy to see how you're doing. In this case, it's easy to determine whether or not you've had the weekly, argument-free conversation with your father—and the decrease in your stress level will be another sign of success!

Appropriate: The outcomes you seek should also be in line with your values. If a strong relationship with your father is important to you, then this goal of having an argument-free conversation with him once a week is appropriate. On the other hand, if you set this goal because your father is on death's door and you want to ensure you inherit your fair share of his estate, it would fail the test.

Realistic: If the outcome you seek is in your control or is in some other way doable, then it meets the "realistic" hurdle. For example, if you are committed to avoiding an argument with your father by actively changing the subject whenever something likely to cause conflict comes up, and he's willing to cooperate, then your desired outcome is realistic. If, however, he insists on picking a fight anyway, no matter how badly you try to avoid it, your desired outcome isn't going to happen.

Timelined: Think about how long it might take to get the outcome you want. It's useful to know in advance that it may take three or four conversations with your father before you have one that's argument free. Putting a time frame around your goal will also infuse it with a greater sense of urgency.

Other Situations Where a SMART Approach Might Be Helpful	
Situation	**Possible SMART Outcome**
Your husband doesn't like your best friend.	You agree to disagree about her and acknowledge that you will spend time with her that doesn't involve him.
The insurance company has denied a claim you have submitted.	Because you want to appeal the claim decision, you need to understand the process and to get the required forms.
The night you spent in the hotel was miserable because the guests across the hall were having a loud party. You called to complain but the noise continued.	You want a partial refund or an extra award of points to compensate for your sleepless night.

MAKE IT WORK FOR YOU

- **Use the SMART approach to craft your desired outcome.** It's easy to remember and covers all the bases. Write down the five elements on a small card and keep it handy for reference.

- **Ask around.** If you're having trouble determining the specific outcome that will meet your needs, do some research about what others have asked for in a similar situation. You don't always have to reinvent the wheel.

- **Talk with the decision maker.** You'll never get what you want if you don't ask the person who has the authority to give it to you. Ask yourself, "Can the person I'm dealing with satisfy what I need?" If not, then find the person who can. Nice girls often fail to take a request to the top because they're afraid they'll be insulting the person they originally asked by going over his or her head. Get over that one—quickly.

PARLAY YOUR NICHE OF EXPERTISE

Consider these two women: Hope is a child whisperer. From the time she was old enough to babysit, she was terrific with kids. So, when she was ready to pick a career, teaching was the obvious choice. Linda's organizational skills are her forte. So when she decided to work at home for a few years while her children were young, she parlayed the skills she'd honed as a project manager to start a "virtual assistant" business. Now she works hours that are convenient for her, keeps up with the work world, and makes money all at the same time.

Knowing what you are good at in your professional life and parlaying that into your personal life—and vice versa—can work wonders. Consider Emma's dilemma. Newly married, she desperately *wanted* to have a good relationship with Joanne, her mother-in-law, but was finding it difficult to even *like* the woman. In fact, Emma found herself dreading spending any more time with her than absolutely necessary. Sure, Joanne was both well-meaning and smart, but she was also high-strung and dramatic. Joanne needed to be the center of attention and tried to dominate every conversation. She also had a terribly annoying (to Emma) habit of cradling Emma's face in her hands. Other than rolling his eyes behind his mother's back, Emma's husband wasn't much help. So Emma, knowing she'd been very successful in coaching people in her office, decided to try to gently "coach" her mother-in-law, by reinforcing the things she did like about Joanne, and discouraging the things she didn't. For example, since she liked that Joanne was well-read, she suggested books they could read and movies they could attend and then discuss together. And when Joanne lapsed into her annoying habit of trying to dominate the conversation, Emma would gently coax the conversation back, just as she often did when the colleagues she coached got off track. Although Joanne will never be someone Emma would choose to have in her life, Emma was pleased that she had adapted her skills to get what she wanted—a comfortable relationship that didn't drive her too crazy.

Whether you are a CEO, a stay-at-home mom, an entrepreneur, or anyone in between, knowing what you do well builds confidence. And confidence is one more factor that distinguishes winning women from nice girls.

MAKE IT WORK FOR YOU

- **Think about what you *like* to do.** Chances are good that if you like to do something, you're good at it. We naturally put more time and energy into things we enjoy—and that pays dividends in terms of getting the outcomes we most want.

- **Recall compliments you've received.** What things do others say you do well? If you can't remember, ask people whom you trust.

- **Keep a success log.** Note not only your areas of strength but specific examples of your success. If you receive a performance evaluation at work, the log will be invaluable because you'll be able to weave your accomplishments into your self-evaluation, whether written or during a conversation with your boss. And, on a personal level, if you ever need a boost, it'll be there for you.

- **Get creative.** Think about any other realms or situations where your expertise might be useful, and brainstorm ways to apply them. You may well find that the very same skill that landed you your last promotion could be the key to solving that personal problem that's been hanging over your head, and vice versa!

CLOSE YOUR ACTUAL GAPS

Nice girls often work too hard to close the gaps *other* people think they have. They diet obsessively in response to friends who keep making comments about their weight. They try to climb the corporate ladder because their husbands think they should, even though they know they don't want the corner office. They expend hours boiling and mashing vegetables for the baby because their meddlesome mothers-in-law aren't shy about insisting that their grandchildren deserve nothing less. But when you spend so much time and energy trying to close gaps that *others* think you should, you'll have little time or energy to close the gaps you yourself find are holding you back.

In short, if *you* don't think its broken, don't try to fix it. If, for example, you are happily single, then there's no reason to join Match .com, no matter how many times your mother suggests it. But if *you'd* prefer to marry, then you've got to put yourself out there.

Jen's math was so poor (the technical term for it is *innumeracy*), she felt overwhelmed with the money matters in her life. She always let someone else take care of checking the bill at the restaurant and calculating the tip because she didn't trust herself to do it correctly. Her husband paid all the bills, managed their investments, and did the taxes. This gap in her abilities bothered her, so she went back to basics, and relearned and practiced simple math. Identifying the gap *she* wanted to close empowered Jen to participate in her finances. That's what closing your gaps is all about—not allowing *perceived* deficits or challenges to get in the way of overcoming actual ones.

MAKE IT WORK FOR YOU

- **Know what you don't know.** If you want to be more socially confident, you may need to know more about the rules of etiquette. If you want to know more about saving for retirement, you may need to learn more about how your 401(k) plan works. There's no shame in acknowledging your gaps—only in not addressing them.

- **Exercise the muscle.** Sometimes a gap is a skill that can only get stronger with practice. For example, if you are less assertive than you'd like to be, practice speaking up at meetings. If you struggle with writing, start by putting words on the page—you can always go back and edit.

AIM FOR THE FAR CORNER

Have you heard the Laurel Thatcher Ulrich quote: "Well-behaved women seldom make history?" You don't have to want to find the cure for cancer or be the first woman president to appreciate the message. Nice girls live their lives in a narrowly defined space—a space usually outlined by others. Their fear of displeasing those around them prevents them not only from aiming outside those lines, but from even getting *near* the lines. Better to play it safe, they reason, than risk going out of bounds.

Think about any sport. Are games won by playing squarely in the middle of the playing field? Nope. They're won at the *edge*. Take tennis, for example. If you continually hit the ball smack dab in the middle of your opponent's court, you won't win many points. It's too easy for your opponent to return the ball. But when you hit the ball to the edge of the far corner, the shot has a better chance of being a winner.

Of course, the risk of aiming for the corner is that if you miss, and hit the ball out, you'll *lose* the point. Are you willing to take that risk for the sake of possibly winning the point, game, or match? Is your forehand good enough that you're likely to keep the ball in bounds? Are

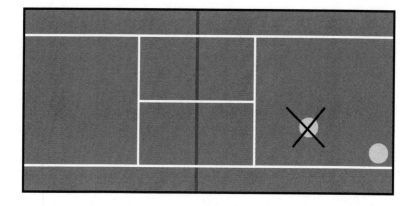

you far enough ahead in the game to lose one point and still not lose the match? These are the kinds of questions you should ask yourself when deciding whether to aim for the far corner in life, as well. More often than not, it'll be worth the risk. The following are some tips for translating these questions into ways to do more of what *you* want, and less of what *others* expect of you.

MAKE IT WORK FOR YOU

- **Determine the level of risk for going out of bounds.** It's not hard to determine whether something is a winning shot or a foolish risk. Do you know what the consequences will be if you miss? The payoff if you nail it? The likelihood your gambit will work? If the payoff is bigger than the consequences and the probability of success is decent, go for it.

- **Develop the skills needed to make the shot.** If you don't have the skills needed to hit that far left-hand corner, start by aiming a little closer to center court. Then once you've mastered those shots, start aiming farther and wider.

TAKE IT ONE DAY AT A TIME

Stephanie, who was on a limited budget, didn't eat out very often. When she did, she was always reluctant to send a meal back if it wasn't prepared the way she had ordered it. But then Stephanie decided that if she could eat out only once a month, she deserved to have her meal served as she wanted. So the next time the situation arose, she politely described the problem to the waiter and sent the meal back. It may seem like a small thing, but it made Stephanie feel much more in control of and better about herself—and in turn gave her the confidence to be more assertive in other areas of her life.

The point is, while you might want to be more assertive in a number of areas of your life, don't try to work on everything at the same time. Pick one or two smaller areas and address them first. A change doesn't have to be dramatic to move you closer to your goal.

Take Melanie. She had noticed her husband never agreed to anything he didn't want to do, but that she, like many nice girls, said yes to almost everything. Determined to stop, Melanie started by practicing saying no just in situations she considered "low risk"—for example, when asked by the cashier at the supermarket to make a charitable donation to a cause she didn't want to support. Although at first she still had trouble declining when asked for a favor by a friend or family member, her practice eventually paid off. Melanie transformed herself from the "yes-girl" to a winning woman who was able to say no without damaging relationships.

Finally, whether the change you want to make is big or small, it still takes dedication and discipline. Hang in there—winning the life you want is a journey, but it's worth it.

MAKE IT WORK FOR YOU

- **Accept that old habits die hard.** It's been widely reported that it takes at least thirty consecutive days to break a habit. Be kind to yourself. Be patient with yourself. If you slip, start again, *without* negative self-talk.

- **Be your own coach.** Be conscious about what you are doing each day to move you closer to making the change you want. Take note of situations where you falter today so that you can better anticipate where you might have trouble tomorrow and plan accordingly. When things don't go according to your game plan, make adjustments and get back on the field.

- **Count every success.** Stop to celebrate what you've accomplished as you accomplish it. Melanie made it a point at first to reward herself every time she delayed saying yes, even if she eventually capitulated. This is more than just a "feel-good" strategy. Focusing on success breeds future success, particularly when long-term change is the goal.

BUILD RELATIONSHIPS THAT WORK FOR YOU

THE TACTICS IN STRATEGY II FOCUS ON

- Determining the circumstances under which and with whom you need to build relationships.

- Balancing your needs with the needs of others.

- Acknowledging the ebb and flow of relationships and the importance of reciprocity in lasting relationships.

*I*f you remember one lesson from this strategy, let it be this one: when you need a relationship, it's too late to build it. *This is why part of every single day should be spent building strong relationships—with neighbors, your child's teachers, colleagues, family members, friends, and even random people you meet along the path of life whom you think you might never meet again. That way, the relationships will already be in place when you need them. The story of how this book came to be published is a wonderful case in point.*

We receive many soon-to-be-published books in the form of ARCs (advance reading copies), which editors and authors send to us hoping for a cover quote to promote the book. Even if we're not major fans of a book, we try hard to find something legitimately good about each one and respond with a positive endorsement. Yes, it takes time to read the books and write the quotes, but we know how much we appreciate it when others do the same for our books, and we know that responding in kind is the right thing to do.

Talia Krohn and Roger Scholl at Random House have sent ARCs to Lois for a number of years, although until recently they had never spoken by phone or met in person. So when our literary agent sent them a proposal for a book we envisioned, they immediately read it and, although it wasn't exactly a book they wanted to publish, they took the time to think about how the concept could be improved. Eventually, they asked if we would consider writing another in the Nice Girls *series. After a number of e-mails, meetings, and phone calls,* Nice Girls Just Don't Get It *was born. And it happened precisely because of the relationship of mutual respect and candor we'd all built through past dealings. In short, an intermittent e-mail relationship ended up resulting in a book deal that would turn out to be beneficial to all involved.*

Some people are easy to build relationships with, whereas others make it more difficult. As you'll learn in this section, relationships take all forms, and all are valuable in different ways. You don't have to be best friends with someone from whom you purchase a car once every few years, but even these interactions can be characterized as relationships and are worth investing with a certain amount of time and effort. But as you'll read in this section, not all relationships are created equal. Nice girls want everyone to like them, so they treat every relationship with equal gravity. Winning women differentiate among various kinds of relationships, determine what's needed in each, and make the appropriate amount of effort to ensure that every relationship works in their favor. This strategy will show you how.

RECOGNIZE THAT NOT ALL RELATIONSHIPS ARE CREATED EQUAL

Nice girls are often plagued by an inordinate need to be liked. As a result, they mistakenly believe they need to devote equal time and energy to *everyone* with whom they come in contact. They spend as much time chatting with the sales clerk at the department store as they do with their next-door neighbors. Or they go as far out of their way to do a favor for a coworker they barely know as they would for a close friend or family member. Although all relationships are important and need to be carefully tended, to be a winning woman you also need to be able to tell the difference between a personal relationship and a transactional one.

Let's say you're going to make a major purchase—like a car. It's pricey enough to warrant investing time to prepare for the interaction, so you do research online. Once you decide which vehicle is the best choice and learn the price range, you head to the nearest car dealer who sells the make you want. Before you step into the showroom and begin the interaction with the salesperson, ask yourself: "What is my ideal outcome from this interaction?"

While you should certainly be polite, your goal should not be to forge a close friendship with the car salesperson. He doesn't have to like you. You're not going to invite him for Thanksgiving dinner. You simply want him to sell you a good car at a fair price. You are realistic enough to know the extent of your relationship—he is there to sell cars and you are there to buy one. This is what's known as a transactional situation.

If you are clear about the fact that the relationship is transactional, you will

- Be better prepared to enter into the inevitable price conversation.

- Not be pressured to make a decision before you are ready to do so.

- Be able to walk away if you don't get a good price.

Once you know what you're looking for, it's easy to recognize transactional situations and respond accordingly. Other examples might include an encounter with a store associate who won't give you the refund you deserve. Because this is a transactional situation, you won't have any hesitation about calmly asking to speak with the department manager to get the outcome you want. Or, in another situation, if it becomes clear to you that you know more about solving your computer problem than the tech support person on the other end of the line, you'll save time by quickly requesting that your case be escalated to a higher level. Finally, if you are dealing with a customer who's loudly demanding something she is not entitled to, you politely stand firm.

In short, you'll be much more likely to get what you want if you're not working overtime to build a relationship where one might not be appropriate or necessary, simply because you want to be liked.

But there are other situations where having a personal relationship *is* more useful in getting you what you want. Take, for example, your child's teacher. She doesn't have to become your best friend, but it's helpful to cultivate a relationship with her—by making small talk when you come to pick up your child, or volunteering to chaperone class trips—even if it's only until June rolls around. Why? Because being on her good side is likely to make things easier for your child. Of course, in some cases you may not be able to accept a particular teacher, and in Strategy III: Manage Expectations we'll talk about how to handle similar situations. Another example of someone with whom having a personal relationship, even a shallow one, can be beneficial, is the receptionist at the dentist's or doctor's office. If she's the gatekeeper who can make it either easy or difficult to get an appointment time that works for you, it's smart to invest in the relationship, even if it's just with a warm smile and a few questions about her weekend. Again, this isn't about being liked. It's about investing in a relationship that has value to you.

MAKE IT WORK FOR YOU

- **Differentiate transactional and personal relationships.** Only nice girls try to invest equally in every relationship with everyone and anyone. Assessing the significance, anticipated term, appropriate depth, and goals of your interactions with someone should inform how much you invest in the relationship.

- **The shorter the time frame of the transaction, the less important it is to build a relationship.** You never want to be rude or discourteous, but if the interaction is brief (e.g., buying a scarf on a street corner in Manhattan), a huge investment of time isn't only unnecessary, it could work to your disadvantage if it makes you seem like a pushover who can be taken advantage of. The question to ask here is "How likely is it that I will ever see this person again?" Conversely, the more likely it is that you will have continued dealings with this person, the more appropriate it is to invest time and energy in building a relationship. These typically include people we work with, people who provide us with services (e.g., doctors, mechanics, our children's teachers), and, of course, friends and family.

- **The more it matters, the more you should invest.** This seems obvious, but you'd be surprised how many nice girls forget this. Think about it this way. No matter how attractive that scarf you see on the street corner, your life will go on as usual if your attempt to bargain it down to $5 doesn't work out. On the other end of the spectrum, without family and friends, we would probably be miserable. These are the relationships that warrant a greater investment of time and attention.

CHOOSE YOUR INNER CIRCLE
WISELY AND WELL

When you think about how to win at life, the close relationships you keep may be the most critical factor. Although we don't get to choose some of the relationships in our lives—parents, siblings, and coworkers, for example—we do have choices about many other affiliations in our adult lives.

Most important are romantic partners and friends, but anyone in your life who has the power to cause you joy or suffering—your boss, your babysitter, your business partner—is someone you should select carefully. And don't trick yourself into thinking that they'll change after you get involved with them. That's a nice girl belief, and it's false. The potential boss who keeps you waiting forty-five minutes for an interview and doesn't have the courtesy to offer an apology or an explanation probably won't give you the respect you deserve once you accept the job. The landlord who has a reputation for avoiding responsibility to tenants almost certainly won't see the light when it comes to fixing *your* heat. Chances are the married man who tells you that his loveless marriage is merely a convenience won't leave his wife for you and, even if he does, what makes you think he won't be telling the same story about *you* to another woman in the future?

Winning women pay careful attention to character. But how can you assess character? By observing behaviors. If he says he'll call, does he? Is she habitually late to meet you even after you've told her it makes you angry? How do you feel about his friends (birds of a feather really *do* flock together)? How does she treat the bellman, waitress, and office custodians? Does he return the grocery cart to the right place in the parking lot when he's finished with it or let it roll into someone else's car? Does she brag about taking short cuts on her taxes? These are all observable measures of character. As the cliché goes, it doesn't take much to talk the talk; the people you allow into your life must walk the walk.

Indrah is the perfect example of a twenty-something woman who hasn't yet learned the art of choosing her inner circle wisely and well. She's a beautiful, energetic, and intelligent woman who has no problem attracting men. Her problem is letting go of the ones who are just plain jerks. Despite the fact that a man she was seeing texted her and suggested they meet at a certain place for drinks, then didn't show up, she gave the guy more chances—and sure enough, he did it again! He didn't respect her time, and yet she allowed him to remain in her life.

And now a word about the relationships in your life that you *didn't* have the opportunity to choose—like in-laws or neighbors. If they become too toxic, you may have to make the painful choice to sever them. Nice girls remain trapped in abusive or disrespectful relationships far too long, whereas winning women realize they have other options.

MAKE IT WORK FOR YOU

- **Do some scouting.** The Internet offers a wealth of information about pretty much anyone. Use it! If you are considering letting someone into your inner circle—whether it's a new man you're deciding whether to keep dating, a colleague you're considering asking to join your team at work, or a new doctor or therapist you may want to visit—start by Googling them. But don't stop there—use your personal network to learn as much more as you can.

- **Pay attention to red flags.** Even a hint of something illegal or immoral should send you running in the opposite direction. Likewise for violent behavior or substance abuse. Flashes of anger, aloofness, or unwillingness to discuss troublesome issues don't bode well either for healthy long-term relationships.

- **Be skeptical of too-fast friends.** It's easy to be so flattered by the attention proffered that you throw caution to the wind. If someone wants too much too soon, proceed carefully.

- **Don't settle for "except for's."** We often hear women say, "This guy is perfect except for _____" (fill in the blank with any red flag). She then goes on to say how she knows that with her love and support, he'll change. Right. If you believe that, you're setting yourself up for heartache and failure. A leopard never changes his spots.

- **Pay attention to your own "hooks."** For example, if you need to be needed, you're going to find a lot of needy people in your life. If you're forever saving people, you'll be taking care of a lot of losers. Make sure you understand *why* you choose as you do and why you tolerate relationships from which you should run the other way.

LOVE THE ONE YOU'RE WITH

Look, life can be unfair. As we've already said, we don't always get to choose the people we have to deal with on a daily or weekly or yearly basis. Nice girls, faced with this reality, passively accept it. They don't realize that although they may be stuck in a relationship they didn't willingly choose, that doesn't mean they have to sublimate their interests and needs.

Take, for example, the teacher who isn't a good fit for your child. She isn't abusive but she intimidates your child to the point that he doesn't want to go to school. You've spoken with the principal and learned that the school's policy is to deny reassignment to another teacher in these circumstances. So what can you do? You could appeal the policy, but that will take time. You could move your child to a different school, but that would undoubtedly cause a great deal of disruption in his life and doesn't guarantee that he will click with the new teacher either. You could home-school your child—but you realize that as much as you love your child, you also value your own sanity. Or you could work to create a relationship with the teacher that's "good enough" to get your child through the school year. In short, you can decide to love the one you're with.

We often find ourselves in similar situations where the options for dealing with those people with whom we'd rather not have a relationship are either limited or unattractive. It might be that you inherited a roommate you never would have chosen, yet the apartment is conveniently located, the rent is reasonable, and moving would be time-consuming. Or you might work for a boss who's difficult, yet the job pays well, the benefits are good, and you're learning new skills. Or you may be married to someone with whom you're no longer in love, but don't want to divorce for any number of legitimate reasons.

That was Jill's case. She and Dan had never been madly in love, but were content in their marriage. Once they had children, though, they seemed to drift further and further apart until no real relationship remained. Jill decided, though, that she had no desire to divorce Dan, for several reasons. Jill, a product of divorce herself, wanted her children to have an "intact" family. Plus, both she and Dan were mild-mannered people who rarely argued, so there was no daily rancor or drama. And she knew the financial reality—even if the costs of divorce are contained, each party's standard of living is likely to decrease postdivorce. From Jill's point of view, the situation she was in was preferable to the alternative. So what did she do? She didn't just sit back and wallow in self-pity. That would have been the nice girl move. She made the best of it. Jill stopped expecting romance from Dan and settled for friendship instead. She and Dan made joint decisions about their children and their money but kept one another emotionally at arm's length.

When their alternatives aren't good, winning women make the situation in which they choose to remain work. The fact is, not making a choice *is* a choice. And a perfectly okay one, if made for the right reasons. That said, if you elect to maintain a less than ideal relationship for any reason, then you have the responsibility to make peace with it.

MAKE IT WORK FOR YOU

- **Know what your alternatives are.** Before you decide you have to make lemonade out of lemons, do some brainstorming. Ask yourself, "What else might I do about this?" In some situations, you have to know what your rights are—knowledge gives you power. Then eliminate the impractical options or choices less desirable than the status quo.

- **Accept that you've got lemons.** Once you've made a decision to stick with things as they are, get over the fact that the situation isn't ideal. Few are.

- **Make the lemonade.** Winning women don't just make the best of an imperfect relationship, they find a way to motivate the other person to do so as well. For example, while it may seem that the teacher holds all the cards, she probably would prefer that you not visit with the principal to express your concerns, so letting her know that's a possibility could go a long way in getting her to clean up her act. Or because the roommate you're not crazy about may need your portion of the rent to afford the apartment, she may be willing to stop leaving her clothes all over the living room.

- **Reconsider now and again.** Life is dynamic. Periodically reconsider your alternatives to determine whether anything has changed. If your roommate starts dating a guy you like even less than you like her and he begins to spend a lot of time at your apartment, plan B might suddenly become the more attractive choice. Or if you win the lottery, you can put your child in the most exclusive private school in your neighborhood. Then again, if your choices remain the same after reconsidering your options, learn to love the one you're stuck with.

HATE THE SIN BUT LOVE THE SINNER

We *strongly* believe that there is *never* a need to treat anyone with disdain, disrespect, or derision. Regardless of how poorly *you* are treated, responding in kind only brings you down to the ill-mannered person's level. With that said, we also know how hard it is to take the high road all of the time. Sometimes you just want to get in the last "F_ _ _ you!" for your own peace of mind. And don't think there haven't been times when we've stooped to it (we never claimed to be saints). But each and every time we've taken the high road and given the person the benefit of the doubt for having a bad day or just being ill-prepared to handle a confrontation the way we might like, we haven't regretted it. We can't say the same of situations where we let our tempers get the better of us and treated someone less than respectfully.

Unconditional positive regard is a term coined by psychologist Carl Rogers that refers to unfailing respect for other human beings despite how hard they make it for you or how they treat you. Another way to think of it is the old maxim Hate the sin but love the sinner. The importance of exhibiting unconditional positive regard in every relationship, no matter what, can't be overestimated. This doesn't mean to say you should accept inappropriate behavior or have to make everyone with whom you come in contact your best friend, even if they treat you badly. To the contrary. That's what nice girls would do. It means that you treat others with respect no matter what they say or do. This isn't just about taking the moral high ground (though it is that, too); it's also the best way to ensure that others come to trust you and ultimately show respect in return. Surely you've been verbally abused by someone who later became contrite or apologetic when he or she realized you weren't going to engage in a spitting match. Or perhaps someone to whom you showed respect even though he treated you poorly later came around to your side or defended you when you least expected it.

As simple as it may sound, loving the sinner is hard to do. On the surface it may look like this is what nice girls do, but in fact they respond to being treated disrespectfully in one of several unhealthy ways:

- **Passive-aggressive behavior:** This is when they smile to the person's face but talk about them behind their back, or agree to do something but then don't follow through. Nice girls revert to this behavior when they feel powerless and don't want to take the risk of saying what they really think. It's an indirect way to get what you want or "get back" at someone.

- **Withholding behavior:** This is when they intentionally don't give the person the response, information, love, or attention they need. This is yet another way to avoid having a difficult conversation. At first blush it appears nonconfrontational, but it causes rifts in relationships because it places an unspoken elephant in the middle of the room—that elephant being what's really bugging the nice girl.

- **Passive behavior:** This is when they do nothing, causing them ultimately to be depressed or feel unworthy of getting the things they most want.

To see what a vicious cycle these responses create, consider the woman whose sister-in-law alternates between disparaging her (or her children) in front of other family members and completely ignoring her. In turn, the woman withholds attention and ignores her sister-in-law at family gatherings—which only serves to escalate her sister-in-law's behavior. The tension has caused problems in her marriage, as her husband simply wants her to get along with his sister. Or consider the woman who works for an abusive boss who seems to relish publicly embarrassing her. Her response is often passive-aggressive—to agree to do something, then conveniently forget to do it. As a result, she gets passed over for a promotion. In both situations, nice girls lose. Consider adding the following skills to your repertoire to increase the likelihood of showing unconditional positive regard in any situation.

MAKE IT WORK FOR YOU

- **Consider the circumstances.** People often treat others badly when they're under stress or anxious. When you're not treated respectfully, ask yourself if these factors may be at play. If the answer is yes, knowing so may help you respond to them with more positive regard.

- **Rinse and repeat.** This is another time when a mantra might come in handy. One such as "I am a loving and kind human being who treats others with respect" might work for you. If you say this over and over, the impulse to lash out may fade.

- **Disengage momentarily.** Lois often tells the story of a time when she had contractors remodeling her house. One of the workmen in particular made her crazy with his inability to remember what was agreed upon in previous discussions (if you've ever had work done on your home, you'll be able to relate to this). One day, this man told her what they were going to do that day—something that was the opposite of what they had already discussed. She felt herself about to explode and become verbally abusive until she said, "Please excuse me for a moment." She used the time to collect herself, and that helped her go back and engage with him in a more civil manner.

ASSUME GOOD INTENTIONS

Too often we ascribe negative intentions that aren't really there, or make up negative stories to explain why someone behaves in a certain way. This happens particularly when we lack information to the contrary. For example, suppose a neighbor doesn't reply to your shout-out "Good morning." Without knowing why he ignored you, you assume the worst and think he's being standoffish or just plain rude, when in reality he just didn't hear you. The next time you see him, you ignore him in return. Pretty soon a neighborhood feud ensues for no good reason. Or perhaps someone cuts in front of you in line at the grocery checkout counter. Assuming negative intentions, you say in a stage whisper, "I guess some people think they're too good to wait in line." In both of these examples, you work yourself into a bad mood that colors the rest of your interactions throughout the day—and it does nothing to change or improve the situation. Often it makes the situation worse.

Communications expert Dr. Lisa Schenk provides insight into why we often assume bad intentions rather than good ones in a monthly coaching tip newsletter distributed by Corporate Coaching International:

> Individuals will tend to blame situational or external variables when they have done something wrong and personality traits or internal variables when someone else does. For example, if I cut someone off on the freeway, I see it through the lens of my experience. I just looked down at my phone for one second, I was about to miss my turnoff and had to get home in time to get my son to his tap lesson. However, if someone cuts me off, they are rude, aggressive, even narcissistic—bad people. We understand our own motives to be honorable and justify our behaviors

in that way. When we see bad behavior in others, however, we attribute it to their lack of character.

But what would happen if you said to yourself, "Maybe my neighbor didn't hear me"? Or might you feel better about yourself if you assumed the person who cut ahead of you was preoccupied and didn't see you, so instead of the stage whisper, you tapped her on the shoulder and said, "Excuse me, I think you didn't realize I was next." By assuming good intentions rather than bad ones, we can avoid unnecessarily damaging relationships or escalating situations. Perhaps you're thinking, *but sometimes people really are rude and don't deserve my goodwill.* It's true that others don't act with the best of intentions all of the time, but until you know that for a fact, it does no good to think otherwise.

Judy was developing a new friendship with Cara, who had children close in age to Judy's own. They also shared a love of gardening, reading, and the theater. Judy looked forward to deepening their friendship. But whenever Judy called her, even though she made sure to do so midmorning, when she knew Cara's children were at school and she wouldn't be disrupting their morning routine, Cara always cut their conversations short. Nice girl Judy assumed Cara didn't like her and couldn't wait to get off the phone. Then one day Cara mentioned a class she was taking at the local community college. Judy asked her about the class and when it was held. As it turns out, the class started at noon three days a week. Cara hadn't been avoiding Judy at all. She simply had to leave the house in time to get to campus.

In the best of all worlds, Cara would have told Judy this was why she had to get off the phone, but for some reason she didn't. Without information to the contrary, Judy assumed Cara simply didn't want to talk to her. You can see how this negative assumption could have created quite a rift in the blossoming friendship, when in fact the real reason was benign. It's just one more reason why assuming good intentions is so important to maintaining healthy relationships.

MAKE IT WORK FOR YOU

- **Gather information before jumping to conclusions.** Nice girls can be hesitant to ask what's really going on for fear of appearing too pushy or intrusive. Instead, they assume that something is wrong with *them* or that *they've* done something wrong. Building strong relationships at times requires asking why someone has behaved in a certain way. It can be as simple as saying, "When you passed me in the hallway this morning you weren't your usual friendly self. Is everything okay?"

- **Assume responsibility for your part in misunderstandings.** Without assuming total blame, it's easy to shoulder some of the responsibility when relationships aren't going in the direction you might like. Perhaps a good friend hasn't returned your calls. Rather than write her off, you can always leave a message or send an e-mail to the effect, "I'm wondering if I've done something to offend you? I haven't heard back from you and I'd hate to think I've in some way damaged our relationship." This gives the other person permission to tell you if you *have* done something wrong or to let you know she's just been busy and hasn't had a minute to call you. If the other person chooses not to take the olive branch you extend, at least you know you've done what you can to get to the bottom of the matter.

- **Don't let them off the hook.** Assuming good intentions doesn't mean you have to be a doormat. If someone overcharges you for a service they've provided, for example, you can assume the worst— that they're trying to swindle you. Or you can say, "Surely there's been some misunderstanding. We originally discussed this costing $100 and I've been billed $150. What accounts for the difference?" Setting a positive tone will likely result in a better outcome than putting the other person on the defensive.

- **View others as complex, multidimensional human beings.** We often don't know what's going on in someone's life, or how their past experiences color their behaviors. People are products of their upbringing, life situations, and a whole host of other factors that cause them to act in particular ways. You don't even have to know the specifics of these things to make a conscious decision to cut others slack. Giving the benefit of the doubt costs you nothing and is more likely to contribute to healthy and productive relationships.

BE FULLY PRESENT IN EACH MOMENT

Author Anne Morrow Lindberg once said, "If you surrender completely to the moments as they pass, you live more richly those moments." Building rewarding, mutually beneficial relationships requires surrendering yourself, momentarily, to the person you are with. Yet living in an age where we are constantly bombarded with information, expectations, and demands on our attention, being fully present in each moment is easier said than done.

How many times has your child tried to get your attention only to find you're distracted by the many chores you've yet to do after a long day at work? Or how many times has a friend needed an ear when you had so much on your plate that you couldn't really listen in a way that would provide comfort to her? In our information-saturated, busy world, we think that multitasking is the answer to getting the most out of the time available to us, but in reality it only makes us less effective, and worse, it hinders our ability to build meaningful relationships.

Sarah wondered why she couldn't get her colleagues to cooperate on an important project. As hard as she tried, her coworkers stalled, reneged on their promises, and in some cases even sabotaged her efforts. During her performance review, her boss praised her for her dedication and hard work, but made it clear that others didn't enjoy working with her. It came as quite a shock to her that they perceived her as self-involved and aloof—she was so distracted thinking about her work, she was never fully there. She thought she was friendly enough, but believed the company paid her well to do a job and *that* was her first priority. She didn't realize that she couldn't be effective in her work without taking the time to build relationships.

As Sarah learned through coaching, being fully present in each moment doesn't have to take a lot of time, nor does it have to detract from the task at hand. It simply requires the willingness to make people a priority. Stopping by someone's office to ask how a sick child is doing—and really listening to the answer—is being fully present in the moment. Turning away from the computer to fully answer a child's question rather than giving her a one-word answer as you continue pounding away at your keyboard is being fully present in the moment. And taking a few minutes to attend someone's birthday celebration, rather than work through it, is being fully present in the moment, too. We're not talking about hours each week, we're talking about minutes—and if you don't have time to spare those minutes, you'll never be able to build relationships that make it easier for you to achieve your goals.

MAKE IT WORK FOR YOU

- **Use self-talk to switch gears.** When interrupted, consciously say to yourself, "There is nothing more important than that I be fully present in this moment." It will act as a segue between "doing" and "being" that will eventually become second nature.

- **Practice meditation.** You can't meditate and be thinking about a thousand different things. Meditation can help you to find that centered place inside yourself that allows you to surrender to the moment. It allows you to build your attention muscle. If you've never done it before, take a workshop or join a meditation group to learn the art of being fully present in the moment.

- **Stop being a human "doing."** If it seems as if you have more to do in a day than there are hours, then it's time to recalibrate. You are not a human doing, you are a human being. Filling up your hours with things to do prevents you from interacting with others in ways that help you get the most out of relationships. Identify one or two things you can either remove from the list or postpone until later to free you up to spend those few extra minutes with the people who are most important to your success in life.

- **Hear meta-messages.** Part of being fully present is taking a moment to consider what the other person is saying they need or want from you. Interactions escalate into confrontations when one or both parties aren't hearing the meta-messages being conveyed—those things that are felt or implied, but not expressed. You won't hear those things if you don't surrender to the moment.

- **Let others know when you can't be fully present.** There are times when we just can't stop what we're doing to give other people the attention they deserve. Rather than have someone walk away feeling misunderstood or underappreciated, let him or her know that now is not a good time but that their needs are important to you and you want to give them your full attention. Suggest another time (within hours, not days) to get together and follow up as promised.

ALLOW OTHERS TO SAVE FACE

Getting what you want in long-term relationships means being "nice" enough to let others save face. Tempting as it might be to remind your colleague that you predicted that the client would be displeased with the project time line, it will only make your colleague feel even worse than she already does. Believe us, she won't thank you by supporting *you* the next time you need her help. Pointing out that you were right and the other person was wrong, even when it is the indisputable truth and even if you are doing it with the best of intentions, won't help the relationship.

When backed into a corner, most people get defensive and angry. Worried about protecting their egos, they stick to their positions. If challenged, clinging to what's left of their diminished dignity, they start to figure out ways they can save face and be "right" again. That's what Heidi found when her daughter refused to break up with the guy she'd been dating despite solid evidence that he'd been seeing someone else. Heidi had never been shy about her suspicions about him, and now she realized her daughter's behavior may have been, at least in part, in response to Heidi's lack of self-control. The more Heidi discussed his flaws, the more her daughter defended him. So staying with him was, in large part, an attempt to prove that her mother hadn't been right about him. Of course, this decision hurt Heidi's daughter, and it hurt the mother-daughter relationship—all of which could have been avoided if Heidi had bitten her tongue and allowed her daughter to save some face.

But allowing others to save face doesn't have to mean biting your tongue. It can also mean graciously accepting a sincere apology and letting the other person explain why he did or didn't act differently. When Tonya came down with a serious case of the flu, not only did her boyfriend not offer to help her, he told her he wouldn't come to see her until she was better. When Tonya recovered, her boyfriend apologized for abandoning her, explaining he'd been afraid he'd catch the flu from her, and he couldn't afford to take time off from work for illness. Tonya had every right to stay angry, but instead she was gracious enough to accept his apology and even went the extra step to say she completely understood and probably would have done the same thing if she had been in his place.

Winning women are smart not to "rub it in." This isn't about being nice; they garner respect because even though the exchange is all very tacit, others know the winning woman took the high ground and let them off the hook.

Make It Work for You

- **Resist the temptation of "I told you so."** Sure, that retort can be tempting, but consider how your relationship with the other person will be affected. It's likely he or she will begin to resent you and, like Heidi's daughter, continue the unwanted behavior just to prove a point.

- **Don't confuse allowing others to save face with giving in on things that are important to you.** They're not the same. If, for example, your partner said something hurtful to a friend of yours, you would probably want to have a conversation with him about it. Your concern about her feelings trumps the risk of hurting his. On the other hand, if his eighty-five-year-old mother keeps calling you by the wrong name, you would most likely choose to let it go.

- **Too much face-saving can signal a problem.** That said, if you find yourself constantly allowing someone to save face, it could be a sign of a bigger problem, and it might be time to speak up—for his or her sake. If your brother routinely has too much to drink and insults your husband at family gatherings, for example, he may have more than a need to save face—he may have a drinking problem. He might initially resent you for confronting him, but if he gets help he'll ultimately realize that you were the only one brave enough to speak up, and respect you for it.

GO OUTSIDE YOUR RELATIONSHIP
COMFORT ZONE

At a very young age, girls build relationships by focusing on what they have in common with others. Unlike boys, who are less discriminating about whom they allow to join their social circle, girls have often formed cliques by the time they reach high school. Boys may be bullies on the schoolyard, but girls use far more insidious weapons—psychological ones—to demean and exclude those they don't deem worthy of their friendship. It's part of what's become known as the "mean girls" phenomenon.

Often, these same behaviors carry over into adulthood, though hopefully to a lesser extreme. But most of us still tend to immediately gravitate toward those who remind us of ourselves—people who typically share our values, beliefs, or interests. It's easy to build relationships with them because they are so much like us. Then there are those people in whom we see no redeeming qualities, most often because they are so dissimilar to us. They're the people we wouldn't cross the street to spit on if they were on fire. And that's a mistake.

But this isn't just about needing to be liked by everyone, or making the girl from the unpopular clique feel included. When we surround ourselves only with people who are closely aligned to our own viewpoints and values, we miss out on valuable opportunities to see the world from different perspectives. As a result, our worlds become artificially narrowed, lacking in the diversity we need to make informed decisions, the talent to complement our own, and the connections to achieve our personal and professional goals. Winning women know not to judge a book by its cover, and cast their nets widely when it comes to bringing others into their circles.

Lois tells the story of flying back from Denver one Friday night nearly thirty years ago when an impeccably groomed and distinguished-looking older woman took the seat next to her. Tired from a long day of work, Lois thought to herself, *This woman looks like she hasn't worked a day in her life. I hope she doesn't expect me to spend the entire trip chatting with her*. With that, Lois immersed herself in a book and didn't look up until the plane landed. When she closed her book, the woman looked over and remarked that she noticed Lois was using her ARCO business card as a bookmark. Lois nodded and the woman said, "What a small world. My husband is the president of ARCO. He'll be meeting me at the gate."

It was, as Carol often says, a V-8® moment (which you'll learn about in Tactic 66). Prematurely judging this woman prevented Lois from interacting with someone who not only seemed quite pleasant, but who also could have made an introduction that could have helped her career. It was an important lesson for Lois and a mistake she didn't make twice.

MAKE IT WORK FOR YOU

- **Suspend judgment when meeting new people.** Making quick judgments without information is never a good idea, but is particularly unwise when meeting people who may not look or sound like you. If something strikes you as off-putting about a person, see this not as an excuse to shut them out, but as a sign that you need to learn more.

- **Don't dismiss the "lunatics."** Let's say you're in a Neighborhood Watch meeting and one of the members, whom you don't know, makes a suggestion that is so far off the wall that it causes others to groan and roll their eyes. You think it's pretty far out too and are tempted to write him off as a lunatic. Rather than remain comfortably ensconced in groupthink, however, you probe more deeply as to why he made the suggestion and what he thinks it might accomplish. It could be that his unique experiences hold the key to an idea that isn't so crazy after all.

- **Exercise your tolerance muscle.** So your husband's best buddy isn't someone you would normally choose to have in your inner circle.

Sure, he has a good heart, he's good to your kids, and he and your husband go way back—but he just doesn't know when to stop talking! Even though he can suck all the air out of a room, the good outweighs the bad. In this case, do as our friend and colleague Dr. Pam Erhardt often suggests: "Build a bridge and get over it." Find ways to connect that let you maintain your boundaries while at the same time exhibit respect for his unique way of being in the world.

UNDERSTAND THE QUID PRO QUO

Inherent in every relationship, whether it's a marriage, a friendship, or a professional partnership, is a quid pro quo, which translates from Latin as *what for what* or *something for something*. This legal term refers to the concept of getting something of value in return for giving something of value. We don't just mean money. It also includes things like attention, affection, time, or favors. As we use the term here, it simply means the natural reciprocity that develops within relationships of all kinds.

When Sasha and Andrew fell in love, became engaged, and dreamed about having a houseful of children, it was never a question that Sasha would be the one to stay home to raise them. They both came from large families with stay-at-home moms and breadwinning dads, so it was a familiar and comfortable lifestyle they envisioned. Ahhh . . . a marriage seemingly made in heaven. Now, fast-forward five years to the day Sasha and Andrew learn they're going to have their first child. They are overjoyed by the good news, but Sasha has been keeping a secret: after being in the workforce for seven years, she's not so sure she wants to be that stay-at-home mom they discussed all those years ago.

From speaking with close friends who left their careers after having children, she'd learned that most of them felt marginalized, out of the loop, and, in some cases, depressed. As much as they loved their children, they longed for what their professions provided them. Not wanting to fall into the same trap, Sasha realized she wanted to be a mom *and* maintain her career. She was about to renege on the quid pro quo to which she and Andrew had agreed before they were married—that once children were born, he would continue working and she would stay home to raise the children. This change in the quid pro quo created a period of tension in the marriage because Andrew felt he wasn't getting what he "bought into" when he married Sasha. Tension, disappointment, anger, or disillusionment are typical feelings when the quid pro quo is altered by one party in a relationship.

An easy-to-understand quid pro quo is the relationship your have with your employer—your efforts in the workplace are rewarded by a paycheck every two weeks. In other relationships, the quid pro quo is more complex, subtle, and prone to misunderstandings—like the one between Sasha and Andrew. He believed that in exchange for being the breadwinner, Sasha would stay home with the kids. But once those kids rolled around, her expectations were different.

Nice girls often find this overt give-and-take distasteful, but winning women put the quid pro quo on the table unself-consciously. A client of Lois's recently called to ask if she would do a keynote address for free. This client works for a big company with plenty of money, but getting Lois to speak to their employees at no charge would make the woman look good to her superiors and further her career—something Lois was well aware of. During the discussion, Lois said in a lighthearted yet pointed manner that she would waive her usual speaking fee if the woman would remember the favor when Lois needed one in return.

If you don't understand the quid pro quo associated with each of your relationships, then you're just setting yourself up for the implicit or explicit exchange to go awry.

Make It Work for You

- **Identify the exchange rate in each of your relationships.** Take a moment now to think about the most important people in your life. What do they get from *you*? What do you get from *them*? Is the exchange equitable? If you feel as if you're giving more than you're getting, then you're being swindled. And if you're receiving more than you're giving, it will eventually breed tension and resentment, possibly damaging a relationship you value.

- **Uncover the implicit quid pro quo.** Perhaps you have a girlfriend whose tab you always pick up for dinner because she's unemployed.

You expect that, in return, she will go out of her way to do you certain favors. But when you call her to ask if she could sit with your kids one evening, she tells you she's too busy, and you begin to harbor ill feelings toward her. Instead of being selfish, she may simply have had a different understanding of the implicit quid pro quo of the relationship. We'll provide you with tips for how to address these kinds of sticky issues in a productive way a bit later. For now, just keep in mind that a misunderstood or unacknowledged quid pro quo can be the source of tension in *any* relationship.

• **State the quid pro quo aloud.** Don't be afraid to say, flat out, what you have to give and what you expect to get.

GIVE MORE THAN YOU GET

After reading Tactic 23, you may have gotten the impression that the goal in relationships is to strive for equal reciprocity at all times. In reality, that's simply not possible. You don't want to be the proverbial giving tree (from the classic Shel Silverstein story), but winning women know that the more you give, the more you get. Maybe not right away, and maybe not from the same source to which you gave, but in the end generosity of spirit always wins out. We've experienced this time and again in our own lives, and others have told us the same holds true for them.

Our friend Eleanor is someone who gives so much you'd think she was a saint—but she'd be the first to tell you she's far from it. She sits on numerous boards, mentors young people, donates both time and money to causes she believes in, and tithes generously at her church. But if you ask her, she would tell you that each time she gives, she ultimately receives more in return. Sometimes it's in the form of a raise she didn't expect, or an offer of help when she needs it most, or an unanticipated gift. Eleanor knows this is the way the world works. You don't build valuable relationships with a closed fist or heart.

Here are a few other examples of people who know the art of giving more than they get and, as a result, enjoy rich relationships:

- Jeremy is a professor at the Drucker School of Business in Claremont, California. His students love him because he's always willing to take time to speak with them about projects they're working on or problems they're encountering. When Jeremy learned he had to have a kidney transplant, no one in his family was willing to donate a kidney to him. Then one day he learned that twenty of his students had gone for testing to see if one of them might be a suitable donor. It turned out one was, and she donated a kidney to Jeremy.

- Winona worked for a large corporation as a strategic planner for one of the business units. A colleague in another unit struggled with her strategic plans each year. Expecting nothing in return, Winona helped her to craft top-notch documents for several years. When Winona left the company to start her own consulting practice, she was discouraged by her lack of progress in attracting clients. Then, out of the blue, the woman Winona had helped called to let her know that a friend of hers at a major manufacturing firm was looking for a consultant and she arranged a meeting. Winona got not only that client, but many more in years to come through this grateful ex-colleague.

- Greta was the kind of neighbor who would always help out in a pinch. She cooked dinner for people who had a family member in the hospital, babysat for children when parents had to work late, and even shoveled snow from the front paths of elderly neighbors. When Greta's husband was laid off from his job in the automotive industry and couldn't find work, they were at risk of losing their home. That's when a cashier's check in the amount of $5,000 arrived in the mail. To this day they don't know who sent it, but clearly someone in the universe had smiled kindly on Greta's generosity.

Winning women don't give more than they get with the expectation of getting anything in return. They do it because they know that giving is the foundation upon which strong relationships are built. The mistake nice girls make is giving for the wrong reasons—because they're scared to say no, they want to be liked, or they feel guilt. Giving for these reasons and allowing others to take advantage of you only depletes your resources and ultimately makes you resentful. We'll talk about how winning women prevent that from happening in Strategy III: Manage Expectations.

MAKE IT WORK FOR YOU

- **Go out of your way.** We're all busy and have limited time and energy. Yet, if you want to build relationships that are mutually rewarding, taking the time to go out of your way pays huge dividends when you least expect it, but most need it.

- **Focus on quality, not quantity.** Giving more than you get doesn't have to take a lot of time or cost significant amounts of money. Instead, make what you do count by giving to those people or causes most important to you.

- **Don't be afraid to ask how you can help.** Too often, when we see someone struggling, we avoid offering help because we're afraid the person will be too embarrassed or proud to accept our assistance. Even if the person declines your offer, he or she will remember your kindness.

- **Collect more reciprocal chips than you cash in.** When you go out of your way for someone, you collect a reciprocal chip—it's like accumulating equity. You want your goodwill account to be overflowing with chips so that when you need a favor, you can cash in.

INCUR INCONSEQUENTIAL COSTS

In an ongoing relationship, each party accumulates equity. *Winning women* not only leverage that equity to get what they want (more on that a little later), they also know others have earned equity as well and cut them slack whenever possible. Consider these examples:

- Allison's husband had a bad habit of "correcting" her whenever she told a story at dinner with friends. If Allison said the incident happened on Tuesday, Dennis would interrupt to recall it had really happened on Wednesday. While the details weren't a big deal, Allison felt that he was undermining her, and they argued about it many times. Then, Allison realized that Dennis's intention was only to set the record straight and thought about how many good qualities he had. Suddenly she didn't mind his interruptions as much. So she decided to let the "correction" stand the next time he did it. It didn't really cost her much to do it, and it built up goodwill in the marriage that benefited them both.

- Donna was on a road trip with a friend to a city she'd visited before. But her friend, who was driving, had not, and so she relied on her GPS, which guided her on a circuitous route, taking them an hour out of their way. Donna considered the costs inconsequential when she stepped back rather than insist her friend was taking the longer route. The extra hour on the road was not a big deal to Donna, so she let it go.

- Carey had a coworker who habitually arrived ten to fifteen minutes late for work. As a result, Carey had to cover her phones during that period. As annoying as this was, the coworker was a delight to work with in all other ways. She was the first to offer help when Carey was swamped, she supported Carey's ideas in meetings, and she would cover for Carey when Carey had to leave early to attend to a sick child. In the scheme of things, the cost of answering the phones was minimal, since the coworker more than made up for it in other ways.

Winning women make conscious choices about what certain sacrifices in life are worth. If the cost is minimal and the payoff is big, that's generally what we'd call a smart investment.

Make It Work for You

- **Drawing on accumulated equity is not the same as asking for a favor.** Drawing on accumulated equity means trading on a relationship when you have been giving more than you've been getting. There is a legitimate expectation that you deserve to get something in return. A favor, on the other hand, is something someone does for you out of sheer goodwill. If you ask for a favor, you must be emotionally prepared to deal with a refusal. If, however, your request for something is declined, even after you've invested in the relationship, this may indicate a fissure in the relationship.

- **Don't bounce a check.** If you make a withdrawal from an account with insufficient funds, you'll incur fees and, if the amount is large enough, the bank may even close your account. The analogy works here too—expecting too much or expecting it too soon will damage the relationship.

- **When you decide to cut someone slack, consider the advantage of telling them.** Sometimes it's useful to tell the person that you've decided to let something go and why—otherwise, they might not even notice, and you've lost an opportunity to build equity. For example, Allison explained her rationale to her husband because she wanted to let him know she appreciated the other things about their relationship enough to let this go. He, in turn, was grateful, and that gratitude was equity she could draw on later.

BE GRACIOUS

If you ask us, graciousness is what's missing from most relationships, of all kinds. For example, Caroline wonders why she can't get the co-operation she needs from the other members of a nonprofit board that she chairs. There's no doubt that she's committed to the cause and puts in more than her fair share of time. But when she asks for volunteers to work with her, hands don't exactly go flying up in the air.

If you watched Caroline in a meeting, you'd know why. She's opinionated, curt, and at times downright rude. When another board member makes a suggestion with which she disagrees she doesn't hesitate to say, "That's a stupid idea because . . ." And when she hosts a fund-raising event, she neglects to give credit to the others who have also contributed to making it happen. Caroline winds up working twice as hard as she should because people don't want to fall victim to her sharp tongue and lack of diplomacy.

Graciousness is one of those things that's hard to describe but you know when you see it, and Caroline's behavior certainly doesn't qualify. The term derives from the word *grace*, which, by one definition, is an "unmerited favor." A tired commuter relinquishing her seat to an older person, a coworker who refuses to assign blame for a mistake, and a man allowing a woman with a sleepy child to go ahead of him in the grocery line so she can get the child home for a nap are all demonstrating simple acts of graciousness.

Graciousness isn't exactly the same as going out of your way. It's more about thoughtfulness than about action. For example, Desiree found herself in an uncomfortable situation at a gathering of friends at lunch. One friend, a women who was formerly obese but had recently lost quite a bit of weight, turned to Desiree and said, "I have a closet full of clothes that don't fit me any longer. Would you like them?" Desiree, who was not much larger than this woman at the moment, was insulted and embarrassed and wanted to reply, "I would never fit into your old clothes—they'd be *way* too big for me!" But she didn't. Instead, she smiled and said, "Let me think about it." And with that the conversation continued and a scene was averted. That was gracious.

If Desiree had been a nice girl she might have felt compelled to say yes because the woman had made the offer. But at the same time, she felt humiliated by the assumption that these large clothes were actually her size. Giving up self-respect is more than what graciousness requires. And, of course, Desiree could later have spoken with the woman privately about how the remark made her feel, and it still wouldn't have detracted from her act of graciousness.

Graciousness takes many forms, including giving credit where it's due, resisting the urge to call public attention to someone's shortcomings, expressing yourself diplomatically, and sometimes just holding your tongue until there's a more appropriate time to voice your opinion. Being gracious costs you nothing but boosts your self-esteem and helps build relationships. After all, who *doesn't* want to be in a relationship with someone gracious?

MAKE IT WORK FOR YOU

- **Don't sweat the small stuff.** Your sister-in-law makes a sarcastic remark about your cooking abilities (or lack thereof) at a Christmas dinner you've worked hard to prepare. You *want* to retort that she's no Julia Child either, but instead you make the self-effacing comment, "I may be a slow learner, but I am learning!" That's gracious. Making a scene would only ruin the dinner for everyone. Plus, you know in your heart of hearts you've actually done a pretty good job.

- **Be tough on problems, gentle on people.** As this Japanese saying suggests, it's fine to aggressively attack mistakes and how they were made, but pointing fingers only causes unnecessary embarrassment and damage to relationships. Next time your husband forgets to pick up the bread and milk on the way home from work, try saying, "I guess you had a busy day. Is there something I can do to help you remember in the future?" That's gracious. Becoming angry or demeaning him for once again forgetting to stop at the market won't put the groceries on the table.

- *Never* **publicly humiliate someone.** We can't think of one instance when public humiliation is appropriate. A private discussion where you air your concerns may be called for (and we'll soon tell you how to have a productive one of those), but humiliating or embarrassing another person isn't. Once, during a meeting, June was blamed for something she knew someone else in the room had actually done. She listened quietly, without accepting the blame or pointing the finger at the person who was actually at fault. That was gracious. Immediately after the meeting, she went to the other person and told him that she didn't appreciate him throwing her under the bus. Although he didn't apologize, you can be certain it didn't happen again.

- **Don't stoop.** There are those people in our lives who are best described as bulls in a china shop. They lack self-awareness or self-discipline and, as a result, are basically incapable of anything that resembles graciousness. When you try to go toe-to-toe with them, you rarely win and wind up stooping to their level. Winning women are gracious even in the face of not-so-gracious behavior.

SEEK TO UNDERSTAND WHAT'S BEHIND THE NEEDS

As we pointed out in Tactic 23 (Understand the Quid Pro Quo), each person must get his or her needs met to some degree or the relationship will flounder. But how do you meet your needs and those of others when they are seemingly irreconcilable? Well, you must first understand *why* people need what they say they need before you can work together to meet their needs. A story (which first appeared in Robert House's *Experiments in Management and Organizational Behavior*) illustrates this concept:

> Two sisters were baking their signature desserts on the eve of a holiday for the celebratory family dinner. It was late in the evening when they realized that each of them needed an orange for her recipe but there was only one orange in the pantry. Of course, all the stores were closed. The older sister said she should get the orange because her fruitcake was the family favorite. Naturally, the younger sister disagreed; she believed everyone enjoyed her orange chiffon cake more than they did the fruitcake.

Even if they had been wise enough to stay away from the issue of whose dessert the family liked more (*that* argument never ends well), each sister still stuck to her position that she needed the orange. What could they do? In an attempt to keep peace and to resolve the issue fairly, they could have decided to split the orange in half—but that wouldn't solve the real problem because each of their recipes called for a full orange.

But these sisters were winning women, determined to both deliver dessert and remain on speaking terms. So instead, they asked each other questions to get to the reason behind the position each had taken—that *she* needed the orange. As it turned out, the older sister needed only the rind for her fruitcake and the younger sister only the juice for her cake. A lucky coincidence, but still, it was only by asking questions that they were able to learn that neither sister actually needed to take the entire orange. The result? A win-win solution.

Lauren used this same principle after waiting five years for her boyfriend to finally pop the question. Her patience running thin, she probed about his reluctance to get married despite his declarations that he couldn't imagine life without her. She learned that he, a product of divorce and someone who worked hard to accumulate his money, was worried that if things didn't work out, she'd end up with half his assets. Now that she understood the reasons behind his position and still wanted to marry him, she offered to sign a prenuptial agreement.

Less life altering but similar was the situation Ashley and her roommate faced. They'd agreed to get a pet, but couldn't agree on what kind. Ashley wanted a dog; her roommate wanted a fish. This argument could have gone on forever, but after some discussion, it became clear that her roommate's primary concern was that the pet not demand a lot of work because she didn't have time to devote to it. Ashley's interest was to have a pet she could cuddle up with after a long day. Their solution was to get both and each would care for the pet she had selected.

MAKE IT WORK FOR YOU

- **Share your interests.** Don't stubbornly stake out a position and don't assume the other person can read your mind. Talk about not only what you want, but also why you want it.

- **Ask about what's important.** Don't assume you know what's on other people's minds, either. Encourage them to explain their thinking to get behind their positions.

- **Create solutions together.** When people commit to honoring each other's needs, relationships thrive. Don't take on the responsibility to solve the problem alone. When you take it upon yourself to solve a problem, it becomes *your* solution, and the other person doesn't have as much investment in making it work.

'FESS UP

Beth and Amy were cochairing the Kindergarten Workshop for the PTA. Designed to offer a preview for incoming students and their parents, it was a high-profile event in the local community. It was also a big job with lots of details to keep track of and a tight time line. To accommodate the printer's schedule, they approved the "Save the Date" postcard describing the event without getting input from the rest of the committee or from the school principal. Of course, there was an error on the card. Annoyed that people seemed to be blaming them even though they were working so hard, Beth and Amy tried to sidestep their mistake and didn't apologize. Even though the event went off without any more glitches, Beth and Amy weren't asked to cochair it the following year, and this incident was likely why.

Being able to admit your mistakes is important in any relationship, and even more so when it comes to family, friends, and partners. Remember that line from the movie *Love Story*: "Love means never having to say you're sorry"? Well, it's just not true. Strong and lasting relationships require honesty and trust to thrive, and part of that means being able to admit when you've been wrong.

Consider Nora and Margo. Their long friendship came dangerously close to imploding because Margo couldn't admit that she'd been envious of Nora's career success. When she finally realized she'd let her jealousy affect their friendship, Margo had the courage to admit it to Nora, who forgave her. Had she failed to apologize, it would've always come between them.

Nice girls sometimes 'fess up to their transgressions, too. What distinguishes winning women from nice girls, however, is that the former know how to admit their mistakes gracefully *without undermining themselves*. They understand that admitting a mistake doesn't require losing self-respect or groveling. Merely stating that they've made an error and regret it is sufficient.

MAKE IT WORK FOR YOU

- **Don't delay.** Admit your mistakes as soon as you know you've made them. The longer you wait, the harder it will be. And not just to adults, either. If you're a parent, be certain to admit your mistakes to your children as well. It's an excellent way to teach your children to admit theirs.

- **Don't over- or under-do it.** The kind of mistake you made and the impact it had on the other person should dictate the type or form of apology you offer. For example, if your mistake was to disappoint a colleague by producing work late, say, "I missed the deadline. I know that put you in a difficult position and I'm sorry. Here's what I propose we do now. . . ." Or, if you lost your temper at work, "I overreacted and I regret it" will probably suffice. On the other hand, if you've made a *big* mistake that caused the other person harm, great inconvenience, or heartache, your apology should probably take the form of a longer conversation or conversations in which you convey that you understand how serious the situation is and that you sincerely want to make amends.

- **Don't just talk the talk.** Sincerity matters a lot when admitting a mistake. Be certain that your tone and body language convey that you mean it. For example, if you say, "I'm sorry," but don't look the other person in the eye while you say it, the apology won't come across as authentic.

IF THREE PEOPLE SAY YOU'RE DRUNK, LIE DOWN

Margaret was beginning to wonder why friends had stopped returning her calls, and why she seemed to always be the one extending invitations to go out to dinner or a movie. Finally, one friend did return her call, but not to accept her request to get together. Instead, the courageous friend told Margaret honestly what it was about her behavior that people found off-putting and unpleasant to be around. Apparently, Margaret was prone to taking over conversations, showed little or no interest in what others had to say, and was quick to gossip about other so-called friends.

As difficult as this was to hear, it forced Margaret to think back to recent interactions with some of her other friends who didn't return her calls. She recalled one of them jokingly saying that Margaret "took up all the air in the room" and another responding to a comment Margaret had made about a mutual friend by saying she didn't really want to gossip about other people. At the time, Margaret had thought these were small things, certainly not enough to damage her relationships. Yet, now that three friends had made these kinds of comments, she realized that perhaps she should have taken them more to heart.

Hearing what others don't like about us can be painful, but it's a necessary evil for building those winning woman relationships that will work for you. You'll recall in Tactic 6 (Beware of Your Achilles' Heel), where we explained the Johari window model for understanding behavior, that the only way to get rid of those blind spots that prevent us from maintaining strong relationships is to get feedback. At this point you might be thinking, why should I care what others think of me? Isn't that a nice girl mistake? Well, no, because the fact is, perception is reality. It's fine to ignore the occasional one-off comment that doesn't really fit, but when you hear the same thing from a number of sources, it's time to pay attention. In other words, *when three people say you're drunk, lie down.*

MAKE IT WORK FOR YOU

- **Observe body language.** People give us messages about their perceptions of us all the time, and not all of them are spoken. Winning women are wise enough to pay attention to *and* inquire about nonverbal clues that suggest what others really think. For example, if several people roll their eyes when you start talking about your child for the umpteenth time during a conversation, you *could* just ignore it, but it would be smarter to take the cue that you're being annoying, and move on to a topic of mutual interest. Similarly, if you're at a party and one person after another continually excuses him- or herself because they've just spotted someone they want to speak with, read this as a message that either your antiperspirant wore off or there's something wrong with your conversational abilities!

- **Don't just ask for feedback, probe it.** We've already talked about the importance of asking for feedback if you want to prevent your Achilles' heel from getting in the way of achieving your goals. Well, when it comes to relationships, you need even more information. When Margaret was told she "takes up all the air in the room," a good response would have been, "Can you help me to understand how I do that?" Avoid asking, "Like how?" or "When did I ever do that?" These questions usually elicit defensiveness rather than promote understanding.

- **Turn the camera on yourself.** Once you're given feedback, the next step is to become self-aware about when and why you in engage in particular behaviors. Imagine you are watching a videotape of yourself going through your daily activities. Can you catch yourself interrupting others? Do you see how you use too many words when fewer would communicate your message just fine? Only after you experience yourself as others experience you can you develop a plan to change.

- **Let them be critics.** Let's face it, most people like to criticize. This is one time you should let them. Let people close to you know that you're trying to make a change, and that when you slip up, you'd love to know about it. Imagine how delighted your husband would be if you said something like "I realize I bombard you with questions and information the minute you walk in the door and that annoys you. I'm trying to find a better time for us to talk about our day. It would help if you would let me know when I'm falling back into old habits so that I stay on track."

TRUST YOUR GUT

Some nice girls have ignored their instincts for so long that they barely even know what they sound like anymore. Others may still be in touch with their instincts, but have so little confidence that they second-guess themselves to the degree that they ignore their better judgment. Take the situation where, despite concerns about being able to work for a boss who demonstrates during the interview process that she'll likely be a micromanager (and you can't stand micromanagers), you take the job anyway. It's a good job and pays fairly well. How would you explain turning it down? Or, if instead of listening to that voice in the back of your head that tells you that your romantic partner is *never* going to take your opinions into account, you keep wishing and hoping that he'll change. Have enough faith in yourself to listen to that voice.

Many of the decisions we face in relationships have no "right" answer—only an answer that is the right answer for us. While you certainly do want to gather as much information as you can, rarely does this provide all the pieces of the puzzle. When you are trying to decide whether you should enter into a relationship, stay in one, or determine what you have to do to salvage one that is going south, you have to trust your gut.

When Kris found incontrovertible evidence that her husband was having an affair, she was devastated. She confronted him, he admitted it, and they separated. But she still loved him and wanted him back. Despite the fact that some of her friends expressed skepticism and others, outright opposition, Kris's instincts told her he could change, and she proceeded to woo him carefully. Eventually she welcomed him home, with the promise that he'd attend marriage counseling with her to help heal the relationship. It's been three years now and although Kris will never forget the pain she suffered, she and her husband are happy.

How did Kris turn such a troubled situation into a "happily ever after"? She was self-aware enough to know that despite what had happened, she still wanted to stay married to him. She believed in her gut that he really loved her and wouldn't stray again (even though he was behaving as if he were temporarily insane). She did seek advice from a lawyer to protect her financial interests and from her very close friends to gain their insights. But in the end, she followed her instinct and got what she wanted. Although the right decision for another woman in a similar situation may have been very different, it was the right one for Kris.

When we ignore our gut feelings about relationships there is no upside, only two possible downsides. One is that we deprive ourselves of wonderful opportunities. The other is that we ignore the red flags warning us that danger lies ahead. Lost opportunities can mean, for example, that we lose in love. Often, nice girls ignore their feelings for someone who isn't considered "right" for them—maybe he's the wrong height, religion, or socioeconomic group—because they live by "the rules." Carol's father, for example, once told her, "People in our family only marry other Irish Catholics." Good thing she wasn't a nice girl and didn't listen, because Carol has been blissfully married to her husband, not an Irish Catholic, for thirty-three years! Women who win at life weigh the facts; seek insights from their families, friends, and advisors; but in the end, follow their hearts.

Nice girls can also overlook business or career breaks when they downplay their instincts. Let's say you meet a potential client or mentor, for example, and feel a connection but fail to follow up because you don't trust your instinct that the other person will be receptive. Even worse than missing an opportunity is the risk a nice girl takes when she disregards alarm bells. If, for example, she gets a gut feeling that someone is out to sabotage her at work but chalks it up to her imagination and ignores it, she's likely putting her job in peril. Or, if she gets a sense that the day care provider isn't being attentive enough to her child yet represses her feelings, she puts her child at risk.

Women who get what they want from life know that their gut feelings count—a lot. They pay attention to their feelings and, if they get the sense that they are being left out, undermined, or otherwise disrespected, they don't just passively hope things will change; they take action.

MAKE IT WORK FOR YOU

- **Identify those who are making lots of noise.** Who are the people in your life who talk so loudly, they drown out your inner voice? Does your best friend think she knows better than you what kind of man you should be dating? Does your dad believe that he knows more than you about what will make your boss value your work? Their input may be helpful, but at the end of the day, your gut knows best.

- **Look for patterns.** Ask yourself whether you are less trusting of your instincts in some areas of your life than others. Some women trust their instincts at work completely, but are ill at ease when it comes to romantic relationships. Others aren't comfortable in a parenting role so they may depend on "how-to" books or simply mirror the way their friends are raising their children. If you can identify where you are vulnerable, you can pay more attention to decisions in that area.

- **Take your time.** When you are struggling with a difficult decision, don't let anyone push you to make it until you've had the time you need to consider what you know and how you feel.

- **Don't overthink things.** Often, the more you ruminate, the greater the chance that you will second-guess yourself. You know what they say about multiple-choice tests—your first answer is usually the right one.

WALK AWAY WHEN IT'S TIME

It's difficult to walk away from meaningful relationships—sometimes even transactional ones—after all we've invested in them. The classic "sunk cost" dilemma is the psychological phenomenon that drives us to keep investing in projects (or in this case, relationships) whose upside is uncertain (or even those likely to fail) because we are trying to protect our initial investment—whether of time, money, or effort. The classic example that everyone falls prey to once in a while is waiting for a late bus or train. Even once we realize we could get to our destination faster if we cut our losses and walked or took a taxi, because we've already invested so long waiting on that platform we continue to wait . . . and wait. Of course, if we were behaving rationally we'd realize that, except in rare instances, our sunk costs should have no impact on our decisions.

Take the example of shopping for a computer or a car. Once it becomes clear that the salesperson isn't amenable to your bottom line, spending more time and energy to try to convince him to change his response is just wasting more of each. You'll never recoup the gas you used to get to the store or the sleep you gave up to get to the dealership early, so it's best to cut your losses and move on.

It's even more difficult to do this in a more personal context, when emotions are on the line. Few of us (except perhaps sociopaths) walk away easily once we've invested time and emotional energy in relationships—even a marginally important one. The challenge for nice girls is to resist the expectations others may have that they'll remain committed for the long term regardless of the quality of the relationship. Winning women know that some relationships are worth investing more time and effort, and some aren't.

Allison faced this problem when her friendship with Melody deteriorated. They had been great friends at school, but since then their lives had taken different directions. Now, from Allison's point of view, they had nothing in common except the past. Yet Allison continued the relationship out of respect for their history together. Although she resented every minute, it was the nice girl thing to do.

Winning women invest in relationships and do the best they can to strengthen them, as long as the relationship includes reciprocity, mutual respect, and authenticity. And when it doesn't, and they're convinced that it never will, they know it's time to walk away.

Morgan had worked long hours at her company for several years, and she was delivering terrific results. Each year her boss promised her a promotion, yet it never happened. When Morgan raised the subject, the boss stalled with excuses, such as the timing wasn't good or the economy was putting pressure on the department, and so on. Year after year, she promised she'd try to make it happen the following one. Finally, Morgan accepted the reality that things weren't going to change and landed a new job with a more delineated career path. Her only regret was that she waited as long as she did.

Recall Lauren, whose boyfriend didn't want to get married because he was afraid he'd be left financially high and dry if the marriage didn't work out. She offered to sign a prenuptial agreement to meet his need to protect his assets in the event they were to divorce. It turned out that still wasn't enough to convince him, and because Lauren did want to marry, she had no choice but to walk away.

Winning women don't apologize for cutting the cord when they realize they can't get what they need from a relationship. They know that hope is not a strategy.

MAKE IT WORK FOR YOU

- **Make every reasonable effort.** Ending a relationship is hard. If you've done all you can on your own and you're still having trouble, you might want to involve a trained third party (like a marriage counselor, or if it's a workplace relationship, an HR professional) to assist. Of course, check credentials carefully and proceed cautiously—nobody knows your relationships better than you do.

- **Take away the good.** It's a truly disastrous relationship that didn't have any good times. Take the time to remember them, even as you mourn the loss. Make a list of what you enjoyed about the relationship and what you learned from it, including the mistakes you won't make twice.

- **Don't look back.** Tempting as it may be to try to reconcile if ending the relationship has left you bored, lonely, or with a hole in your life, don't second-guess the decision you made. Ninety-nine percent of the time, an ex (ex anything: spouse, friend, boss, etc.) should stay that way—if you go back you probably won't be any happier with the relationship than you were before you ended it the first time. Returning to old relationships often happens between Thanksgiving and New Year's. We call them "holiday hook-ups" because people tend to unwisely rekindle relationships that best belong in the past because they don't want to be alone during the end-of-year holiday season.

MANAGE EXPECTATIONS

THE TACTICS IN STRATEGY III FOCUS ON

- Defining what is acceptable to you.
- Asserting yourself and sharing your expectations.
- Standing firm for your interests.

Perhaps the biggest mistake made by nice girls everywhere is the mistaken belief that they must be all things to all people all the time. Suffering from the disease to please, they say yes when they should be saying no, allow others to take advantage of their kindheartedness, and do things they don't really want to do so as not to create friction in relationships. Nice girls often lack the language to express what's most important to them, are reticent to ask for help when they need it, and expect that others will treat them with the same courtesy and respect they themselves exhibit.

Winning women, on the other hand, know that time, expertise, and money are limited commodities and must be doled out with the utmost care and consciousness so as not to lose sight of their own goals. They make decisions about what they do and don't want rather than allow others to make decisions for them. It's not that winning women are selfish or self-absorbed; they simply factor their own needs and wants into the equation.

Managing expectations may be difficult for you if you've unintentionally "trained" others that their needs come first and yours come second. The tactics we provide in this section will feel awkward if you haven't yet found your voice. Not only will you feel as if you're letting other people down, those people will make sure you know they agree with you! But not to worry—we'll give you tips for how to handle resistance as you change in Strategy V: Prepare for Pushback. For now, we encourage you to learn the critical skills covered in this strategy as yet another means of expanding your toolkit.

KNOW YOUR BOUNDARIES

The boundaries surrounding nice girls are amorphous and penetrable. Your children know how to get you to do what *they* want, even when it's against your better judgment. Your mother knows how to make you feel guilty, even when you've done your best to meet *her* needs. Your best friend knows how to play on your compassion, even when your own priorities aren't being met. That's because you haven't established your own boundaries and remain intent on putting others first and yourself second. Eleanor Roosevelt said, "No one can make you feel inferior without your consent." Not establishing boundaries in effect gives others your consent to believe their needs supersede yours.

Not only are boundaries essential for mental and physical health, they contribute to healthy relationships. They help you by circumscribing what you can and can't do, what you will accept and what you won't. Boundaries also provide others with a clear understanding of how much you can do, when you can do it, and if you will do it. But for nice girls, a boundary feels like something that will disappoint others. And sometimes that's true. Boundaries can lead to disappointment, but they also allow you to be authentically you.

Natalie is a twenty-six-year-old Iranian Jewish woman who works as a stockbroker on Wall Street. She comes from a traditional household where Mom worked inside the home and Dad worked outside the home as a tailor in the New York garment district. They're proud of all that Natalie has achieved, but each Friday night on the Sabbath they lament the fact that she isn't yet married with children. It's reached the point where Natalie doesn't want to visit them for Friday dinner because she doesn't want to be harangued. She knows she wants to start a family someday, but her career is also important to her, and now is the time to establish her reputation. To avoid confrontation, Natalie has begun to tell her parents that she has to work late, even though that's not really true.

Natalie is a good example of a nice girl who has not yet established boundaries. Lying about her workload will only add to the burden she already carries about disappointing her well-intentioned parents. The better tactic here would be to acknowledge her discomfort and express her feelings to her parents with a tactful comment such as "Believe me, I want to be married and have children, but now is not the right time for me. This ongoing discussion doesn't change that fact and makes me want to avoid our family dinners. I'd appreciate it if we could let it go and let me enjoy our time together."

Make It Work for You

- **Identify what makes you uncomfortable.** You know when someone has crossed your boundaries because you're ill at ease with the person or the discussion. Stay tuned to your feelings and avoid the inclination to gloss over them. If you're uncomfortable, it's a good sign your boundaries haven't been honored.

- **Maintain equanimity.** There's no need to minimize or amplify the situation when setting boundaries. Simply keep your emotional balance and state your thoughts and your needs. No need to move into drama mode or to be stoic. Keep it simple and remain true to yourself.

- **Consider silence as a good boundary setter.** If you feel you're being put in a compromised situation because of the content of a conversation or because of what's being asked of you, it's acceptable to not respond. You can always say, "Let me think about it," and then allow your silence to be the answer. If the person comes back to you, an appropriate response might be "You know, I thought about what you suggested, and I'm just not comfortable with it." If the person still won't drop the matter, you can either explain why you're not comfortable with the request or simply say, "I'm sure you can understand that I don't want to discuss this anymore."

- **Know your triggers**. Become more self-aware of what pushes your buttons. Some women can be asked their age and the question feels perfectly fine. For others, it feels like a boundary crossing. Pay attention to your *true* self, not the self you think you should be or were required to be as a child. Tune in to the adult self you have grown to be and who continues to grow.

ASSESS APPROPRIATENESS

The line is not very fine when it comes to appropriateness or lack thereof. Winning women have no problem rebuffing inappropriate behavior. Consider what happened to Camille, Angie, and Olivia when they went on vacation. The day they arrived at the resort, they were having lunch at an oceanside restaurant when another guest, who'd clearly had too much to drink, sat down, introduced himself, and began to monopolize the conversation. Camille politely told him they were having a private conversation and asked him to excuse them. Shocked, he asked if she really meant what she said. Camille assured him that she did and he left. Angie and Olivia were stunned but delighted that Camille said what she did. The man was annoying them, too, but they would have just put up with him.

Julia, on the other hand, is still tolerating inappropriate behavior. Admittedly, her situation is more difficult to handle because her mother is the problem. An architect in business with her husband and another partner, Julia has two young children. She's leaning toward making a decision to reduce her work schedule to a three-day work-week for the next few years so she can spend more time at home. Her husband favors the idea, as does the other partner. The move would actually make things easier for the business because work has slowed with the economic downturn. So what's the problem? Julia's mom is vehemently opposed to her plan. She believes Julia shouldn't step off the fast track even for a short period of time.

Although Julia originally appreciated her mom's advice, she's heard it so often now that it's causing her to doubt herself. Not only did she start rethinking the decision itself, but she worries that if she does step back, her mother will be disappointed with her and their relationship will suffer. Julia's mom's behavior is inappropriate and Julia's reluctance to discuss it with her enables her mom to keep it up.

Another example involves Chloe's friend Hannah, who is

exhausting her. Hannah calls at least daily to complain about how miserable she is. Her marriage is falling apart, her kids are running wild, and she hates both her job and her boss with a passion. Hannah expects that Chloe will drop whatever it is she's doing to lend a sympathetic ear. Chloe feels bad that Hannah is so unhappy and has suggested that Hannah seek professional advice. Hannah ignores her and keeps on calling.

When someone else's inappropriate behavior gets between a winning woman and the things she wants (including respect, appreciation, or things more tangible), she takes action. If she can't convince the other person to behave appropriately, she has to set boundaries. Regardless of the source of inappropriate behavior—a son or daughter in middle school who starts to question your intelligence, a colleague who's rude at a meeting, or a customer who berates you loudly—it is highly unlikely that the ongoing behavior will just stop. And the sooner you address the problem, the better.

MAKE IT WORK FOR YOU

- **Consider the tenor of the relationship before you act.** If the situation is more transactional than personal, your threshold of tolerance for inappropriate behavior can and should be lower. Camille didn't have to struggle very hard with her decision to politely ask the rude hotel guest to leave her and her friends alone. If, however, the person exhibiting bad behavior is your boss, a colleague, a customer, a family member, or a friend, the conversation will require more preparation and diplomacy.

- **Reflect on the consequences of inaction.** If you tolerate inappropriate behavior, it will have an impact on how you feel about yourself and on your ongoing relationship with the other person. If, for example, Chloe doesn't have a frank talk with Hannah soon to let Hannah know she can't continue to spend hours listening to an unrelenting litany of complaints, chances are her instinct for self-preservation will kick in and Chloe will stop picking up the phone when Hannah calls. The friendship will fade away over time because Chloe didn't take the action necessary to try to salvage it.

- **Be patient with relapses.** If the person has agreed to mend his ways and demonstrates sincerity, don't be surprised if he occasionally slips. Change is a process that takes time for everyone.

CREATE FAMILY BOUNDARIES

When it comes to boundaries, families fall into one of three kinds:

1. **Enmeshed:** In this pattern, family members find it difficult to do things and make decisions without the involvement of other family members. Outsiders find it difficult to get "into" the enmeshed family because the boundaries are impenetrable and they don't welcome outsiders.

2. **Disengaged:** These family members have little or no engagement or involvement in each other's lives.

3. **Engaged:** Family members are appropriately involved in each other's lives but also encourage one another to make decisions and create independent relationships outside of the family.

In the engaged family, each member respects boundaries and supports decisions made by others in the family so there are no boundary problems. Nor does the disengaged family present a boundary problem (though it does present other problems), because the boundaries surrounding each individual member are rigid and well defined, often to the point of excluding relatives from knowing what's happening in their lives. But, if you come from an enmeshed family, chances are you struggle with boundary issues. Most likely, you have one or more family members who continually try to keep you involved in *their* problems and *their* decisions, and continually offer *their* views of how you should think or act.

Television provides an excellent glimpse into the differences between enmeshed and engaged families (by their nature, disengaged families don't make for interesting viewing, so you don't see these on television too often). To understand the machinations of the enmeshed family you need only to watch the ABC drama *Brothers and*

Sisters. Here's a family where the mother is involved in every aspect of her adult children's lives, the siblings can't keep confidences among themselves, and all of them are constantly crossing each other's boundaries. What might be intended as support or concern is in reality inappropriate meddling and disrespect for individual boundaries.

On the other hand, remember *The Cosby Show*? Even if you didn't see it when it originally aired, you may have caught it in reruns. All the siblings on the show had unique personalities that were respected and supported by everyone else in the family. The parents were there for each of their children, but allowed their kids room to make mistakes and become individuals. The process of becoming one's true self, what psychologists call *individuation*, is critical to all human development, and particularly so for moving from nice girl to adult woman. Unfortunately, it's often missing in the lives of women who come from enmeshed families.

This is not to say enmeshed families aren't loving and caring, because they quite frequently are. But it's at a cost. If you want to know whether the boundary issues you experience with your family are due to enmeshment, ask yourself these questions:

- Is my family understanding and nonpunitive when I don't do what they would like me to do?

- Does my family respect my need for privacy in certain matters?

- Does my family fully support decisions I make that they may not agree with or understand?

- Does my family encourage me to build relationships with people outside of the family?

- Does my family welcome nonfamily members (friends, spouses, stepchildren, significant others) into the fold?

- Does my family refrain from interfering with how I raise my children or interact with my spouse?

- Are my family members able to disagree without an ensuing drama?

- Are my family members respectful of individual differences such as sexual orientation, education, or socioeconomic status?

If you answered no to three or more questions, then it's time to establish family boundaries that will enable you to move fully into your female adulthood. The following tips focus on how to establish clear, but kind, boundaries.

Make It Work for You

- **Develop a thicker skin.** Nice girls don't like to let others down, but sometimes this is necessary when others' expectations are inappropriate or out of bounds. Get over the notion that your job is to take care of others. Your job is to take care of *yourself*—with honesty, grace, skill, and kindness.

- **Pick your battles.** You'd rather go for a massage than to Aunt Mary's eightieth birthday party, but you know Mary would be crushed. So you forgo the massage and show up at the party. No big deal. The price of family membership means *sometimes* doing things you'd rather not do. In another scenario, let's say that now that you have your own children, you don't want to continue going to your mother's house for the major holidays. But when you say you plan to stay home this year and invite the family to join you, your mother gets angry and accuses you of ruining the family tradition. Now *this* is a big deal—if you have to tolerate anger, guilt-tripping, or the silent treatment for something as inoffensive as wanting to create your own family tradition, this is a battle worth fighting.

- **Make family members aware of consequences for inappropriate behavior.** If old Uncle Harry (or anyone else for that matter) ruins family get-togethers by drinking too much, then making nasty remarks about everything and everyone, you need to make it clear that as long as the behavior continues you won't be attending (or will leave) the events. Simply say (when he's sober), "I'm uncomfortable being in the presence of an abusive alcoholic and choose not to subject myself and my family to this kind of treatment." Notice the use of the "I-message" here. He may become defensive, but people have a hard time arguing with that kind of logic.

- **Nip it in the bud.** As soon as your sister gets a piece of information about anyone in the family, she picks up the phone and starts the grapevine of gossip. If you want the behavior to stop (remember, if she talks about everyone else, you *know* she talks about you as well), you'll have to nip it in the bud. Instead of listening politely (even if you don't intend to repeat it to someone else), say something like, "You know, I'm not comfortable talking about people behind their backs. I'd prefer to focus our conversation on what's going on in our own lives."

DON'T BE A MARTYR

In psychology, there's a concept called *secondary gain*. It applies in situations where it appears on the surface that a person is in some way being harmed or hindered, when in fact they are getting something out of the situation. Take, for example, a woman who is married to a philandering husband. She certainly doesn't like his indiscretions, but she's also not willing to leave him because she's actually getting something that she wants: the lavish gifts and exotic trips he keeps showering on her out of guilt, and the attention from her friends, who feel bad for her. These are examples of secondary gain. We call it being a martyr.

We've known many nice girls who are martyrs, but not many winning women play the martyr card. Nice girls use martyrdom as a means of escaping the inevitable stress, indecision, and responsibility that comes from being in charge of their own lives. For them, it's easier to be a martyr, one who suffers greatly at the hand of another, than to be a woman who makes the difficult choices needed to escape situations in which her needs aren't being met. And then there's always that secondary gain to reinforce martyr behavior. Here are a few examples of how martyrdom plays out in different situations. See if you recognize yourself or anyone you know.

The martyr says or thinks . . .	But receives secondary gain in the form of . . .
"I'm so busy I never get out of here before 8:00 p.m. No one works as hard as I do."	Praise from management, respect from peers, a way to avoid problems at home.
"Tuition for my kids is costing me a fortune. With them in private school, I can't even afford to take a vacation."	The envy of friends and family who can't afford private school, bragging rights.

The martyr says or thinks . . .	But receives secondary gain in the form of . . .
"My friends don't appreciate that I go out of my way to make them special meals for their birthdays."	Sympathy from family who may consider those friends selfish, friends showering her with gifts on her next birthday.
"I'll take the kids to the beach so you can go on your motorcycle ride. I can go out to lunch with my friends another day."	Indebtedness from her husband, appreciation from her children.
"If I don't let all the neighborhood kids play at my house every day, they'll have no place to go."	Gratitude from the kids' parents, appreciation from the other kids as well as her own.
"I have to pick up the check when I have lunch with my friend because she can't afford to eat out."	Ego gratification that she can afford to pay for lunch, gratitude from the friend, bragging rights.

MAKE IT WORK FOR YOU

- **Ask directly for what you need rather than hinting around.** If your husband doesn't compliment you often enough or friends take you for granted, don't look for sympathy. Just let them know that you'd appreciate positive feedback now and then. It doesn't mean you're high maintenance, only that you're human.

- **Consider your motives.** Sometimes we genuinely want to go out of our way or extend ourselves for others because it makes us feel good to be able to do so. That's perfectly okay. It's only when you resent doing something and find yourself playing the martyr that it's a problem. In fact, you're most likely behaving like a nice girl who wants others to love her for what she *does*, not who she *is*.

- **Look at your array of choices.** Nice girls get stuck doing things they later resent because they can't see the many choices that lie before them. Given that we can't see what we can't see and don't know what we don't know, you may have to enlist a friend to help you identify alternatives. For example, instead of complaining that you are the one everyone always expects to arrange neighborhood potluck dinners, ask someone you trust, "How can I break the pattern without unnecessarily offending anyone?" A good friend will help you develop a game plan to prevent you from being the neighborhood martyr—or any other kind of martyr for that matter.

AGREE ON ROLES—AHEAD OF TIME

Charlotte had done most of the preparation for a client presentation, but when she and her boss met with the client, her boss not only took the lead but gave her no airtime at all. Charlotte felt awkward—the client was probably wondering why she was even at the meeting! It was no wonder that, after the meeting, the client kept calling her boss rather than Charlotte to ask questions about the project. Because the client didn't see her as a credible resource, Charlotte missed an opportunity to further develop that relationship. And, because she was frustrated, her relationship with her boss suffered as well.

The root cause of some of the biggest relationship problems is confusion about roles. In this case, when Charlotte's boss didn't assign her a role at a client meeting, she, being a nice girl, didn't push back. She may have thought her boss would have proactively assigned her a role if he thought she was ready for it. Or she might not have wanted to make a big deal out of it. After all, her boss is busy and she wouldn't want to appear to be high maintenance. But one of the biggest nice girl mistakes is waiting for things to be handed to you. In work and in life, you can't expect to get something if you don't ask for it.

Of course, this works the other way as well. Sometimes we are assigned roles we didn't ask for, and in fact don't want. When this happens a nice girl never complains. She simply takes the roles assigned to her, without questioning why.

That's what happened when Taylor and Madison decided to move in together. Somehow, Taylor ended up as both the chief financial officer (paying all the bills) and chief operating officer (making sure everything worked and making arrangements to get things repaired when they didn't) of the household. They never discussed it—it just happened. Taylor hated doing both roles, but was reluctant to bring it up, so she just kept doing them. Understandably, her resentment built over time.

Winning women know that clarifying roles in advance prevents misunderstandings down the line. Anna had been promoted to run the team she used to be a part of. Not everyone on the team was thrilled—and they weren't afraid to show it. Some of them felt they should have gotten the promotion instead. Others didn't want the job, but didn't want Anna to have it either. Faced with the challenge of getting her former coworkers to take her seriously, she needed to make sure that each person who worked for her understood and accepted that her role had changed. She was now the boss, not just one of the gang.

Anna took two steps. First, she asked her boss to explain to the team why she had been selected for the job—what specifically qualified her as the best person for the role. Then, she scheduled one-on-one meetings with each person in the group to ask for their support. In those meetings, Anna made it clear that while she welcomed feedback and ideas, she'd be making the final decisions. Although one or two people still grumbled, having these conversations helped Anna get the respect she deserved much more easily.

Another example of clarifying roles is that of Lily and her boy-friend. They often fought because he kept making plans to see certain friends when Lily had made a commitment to others and vice versa. So they simply agreed that Lily would be the one to keep the social calendar—a role she was happy to take on. This made their life a lot easier, and saved them from the embarrassment of having to con-stantly admit to friends that they'd double-booked. Of course, the role clarification alone didn't help them agree on *which* friends to see—but that's another story!

Clarifying roles strengthens relationships because each person can select a role that plays to her strengths. It also helps to avoid arguments since people won't be tripping over each other to do the same things or undoing what the other person has just done. Of course, to make this work, whoever is in a particular role should still accept input from the other person (if it's offered), and the parties should periodically assess how well the role assignment is working.

MAKE IT WORK FOR YOU

- **Play to your strengths.** Pick the role that appeals to you. You can make your life easier by taking on roles that leverage things you are good at, as we discussed in Tactic 11: Parlay Your Niche of Expertise. That doesn't mean that you shouldn't try to challenge yourself in the right situations. Even if your forte is organizing large-scale events, always playing that role and no other will limit your ability to expand your skill set.

- **Raise your hand for the role you want.** If the role fits, make it clear you'd be happy to take it on. Don't expect that a role you want will just fall into your lap. For example, if you want to be the executor of your parent's estate because you are the best-qualified sibling, tell them.

- **Get comfortable with relinquishing responsibility.** Agreeing on roles isn't just about taking on the ones you want; it also involves giving up the ones you don't. But to do this effectively, you have to be willing to give up a little control. What tasks are you comfortable delegating completely to the other person? What is it that he will happily let you make decisions about? What kinds of things should you discuss before either of you takes action? Clarifying not only the roles each person will take but also what each one consists of is critically important.

SHARE THE WEALTH

Nice girls take it all on—they do more than their fair share at home, at work, and everywhere in between. Reluctant to say no, they rarely have the luxury of time to themselves because they're too busy doing everything that needs to be done. It's not always because they're being martyrs; it's often because when they see something that needs to be done, they'd rather do it than risk disappointing someone or ask for help.

For example, at work, the nice girl is the one who walks out of the weekly planning meeting with the lion's share of the "to do's." Although her plate is just as full as everyone else's (and probably even more so), she just says yes when asked to do more. If approached for help by a colleague, she immediately runs to the rescue, flattered to be asked. And if there's an unpopular project, one that others won't even go near, she raises her hand for it.

At home, it's the same story. Even if she works outside the home, she does the majority of household tasks. She takes the lead in caring for children, relatives who need help, and even the family pets. With friends, she's the one who always makes the restaurant reservations because everyone else is busy and, to boot, she even does the driving because no one else has had time to put gas in their cars. It's no wonder nice girls are so tired! Winning women, on the other hand, aren't shy about asserting themselves. While happy to pitch in, they also expect others to step up and share the wealth—of responsibility, that is.

Maria, one of three siblings, was the only one who still lived in their hometown, where her mother still lived. As her widowed mother aged, Maria found herself taking on more and more responsibility for her care. But as a working mother herself, Maria struggled to find time to fit everything in and soon realized that something had to give. So she had a talk with her brother and sister to apprise them of the situation and to ask for their help. Her sister agreed to take on the job of helping their mother manage her finances, something she could easily do from afar. Although the conversation with her brother didn't go as well as she had hoped, Maria knew she had done all she could to share the wealth. Remember, being a winning woman isn't about getting everything you want at all times, it's about handling yourself and the situation in a mature way that you can feel good about.

In another scenario, Marianne, who'd returned to work after being at home for a few years, had a heart-to-heart with her husband about their respective roles and responsibilities. Since both were now working full-time, they agreed to hire a cleaning person as well as to alternate driving the kids to various activities, depending on their schedules. Marianne still ended up with more than half the chores, including doing all the laundry, shopping, and meal preparation, but she's satisfied with the way things are—for now at least. And she knows she can have another conversation with her husband later to reexamine the division of labor in the household. In the meantime, her life is manageable.

Negotiating with family and friends is the most delicate kind of negotiation, but it can be done successfully. Win-win agreements will transition you from being a nice girl to being a winning woman.

MAKE IT WORK FOR YOU

- **Know you have the right to change how things are done.** Just because you've always picked up the slack doesn't mean you have to continue to do so. Recognize, though, that it won't be easy to change the status quo because your coworkers, family, or friends are likely very happy that you do more and they do less.

- **Wait for another hand to go up.** Get comfortable with that awkward moment when it's time for someone to step up—don't feel compelled to be the first to raise a hand. If you hang back, you may be pleasantly surprised.

- **Ask for help.** If you know what you want help with, ask for it. Alternatively, engage in brainstorming to determine how everyone can do their fair share. At work, if you take on extra responsibilities, make your limitations clear in a professional way. At home, keep the discussion focused on facts without blaming or shaming.

- **Recognize that others won't do things exactly the way you do them**. And that's okay. You may need to learn to relax your standards. If you don't want to be the one who always does the laundry, then you're going to have to put up with your white bras occasionally turning gray because your spouse mixed colors. Or if you want to share the responsibility for going to the grocery store, you'll have to zip your lip when your daughter comes home with blueberries that cost twice as much as you would have paid for them.

- **Don't take efforts to share the wealth for granted**. Make sure you acknowledge the behaviors you want to see repeated. If you think, "Why should I thank my child for picking up his room when that's his responsibility?" you'll run the risk of extinguishing the behavior. In just a few more pages, we'll talk about the power of positive reinforcement.

PARENT, DON'T BEFRIEND

Nice girls are often reluctant to parent. As mothers, they love their children well but not wisely, confusing the role of parent with that of a friend. They quake at taking a hard stance or setting limits, worried that their children won't like them anymore. But, to their detriment and to that of their kids, such moms fail to garner the respect they deserve.

When Carol's children were young, she often told them that while they'd have many friends in their lives, they'd have only one mother. The attempt she made to teach them the difference between the two proved helpful for them—and for her. For them, it reduced confusion over just how serious she was about enforcing the rules she had established. And for her, it was a reminder that her role as a mom would sometimes put her in the uncomfortable position of disciplining her children. It helped her learn that being a mother means sometimes being unpopular. And that's okay, as long as you're acting with your children's best interests at heart.

Few conversations are trickier than the ones that stem from the inevitable difference of opinion with a child. There's a lot more at stake than the issue itself—such as the residual impact to the relationship. If, behaving like a nice girl, a woman just caves in and gives her daughter what she wants even though she doesn't believe it is in her daughter's best interest, it might solve the short-term problem—the fight—but it will sabotage her ultimate goal—to raise a healthy, productive adult.

For example, Tracy, a divorced mom, had to take action after her eighteen-year-old daughter, Nicki, had a party one night while she was out of town. Not only had Nicki disobeyed her explicit warning not to have a party, but to make matters even worse, Tracy's neighbors had alerted her that the kids were drinking. When Tracy suspended the service on Nicki's phone as punishment, Nicki was simply furious with Tracy, accusing her of overreacting to what Nicki described as a small gathering of friends sharing a few beers before going out for the evening—which was no big deal according to Nicki, because one of the kids was the designated driver. Nicki told Tracy that everyone else's parents let them drink at their homes and that Tracy was ruining her life by punishing her in this way.

Tracy stood firm, unrelenting until she was comfortable that Nicki had learned her lesson. Had she given in to avoid making Nicki unhappy or angry at her, she would have saved herself some grief in the short term, but the message she would have sent to her daughter was that she didn't care enough to enforce the rule she'd made to protect her. Although Nicki might have been happy she got her own way *for the moment*, she'd probably someday look back and wish her mother had been strong enough to do her job as a parent.

MAKE IT WORK FOR YOU

- **Be realistic about the outcome you can expect.** If your teenage son brings up the subject of getting a tattoo, you probably won't be able to extract a promise that he'll never do it as long as he lives. The best you'll probably be able to get is an agreement to wait until he's over twenty-one. You can always have another conversation about it then, but hopefully in the interim life experiences may cause him to think more carefully about doing it *ever*.

- **Pick the right time and place.** Discussing something you and your daughter both feel strongly about and are likely to disagree over as you drive home from soccer practice in traffic, when you are both exhausted from a very long day, isn't a good idea. Set yourself up for success by setting time aside to have the conversation in a place where you'll both be relaxed, refreshed, and receptive.

- **Make like a Girl Scout.** Consider the arguments that will be made to defend a position and be prepared to counter them with not only an explanation of your position but the reasons behind it as well. Your child may still not agree with you, but at least he or she will have more insight about your concerns—knowledge that will likely serve him or her well later in life.

- **Anticipate the buttons that will be pushed.** Although it may seem as if they live on an entirely different planet, your kids have been paying attention. They know you very well and are likely to use that knowledge to get what they want. Don't let them goad you into an emotional response that you'll regret later. When you know your buttons are being pushed, particularly the guilt button, call for a time-out to regroup.

- **Problem solve.** Without ceding authority, encourage your child to work with you to craft a creative solution. What other ways are there to look at the problem? Can you link the outcomes to other issues? For example, your daughter wants a new dress for the dance but you are strapped for cash and believe she has plenty of dresses hanging in her closet. Perhaps through mutual problem solving she'll propose taking another babysitting job to earn the money or consider borrowing a dress from her cousin for the evening.

- **Don't back kids into a corner.** Being a parent doesn't mean being a bully. Just because you *can* force your solution because you are the parent doesn't mean you *should*. Even young kids respond negatively to the explanation "because I said so." Allow your children to have their say and listen respectfully to their points of view.

USE INTERMITTENT POSITIVE
REINFORCEMENT TO YOUR ADVANTAGE

If you've ever played slot machines in a casino, your behavior has likely been shaped by what psychologists call intermittent positive reinforcement—and behavior that has been reinforced in this manner is hard to change. Let's say you sit down at a quarter machine, drop in a few coins, and yank the handle. What typically happens? That's right, you lose. Then you drop in a few more coins and pull the handle, but this time you win, though slightly fewer coins than you've already spent. Convinced that the big payoff is just a few coins away (here you may want to employ Tactic 31: Walk Away When It's Time), you keep it up with the same results—a few small payoffs that don't exceed your investment. Does that deter you? No! Why? Because the intermittent positive reinforcement has caused you to keep playing. Without a doubt, casino owners understand this psychological phenomenon and use it to their advantage.

The beauty of intermittent positive reinforcement is that you don't know *when* you'll get the reward so you continue to try. If a tough boss never provides praise, staff members may become discouraged or unmotivated. If she praises continually, even for the smallest achievements, staff members become immune to it. But, when praise is given intermittently and for specific achievements, it typically yields higher productivity.

Because of their overwhelming need to be liked, nice girls often unwittingly reinforce behaviors they would prefer not to continue. And you can bet that if you are a nice girl, your children, spouse, friends, and family will use this to their advantage. Small children have this one down pat. When your four-year-old asks for a cookie at 5:00 p.m. and you tell him no because it will ruin his dinner, chances are he just keeps asking, albeit in different ways. Finally, out of frustration, annoyance, or because you're being disrupted from what you're doing, you give him the cookie. You've just positively reinforced his behavior. He now knows if he does the same thing next time he'll likely get the same result. Conversely, if his tactics didn't work on you, the behavior will ultimately stop.

Here we've made it sound like intermittent positive reinforcement is a bad thing, but that's only the case when you're not aware that you're shaping undesirable behaviors. Instead, you can use it to your advantage by consciously applying it in more functional ways. For example, when your spouse does a chore in a timely manner, you can make him his favorite dinner. Or the next time your son brings the car home on time, tell him he's now earned the right to use it again over the weekend. Intermittently reinforcing the behaviors you want to see exhibited increases the likelihood they'll be repeated.

MAKE IT WORK FOR YOU

- **Say what you mean and mean what you say.** People learn to trust us and believe in what we say through consistency. If you tell your mother you just don't have time to make dinner for out-of-town family coming to visit, but once she nags a little, you turn yourself into a pretzel to make it happen, you've taught her that you'll cave to pressure. Nice girls do this all the time, then wonder why no one listens to their needs.

- **Resist others' attempts to wear you down.** Perhaps you think you do a good job of establishing boundaries, but find it difficult to stick to them when others cajole, implore, or guilt-trip you into changing your mind. Each time you do, you've taught them that those behaviors will help them to get their needs met—at the expense of yours. Recognizing that these are strategies intended to get you to go along with someone else's program will help you to remain grounded in your own expectations. We'll talk more about this and how to handle it in Strategy V: Prepare for Pushback.

- **Intermittently reward behaviors that meet your needs.** The operative word here is *intermittently*. If you provide rewards (either verbal or tangible) each and every time someone respects your boundaries or needs, they will either come to take that reward for granted or see it as insincere, and eventually it will stop working.

ROCK THE BOAT WITHOUT CAPSIZING IT

Avoiding difficult conversations is but another classic nice girl mistake. Afraid to damage the relationship, when it comes to confrontation, nice girls adopt the Scarlett O'Hara philosophy—"Tomorrow is another day." In other words, they postpone these potentially conflict-ridden talks. But even nice girls get to a point when a heart-to-heart is impossible to delay because the issue just won't go away—no matter how hard they try to sweep it under the rug. And the longer they procrastinate the more frustration, anger, and hurt will build up, exacerbating the problem, and causing an eventual conversation to go wrong quickly.

Take the following situation, one that most of us have been in at one time or another. Valerie's best friend, Karen, seemed to be pulling away. Karen wasn't returning her phone calls as quickly as she always had and when they did make plans to get together, Karen would often cancel at the last minute. Hurt and confused, nice girl Valerie didn't know what to do, so she did nothing. Eventually, more and more time lapsed between their communications and they drifted further and further apart, without ever discussing why. Now social situations where they run into each other are awkward and uncomfortable. Although there is no guarantee that a discussion would have changed anything, Valerie will never know—and that bothers her.

Selena, a winning woman, also faced a difficult conversation but responded differently. Her coworker Tory had recently been behaving badly. She wasn't carrying her weight, was taking credit for Selena's work, and was generally making Selena's life miserable. Selena knew that if she did nothing things would probably get worse, so she scheduled some time to talk with Tory. But Selena also knew that the stakes were high. If she handled the conversation poorly, she might make things even worse. So she invested the time to prepare for the conversation and even enlisted a friend to role-play with her so that she could practice saying the difficult words out loud. It's one thing to know *what* you want to say; it's another *to actually get the words out of your mouth* comfortably. Practice makes it possible.

It's certainly tempting to avoid difficult conversations, hoping that things will resolve themselves. The problem is that they won't. Avoidance just doesn't work. In fact, having a successful, albeit difficult, conversation with someone will typically build mutual respect and make your relationship even stronger.

Make It Work for You

- **Set unintimidating goals.** Ask yourself what you want as an outcome from a difficult conversation. Selena's ultimate goal, for example, was to get her colleague's agreement to shape up, but since this goal made the interaction seem more like a confrontation than a discussion, she set a less intimidating one: to simply understand why Tory was acting the way she was.

- **List the facts.** What are the facts of the situation? What happened? When? By whom? Be careful not to interpret or make assumptions about the facts at this point; just list them.

- **Consider your contributions.** While at first blush it may seem that you're completely blameless and the other person single-handedly created the problem, that's unlikely. Be honest with yourself—what did you do (or not do) that made the situation worse?

- **Think about the other person as a person, not an enemy.** Most people aren't evil. They don't get out of bed in the morning, look at themselves in the mirror, and proactively plan to make someone else's life miserable that day (although we can think of a few exceptions!). When planning a difficult conversation, it's helpful to remind yourself that the other person is only human, with weaknesses and insecurities, just like you.

- **Pick the right method, time, and place.** Be thoughtful about how and where to have a difficult conversation. Face-to-face can be scary but it's almost always best, because you'll be able to observe each other's body language. And, although timing may not be everything, it matters a lot. Don't have a difficult conversation when you are rushed or not feeling your best—and give the other person the same consideration. Finally, the location matters too. Choose a place that's quiet and private.

• **Practice out loud.** Pick someone you can trust who has no stake in the outcome of the difficult conversation to role-play with you. You might even want to tape your session so that you can review it later. Comfort and confidence come with repetition and practice.

SET A RANGE OF DESIRED OUTCOMES

When applying for a new job, Jessica was asked what her salary requirements were. She had done her homework and from researching similar jobs in her area on the Internet and through her professional organization, knew that the pay range was from $62,000 to $78,000. She was earning $68,000 annually at her current employer. To make the move worth it, she knew she wanted at least a 10 percent increase, which would make the new salary $74,800. So she very specifically told the recruiter she would accept anywhere from $74,800 to $80,000. As she suspected, he went to the middle of the range and offered her $76,500.

Realtors do this all the time. Let's say you tell your Realtor that the most you can afford is $325,000. Does she show you listings that are only $325,000 or less? No way. She shows you homes in the range of $325,000 to $395,000. Pretty soon the $325,000 homes are paling in comparison to the more expensive ones, and you're frantically trying to figure out a way to finance a more expensive home. She walks away with a bigger commission and you end up with a home that costs more than you wanted to spend. If, however, you'd given her a range in the first place, say $300,000 to $325,000, she'd have been more likely to show you houses in your budget.

Setting a range of outcomes you'll accept in a situation instead of presenting a single acceptable solution increases the chances you'll get what you want. This doesn't just apply to negotiating a salary—it also holds true when splitting up chores with a spouse, or drafting an agreement with a repairman, or even trying to settle a score with a friend. Not only does it give you common ground from which to begin the discussion, it also requires you to think thoroughly about the least ideal situation that would still be acceptable to you, as well as the best possible outcome.

When determining the range or parameters of desired outcomes, it's often helpful to think in terms of what would be disappointing but still okay and, on the other end, what would make you delighted. For example, you're planning a vacation with some friends. Everyone has ideas about where they want to go and what they want to do—from the ridiculous to the sublime. You've researched different trips and the associated costs and determined that while a five-day trip to Cancun would be ideal, Vancouver and Hawaii are also affordable provided the trip is no longer than seven nights and each person shares a hotel room and the expense for a rental car. When you meet to discuss it, you tell them you would be fine with anything within that range of options and propose these destinations with specific provisos.

This doesn't mean you'll always get the ideal outcome. An employer can come back and say your salary request is too high, the realtor might say it's impossible to find a suitable home in the neighborhood you want at the price you want, and your friends may agree on a more exotic and expensive trip than you can afford. But stating in advance a range of what is acceptable to you does increase the likelihood of an outcome you can live with.

MAKE IT WORK FOR YOU

- **Do your homework.** By its nature, managing expectations requires you to have the facts and figures needed to make a strong case for your wishes. As one friend of ours always says, "Facts are friendly." A fact-based discussion is always easier than a more emotional appeal.

- **Create a range wide enough for wiggle room.** This is especially true when negotiating. If you're selling a used car, you don't ask for the price that's exactly what you want. Typically, you inflate it by about 10 percent so there's room to come down to the least you're willing to accept. Similarly, if you're negotiating benefits in a new job, you throw in a few things that you'd like to have, but that you're willing to give up for more important perks.

- **Be prepared to walk.** When you are clear about the parameters of your desired outcomes, it's easier to know when to walk away, making it less likely you'll make the nice girl mistake of agreeing to something you'll later regret.

START WITH YES

This is a simple trick we use all the time to manage expectations in all kinds of relationships, and it works like a charm. Often, when we travel to give a keynote presentation, we're met at the hotel by clients who want us to change significant portions of our planned talk. It's usually late at night, after we've traveled all day, and the request is completely last minute. However, as firm believers in having the best possible relationships with our clients, we're not going to say no to the request. No one likes to hear "no." It only creates defensiveness from the get-go—something we definitely don't want to do with our clients.

Instead, we start with a resounding "yes." We begin by saying we will be happy to meet their needs. However, we don't roll over and just do what is asked of us, especially not at the expense of a relaxing dinner and a good night's sleep. We're no nice girls! Instead, we provide options the client can accept or decline. It sometimes sounds like this: "We'd be happy to make those changes. We charge $500 an hour for changes made with less than forty-eight hours' notice, so just let us know how much time you'd like us to spend on it." Ninety-nine percent of the time the client decides the changes aren't really needed. As for the one percent of the time they still want them—well, at least we're well compensated for the effort.

It's not only expectations about money, but your time and energy that you need to manage. Consider the scenario where your best friend calls in a panic and just has to come over to tell you about the latest crisis in her love life. You care, of course, but you've just returned from a long business trip, have laundry to do so that you have something to wear to work in the morning, and you haven't yet had dinner. If you say no to her, it will create tension in your friendship. Beginning with yes minimizes any immediate defensiveness so that you can go on to manage her expectations and your needs. "Of course you can come over to talk," you begin. "I've got to let you know, though, that I've got an important early meeting in the morning and I have to get my laundry done so that I have clean clothes for it, so I might have to run some loads while we talk. I want to be able to give you my complete attention for as long as you need it, so if you prefer, I can meet you after work tomorrow when I'll be less distracted." Most likely she'll take you up on that second option, the better one for both of you. Here are several examples of how you can follow a "yes" with another option:

- "It would be my pleasure to host a dinner party for our friends on Saturday. Since I'll be at a workshop for most of the day, I'll have to order out or, if you prefer, we can make reservations at a restaurant."

- "Sure, I can watch your kids on Wednesday night. I won't be home until six and I'm expecting a business call from overseas, so I'll either need you to bring them here and pick them up when you're ready, or I could come to you any time after seven."

The obvious caveat is that this tactic works only if you're willing to do what is requested of you if the other person doesn't bite. Your friend might *still* want to come over, in which case you should still do your laundry, as she was warned. On the other hand, if you weren't willing for her to come over to begin with, this isn't the tactic you should have employed.

MAKE IT WORK FOR YOU

- **Mean it.** It's not appropriate to start with yes if you really mean no. This puts you in the position of having to go back on your original statement, which will cause anger and resentment—on the part of all parties involved. If there's no way you will or can do what's being asked of you, then saying no is a necessary evil. In the following tactic, we tell you how to pull it off diplomatically.

- **Combine "yes" with a range of desired outcomes.** Make sure to provide alternatives with which you can live. It puts the onus of choice on the other person.

- **Don't be passive-aggressive.** Starting with yes isn't a license to manipulate other people. It's a way to maintain positive, beneficial relationships while managing the other person's expectations of what you are realistically willing to do for them. The intention is to assure you aren't treated as a doormat and let others know the ramifications or cost of their requests. If you say yes and then completely ignore the request or conveniently forget to deliver on your promise, that's passive-aggressive.

IF YOU HAVE TO SAY NO, SUPPORT IT WITH A LEGITIMATE RATIONALE AND ALTERNATIVES

Most of the time, starting with yes is your best strategy for managing expectations while at the same time maintaining relationships. However, there are those times when saying no can't be avoided. Given that others become defensive when "no" is the first thing out of your mouth, it's critical that you provide a strong, legitimate reason and alternative options.

When we were in the midst of writing this book, the editor of *Nice Girls Don't Get the Corner Office* called Lois and asked if she could make revisions for the soon-to-be-published paperback version. In three days. Turned out, the editor was just back from maternity leave and things had moved more quickly than she anticipated, requiring a quick turnaround. Not only was Lois busy writing *this* book with Carol, her father-in-law had just that day been diagnosed with terminal cancer *and* she was involved in planning the memorial service for a dear friend who had passed away unexpectedly, *and* she was chairing a fund-raiser for her nonprofit organization, Bloom Again Foundation. As much as she wanted to meet the editor's deadline, she knew it was impossible.

This was one of the few times Lois had to respond with no, rather than her usual yes. So, following her own advice, instead of balking and saying the three-day turnaround was unreasonable, Lois explained all that was going on in her life at the moment and that there just weren't enough hours in the day to write the revisions and get them back within three days; however, with even a little more time, she would be happy to provide what was needed. Within a few days the editor contacted her again and said they could wait two weeks for the revisions. Lois got more time, her editor got the revisions, and most important, the relationship wasn't unnecessarily damaged.

All too often nice girls bow to unreasonable requests because they don't want to disappoint others, but each time they do they reinforce the notion that their needs are inconsequential. In turn, they become resentful, burned out, or passive-aggressive (they say yes, but then don't follow through). Before agreeing to do something that requires you to turn yourself inside out, think about whether it might just be one of those times when saying no, providing a legitimate rationale, and outlining alternatives would be the better choice.

Make It Work for You

- **Give your needs equal or greater weight.** You've probably heard the saying "Your failure to plan is not my emergency." Although you may not want to *say* this, you can incorporate it into your decision making as to whether or not a request is reasonable. There will always be times when you *do* have to suspend your needs because the other person is having a true crisis (and trust us, they'll repay the favor someday), but what you currently have on your plate should be considered a legitimate reason for saying no.

- **Use explanations as a means of humanizing your position.** Although we're not typically big fans of women having to explain themselves, when it comes to managing expectations, it does serve the purpose of letting people know that you're not a human *doing*, but rather a human *being*. Again, it's not something we recommend doing regularly, because then you may come across as uncooperative or unable to handle multiple priorities, but when done every once in a while, explaining all that you have going on in your life lets others know your time and priorities are valuable, too.

- **Seek creative solutions rather than compromises.** When you think about it, compromises are lose-lose situations. Each person ends up giving up something he or she wants, so in effect, both parties lose something. If a friend asks you to attend her birthday dinner at an expensive restaurant that you can't afford, a compromise would be to go somewhere else that is less expensive. But you still end up spending more than you want and she doesn't get to celebrate her birthday at her restaurant of choice. Thinking more creatively, you might explain that although you can't afford to join them, why doesn't she go ahead and enjoy the restaurant she prefers and you'll cook a meal for her in your home at a later date. This way, both of your needs are met, and the relationship doesn't take a hit.

USE FACTS, NOT FEELINGS

When the landlord refuses to pay for repairs a nice girl needs, she may waste time and energy begging and cajoling rather than pointing out the provision in her lease that makes repairs the landlord's responsibility. Or if she's quoted a ridiculously high price for an appliance she's buying, she may simply walk away instead of using the research she's done in advance to show the going rate is lower.

Fact is, facts speak louder than feelings. People can rebut your feelings with their feelings, but facts focus the conversation on the issues. Take, for example, the situation Erlinda faced when she was negotiating with her plastic surgeon's office. Ever since she was a teenager, Erlinda had wanted a nose job. Whether or not she needed it is another story, but she felt it would give her confidence a boost. She visited several plastic surgeons and settled on the one she liked best and who had the best testimonials from patients. The problem was, he wasn't the cheapest, and Erlinda was on a budget. A nice girl might have approached the situation by telling him how important the surgery was to her, and how upset she'd be if she had to wait another year while she saved up the money she needed to afford his rate. These are feelings. Instead, she put together the following facts she could use to negotiate the surgeon's fee:

- His fees were 10 to 25 percent higher than those of other surgeons in the area.

- If he gave her a discount, she would pay with cash up front, not in installments or on a credit card.

- She would be happy to appear in advertising as a "before" and "after" picture (something many patients won't allow).

- She would have the surgery done at a time when his schedule was lighter than usual so that he wouldn't have to turn away a patient willing to pay his full fee to do her surgery.

- She would have the surgery done without anesthesia so that he could give the anesthesiologist the day off. *(Only kidding!)*

Point is, by appealing on a rational rather than emotional level, she could confidently ask for the reduced fees without hesitation or apology. She knew what she had to give in exchange for the discount. Although the surgeon's business manager didn't significantly reduce the fee, she did reduce it enough that Erlinda could afford it.

Because facts aren't in the control of either person, they are friendly to both. They are what they are. When your expectations differ from those of someone with whom you want to reach an agreement, think about how you can use facts to resolve your differences more easily.

| Other Situations Where Using Facts Might Be Helpful ||
Situation	Benefit to You
If you're trying to agree with your husband about the value of your home because you're divorcing, instead of going back and forth about what you feel the house is worth, hire an appraiser, who will be able to evaluate your home's value objectively based on what similar homes in your neighborhood have sold for recently.	When emotions are high (divorce is a terrific example), agreeing to let the facts solve the problem can save you both a lot of money in lawyer's fees.
If a customer or client is requesting to pay your bills in sixty days instead of thirty days, instead of taking it personally, you can point to the industry billing practice of thirty days.	You'll be able to maintain your business cash flow and your customer relationship at the same time.

Other Situations Where Using Facts Might Be Helpful	
Situation	**Benefit to You**
If your dentist is quoting you a huge fee for dental work you need done, instead of playing the pity card, you may agree on "reasonable and customary" fees published by insurance companies in your area.	You'll get your dental work done by the dentist of your choice without paying more than you can afford.

MAKE IT WORK FOR YOU

- **Keep track of the facts.** It's very difficult to recall the specific chronology of events or the details after time has passed, particularly when your emotions run high. Don't put yourself in the position of having to guess or piece them together. Keep a journal—especially if you think you'll later be required to support your position. Note the incident, the date, if there was anyone else present, and as much supporting information as you can.

- **Use facts that will stand up.** Whatever the source you are using, be sure it's credible. Citing "facts" that are unreliable will make you seem careless at best and, worse, dishonest. And, although a wealth of information is available online, be particularly careful to check that the information you get there is trustworthy.

- **If facts aren't available, substitute "standard practices."** Sometimes you can point to "usual policy" or "standard practices" as a way to solve a problem. For example, if you work for a bank that has a firm policy requiring customers to show identification before you can provide information about their account, you can tell a complaining customer that it's the bank's policy and explain that it's for their protection.

- **If you are negotiating compensation, don't even think about doing it without researching what the position is worth.** Women are much more successful at getting paid what they deserve when they have good information. Do your homework regarding what the salary range should be, whether or not bonuses are usually paid, and the customary benefits at companies similar to the one where you're applying.

AVOID PERFECTIONISM

We've met a lot of nice girls who have gotten good at managing expectations in their various relationships, but still forget to manage the expectations they have for themselves. At times, they look outward for the reasons why things aren't going as planned or they aren't getting the things they want when, in fact, the problem lies closer to home—a lot closer. Consider how many of the following statements apply to you (be honest!):

✓ Others often let me down because they don't do things the way they *should* be done.

✓ I'm afraid if I do something less than perfectly others will think of me as incompetent.

✓ I'd rather do something myself than have someone else do it improperly.

✓ It's difficult for me to know when good enough is good enough.

✓ I often spend more time than necessary on projects to ensure I've covered every angle.

✓ When there's a job to do in my area of expertise, I'm usually the best one to do it.

✓ The thought of making a mistake is mortifying to me.

✓ I'm my own worst critic.

✓ My parents expected me to be perfect.

How did you do? If few or none of the statements apply to you, congratulations! You know that you're human and striving for perfection is an exercise in futility. If you think all or most of the statements apply to you, then you're not doing a great job of managing your self-expectations. In fact, you're probably overworked and exhausted. There's nothing wrong with aiming for excellence, but perfection—that's a different story.

Although striving for perfection isn't in the exclusive domain of women, we do tend to suffer from it more than men. Living in a society where women are considered less than perfect simply because they *are* women is one explanation. Other reasons include early childhood messages about the need to be perfect, attempting to compensate for perceived shortcomings (e.g., I'm not that attractive so I can't leave the house looking less than perfect), and buying into the myth that if you're a woman, you have to work twice as hard to be considered half as good. Given that regardless of your reasons it's impossible to achieve perfection, you're only spinning your wheels by trying. Your time would be much better spent managing your own expectations.

It's one thing to want to get something right because it's really important. It's another thing to not be able to let things go—even minor things—until you're 100 percent certain they're perfect. For example, if you're the maid of honor for a friend and responsible for throwing the bridal shower, it would only make sense that you would put extra time and effort into ensuring the event goes well. On the other hand, if you're not sleeping at night worrying about the floral arrangements, the food, and the myriad other things that could possibly go wrong, then you're fighting a losing battle. Nothing is ever perfect—the best we can hope for is a near approximation with an investment of reasonable time and effort.

MAKE IT WORK FOR YOU

- **Consider what is realistic given the time and resources available to you.** If you're given twenty-four hours' notice that you have to make the cake for your parents' fiftieth wedding anniversary party, it's not reasonable to expect you're going to make a five-tiered fondant-covered delicacy from scratch. In fact, this is a time when you might let your fingers do the walking and find a local patisserie to make it for you—even if it winds up costing more due to the tight deadline. Conversely, if you've been given plenty of time, then it's reasonable to put in the time needed to whip up something fancy (but not perfect).

- **Failure to plan is a plan to fail.** We sometimes get caught up in trying to be perfect when we're working under tight deadlines. The adrenaline starts flowing and suddenly everything is of equal and urgent importance. Don't procrastinate on plans or projects that require excellence. Advance planning allows you the time to think things through logically, review your work, and make the necessary adjustments that ensure quality (but not perfection).

- **Resist thinking that if something isn't done your way, it won't be good.** Lois tells the story of the first year she hosted Thanksgiving dinner in her home. She spent hours and hours in advance trying to make everything perfect. But once her mother, aunts, and other women arrived in the kitchen, her best-laid plans were suddenly for naught. With little choice given the strong-willed personalities involved, she had to let go and allow others to have a hand in the preparations. And you know what? It was probably the best Thanksgiving feast ever served on her table (but not perfect!).

- **Get help.** At the extreme, perfectionist tendencies can be a sign of obsessive-compulsive disorder. If you find yourself obsessing over the most minute details, and this gets in the way of achieving your overarching goals or spending time on things and people that are important to you, it might be time to seek professional assistance. There are medications, therapies, exercises, and other resources available to help you live your life more fully and with less anxiety.

WHEN IN DOUBT, DELEGATE

Nice girls who haven't gotten over their guilt wear themselves out by trying to do it all. And, inevitably, things *still* fall through the cracks. Unfortunately, the things that don't get done are often the things the nice girl wants to do for herself. Given that it's impossible to do it all, winning women use their values to guide where they choose to invest their time and energy.

Ellen, a working mother with two middle school daughters and a demanding job, was simply exhausted. There weren't enough hours in the day to give her family, her home, her job, and her husband the attention they deserved, and she had given up the notion of fitting in her friends and hobbies long ago. Her husband did his fair share, but also worked long hours. Overwhelmed, she constantly found herself snapping at her husband and kids—something had to change. When she asked Carol for advice, Carol questioned Ellen about what duties she truly had to do herself, and which she could delegate to others. It turned out that if they made some changes in their spending habits, Ellen's family could afford help—but Ellen wasn't convinced that anyone would do things exactly the way she did them herself. Ellen was a control freak in nice girl's clothing!

At other times, nice girls aren't willing to delegate because they confuse who they are with the tasks they perform. For example, taking charge of every possible domestic chore doesn't necessarily win a mother the respect she deserves—au contraire, she can easily be taken for granted. And while a mother can delegate laundry, shopping, cooking, and cleaning, she can't delegate the really important things that only she can do for her children—like talking and listening to them. That's why some moms hold on to chauffeur duties—they find the bonding time they get while driving their kids is invaluable!

Some nice girls don't delegate because when they've done it in the past, they've been burned. Winning women avoid this trap by making their expectations clearly known. Brooke, an interior designer, hired Danielle to work as an assistant. One day Danielle sent the wrong designs to a client, embarrassing Brooke. Her trust in Danielle badly shaken, Brooke began micromanaging, checking everything Danielle did. Instead of chalking up Danielle's error as a mistake, using it as a coaching moment and then moving on, Brooke let it get in the way of more important things she should have been doing to grow her business.

We believe that the acid test regarding whether you should "do it" or "delegate it" is the following question: Is performing this task the highest and best use of my time? If it is, do it. If not, delegate it.

MAKE IT WORK FOR YOU

- **If someone else can do the task, let them.** Even if you are really good at it, and even if you like doing it, consider assigning it to someone else—especially if he or she can learn from it.

- **Take the time to explain.** Delegating rarely goes well unless you are willing to take the time and make the effort to give the other person the information necessary to be successful. Clearly communicate expectations and encourage questions. Although the time investment may be a challenge, think of it as an investment in time saved over the long run.

- **Trust the person to whom you delegate.** Step back and let him or her get the task done. It may be done differently than you would do it, but as long as you've provided the information needed, the final product will be close enough to acceptable.

CRAFT MEANINGFUL MESSAGES

THE TACTICS IN STRATEGY IV FOCUS ON

- Finding and using your voice to your advantage.

- Preparing critical messages in advance.

- Thinking on your feet.

George Bernard Shaw once said, "The single biggest problem in communication is the illusion that it has taken place." This couldn't be more true for nice girls, who often think they've made themselves clear when in fact all they've done is hint around, skirt the issue, or water down the real message they want to communicate. In our culture, crafting clear, meaningful messages is harder for women than for men. If we communicate in the same way as men, we're accused of being pushy, aggressive, or worse, but we're also more likely than men to be ignored when we don't speak up. We continually walk a tightrope between being perceived as too aggressive and being invisible.

As we often say, winning women have mastered the art of telling others to go to hell in such a way that they look forward to the trip. In other words, they say what they mean, but with as much respect as possible. Communication that works to your advantage requires you to develop a style that suits your personality, the skills to make your point clearly the first time, and the ability to hear unspoken messages of others. This strategy provides you with the tactics needed to do all that—and more—with courage and confidence.

SPEAK EARLY AND OFTEN

All children—both boys and girls—are socialized to be polite. But nice girls take it to the extreme. They wait their turn to be called on. They're intimidated by the louder voices of men. They hesitate to offer their opinions for fear of overstepping their bounds or being ridiculed. And, often, they wait so long to give their opinions that all the good ideas are already on the table. As a result, they're perceived as not adding much value, lacking confidence, or not having opinions of their own. It's a vicious cycle.

This was the case with Ellie, a new clinical director with a large pharmaceutical firm. She was well educated, smart, and capable, but others didn't see her that way. In fact, her management wondered if they had made a mistake recruiting her. The culture at the company encouraged what the CEO described as "noisy debate." Staff meetings were raucous affairs, where ideas were tossed about and debated for hours. That's not to say these meetings weren't productive, because they were. But Ellie, accustomed to the culture at her previous company where people were less vociferous, felt intimidated by her new colleagues.

Speaking early and often is critical not just in the workplace, but in personal situations, particularly when thrown into a new culture. Perhaps you've had the experience of marrying into a family the polar opposite of the one you grew up in—maybe your family dinners are the kind where everyone eats in silence, while your spouse's family constantly talks over one another. As the saying goes, "When in Rome, do as the Romans do." It doesn't mean you have to change your personality, but if you've landed in a culture where you have to fight to be heard, you're going to need to make an effort to speak up. By practicing the following coaching tips, Ellie was able to make her presence known and manage her professional brand *without* losing the essence of her personality. She will always be more subdued than many people, but with just a few minor changes in her behavior, she found the voice she needed to succeed in her new role.

MAKE IT WORK FOR YOU

- **Be among the first two or three people to speak in a meeting.** Early speakers are seen as more self-confident than those who wait until much later. We don't recommend always being the first to speak, because this can lead to the perception that you're overly aggressive. Speaking up doesn't always mean you have to give an opinion; asking a question or supporting what others have said allows you to make your presence known—and that's what's important.

- **Use the "court reporter" technique.** This is something executive coach and communications expert Tom Henschel of Essential Communications suggests. When in a conversation, meeting, or other interaction, pretend you're in a courtroom where a court reporter is capturing everything being said and by whom. You want your name to be on every other page. So speaking up once isn't enough; you have to remain engaged enough in the discussion to appear throughout the court record.

- **Give yourself permission to interrupt.** Whether it's a meeting, a party, or a family gathering, sometimes you just can't seem to find a lull to insert yourself into the conversation. Nice girls don't interrupt, but winning women know how to do it with aplomb. The trick here is to use something that has already been said as your entree. For example, you can say, "Excuse me. Before we move on I'd like to comment on what John has just said about the new marketing strategy." Now, in addition to having your voice heard, you've also built an alliance with John, who knows that at least one person in the room has heard him and wants to build on his idea.

- **Aim for three to five comments or questions in a one-hour period.** Keep track of how many times you speak. If you're the quiet type, you'll be surprised at how few times this is. Keep in mind that silence is not always golden; it can also be seen as disinterested, aloof, or suggesting that you simply have nothing to contribute.

SPEAK IN HEADLINES WITH TAGLINES

I've been researching other school systems—you know, it's great that we're able to do all of this online. I've found so much information that is invaluable to us as PTA members. In fact, I've found more information than we can even possibly use. I found best practices from schools around the country that are doing things in a much more efficient and effective way than we are. The Dallas school system, for example, has an entire interactive website that parents and teachers can use to their advantage. Would you believe that they get over five hundred unique visitors every day while we can't even get a good turnout for our meetings? That's really something that we need to turn around. And the Seattle schools are engaging local businesses to help them design their website and make it more interactive. Of course, they're lucky because Microsoft is in their backyard. Unfortunately, we don't have the same kind of resources in our community. Well, anyway, what I'd like to talk about are a few ideas for how we can improve the quality of education in our own school system.

Was that painful for you to read? It was painful for us to write! And it's even more painful for the people who had to listen to it. Using more words than necessary to convey a message causes great ideas to be minimized, misunderstood, or flat out ignored (case in point: did you even read that paragraph to the end?). The inclination of nice girls is to use far too many words but the more words that are used, the less effect they have. As a result, nice girls often unwittingly sabotage their best efforts to communicate important messages for fear of being too direct or pushy.

Not to worry, though. We've got a method for getting your point across more effectively and succinctly without coming across as brazen or strident. Like it or not, men have more latitude when it comes to short communications. Most women can't get away with short, pithy messages the way men can—we're accused of being aloof or rude, whereas men are just assumed to be busy and efficient. We're expected to not only communicate clearly, but also care about what others think about what we've just said—and that's where headlines and taglines are the ideal solutions.

In the painfully long argument that begins this chapter, the woman made the mistake of not clearly stating from the outset the message she wanted people to take away. She left it until the end, and by then many listeners had mentally checked out. The first thing that comes out of your mouth should be your headline, and it should indicate to the listener what's about to come. In this case, the woman's headline should have been:

> I'd like to present three ideas for how we can improve the quality of education in our school district based on the best practices of other districts.

Now *that's* clear! It gets the attention of her audience. It also sets up what's to come, so people will want to keep listening. She would be wise to continue as follows:

> First, we need to engage more parents in the process. One way to do this is to develop a user-friendly interactive website.
>
> Second, I propose that we develop a process where parents meet more regularly with teachers to better understand their challenges.
>
> And third, our curriculum is outdated and would benefit from a review by an outside expert who can help us to ensure it's state-of-the-art.

These are the key points: 1, 2, 3. But she can't stop there. Because she's a woman, walking that tightrope between being seen as pushy or not being seen at all, she should add the following direct, straightforward tagline:

> These are my recommendations. However, I'd like to open it up for discussion so that we can get other good ideas on the table as well and make a decision as to the most appropriate way to move forward.

Now her ideas have been clearly expressed and she's also indicated that she's open to other options. Regardless of your audience or your message, using headlines and taglines in this way will help to organize your thoughts, present them in a way that is understandable to the listener, and increase the likelihood of being heard.

MAKE IT WORK FOR YOU

- **Prepare your communications in advance.** If the message you want to convey is important, then preparing it in advance is critical. Sketch out the boxes in the following diagram and fill them in with your message. If you have to think on your feet and don't have time to write down what you want to say, mentally picture the boxes and what you want to say within each one. Pretty soon, you'll be able to use the model without even having to write anything down. Make several copies of the diagram and keep them handy as a reminder.

- **Avoid the temptation to share everything in your head.** No one wants or needs to know everything that you're thinking. Operating under the misconception that more is better, nice girls overexplain themselves and provide too much detail. Save the fine points for when and if questions are asked.

- **Use headlines and taglines *everywhere*.** This technique is not only valuable when making important presentations, but also when you're communicating a message to your spouse, child, friends, salespeople, and so on. If you've ever wondered why your husband or friends tune you out, it could be that you're not getting your point across quickly enough. We've found that to be better heard, most women can reduce their messages by at least 25 percent.

- **Cue people when you're thinking out loud.** There will always be times when you just don't have a clear message outlined in your head; that's all right provided you say, "Let me think out loud for a moment." It cues the listener not to expect a fully thought out and succinct communication.

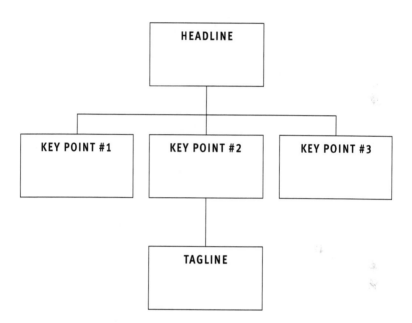

INFORM, DON'T ASK

Nice girls seek approval from others before taking action because they fear conflict. Yet, when a nice girl asks for permission, she gives the other person in the relationship a "one up" in the power equation. After all, no matter how nicely a nice girl asks, she's still giving the other person the opportunity to say no.

Brittney, for example, had accrued plenty of vacation days, but things were always so busy at her office that she hadn't taken any time off in a year. Well overdue for some rest and recreation, instead of informing her boss she'd soon be taking her well-deserved vacation, she made the mistake of asking him *when* it would be a good time for her to take a week off. He said, "Not now. Wait a few months." Now Brittney was stuck.

Don't get us wrong—we aren't saying that winning women make unilateral decisions that affect the people in their lives. We're saying they don't cede decision-making authority to others about issues that really are all about them.

Leah, in her mid-thirties, had always enjoyed a wonderful relationship with her parents. The trouble began when she started dating Dan, whose ethnicity was different from hers. While this didn't bother Leah, it did worry her parents, who kept meddling, telling Leah she should break it off (if you find yourself in this situation, you should also see Tactic 34: Create Family Boundaries). Leah knew she had to do something to stop the madness, so she gently told her parents she loved them but was not going to ask for their permission to date Dan because he was important to her and because this decision was hers alone to make.

When Diana and her boyfriend decided to move in together, she was worried it might interfere with the other relationships in her life. A nice girl might have asked her boyfriend whether he minded if she went out with her friends once a week. But she wasn't a nice girl. So instead she told him that she planned to continue seeing her friends regularly and that she expected he would do the same. They were moving in together; they weren't being joined at the hip. Diana knew that clearing the air regarding the issue of her ongoing independence would make the transition to formal "couplehood" a great deal easier. But she didn't ask permission; she informed him.

Not only do winning women inform rather than ask, they are careful not to undermine themselves when they communicate what's on their minds. They avoid setting themselves up for pushback by cushioning their message with things like, "I know you probably won't agree with me about this but . . .," or, "I'm sorry, but I have to tell you. . . ." Instead, winning women approach the conversation respectfully but from a position of strength. They may say something like "I've given a lot of thought to the issue and here's what I've decided. . . ." Or perhaps "My guess is that we're in agreement about the issue, so here's what I plan to do. . . ." If the issue is so minor that it's really a nonissue, they may even say, "I wanted to let you know I'm going to . . ."

Winning women know that it's better to ask forgiveness than to ask permission. When they want something, they go for it.

Make It Work for You

- **Consider whether this issue is yours to decide.** If so, then you don't need approval from anyone else. You may want to ask for input from others, but that's different from asking for permission.

- **Be respectful of the other person's feelings.** Think about how you would feel if the tables were turned and proceed accordingly. You can inform people about your decisions without being callous.

- **Don't apologize.** If a decision is yours to make and you approach others in a sensitive way about it, don't feel bad for living your life in a way that makes you happy.

ASK OPEN-ENDED QUESTIONS

Given that Melanie had dental insurance, she was shocked when she got a bill from her dentist for hundreds of dollars. It turned out that only a small portion of the work she'd had done was covered, and to make matters worse, her dentist's fees were higher than those considered "reasonable and customary" by the insurance company. Of course, it paid only a percentage of the "reasonable and customary" fees. Melanie hadn't really understood how her dentist worked with insurance coverage and she hadn't wanted to bother the dentist's office manager, who wasn't very friendly, by asking her to explain it.

In another scenario, when interviewing for a new job, Rebecca, reluctant to seem inexperienced, asked very few questions about exactly what she'd be doing. Within the first two days, she realized the job was considerably more administrative and a lot less creative than it had seemed from the posting on the company's website, and that accepting the job had been a mistake.

Winning women know that if they don't ask open-ended questions, they won't get the information they need—whether it's what their medical diagnosis means, where their teenagers are going when they say, "See you later!" or how the men they're dating feel about them. And they also know that *just* asking questions isn't enough. They ask the right kinds of questions and ask them in ways that encourage people to open up.

There are two kinds of questions—open-ended and closed-ended. Closed-ended questions can be answered with one word (usually yes or no) or a phrase (such as, "I don't know"). Ask any teenager if he had a good day at school and you know what we're talking about. Open-ended questions, on the other hand, are designed to invite a more useful response. An example: "Tell me about your day."

Examples of Open-Ended and Closed-Ended Questions	
Closed-Ended	**Open-Ended**
"Did you go to the party?"	"Tell me about the party."
"Will you agree to . . . ?"	"What's your thinking about . . . ?"
"Is that the right way to do that?"	"How did you do that?"

Think back to Melanie's situation. If she had asked an open-ended question like "What's the policy regarding coverage for this procedure?" instead of the yes/no question, "Is it covered?" she would have gotten the information she needed and spared herself a very expensive lesson. Although closed-ended questions are efficient and can be useful in the right circumstances, they have a couple of downsides. The first is that they fail to elicit the information we need. Then, to make matters worse, we follow up with more questions, and as a result, the person with whom we're talking can perceive the questioning process as an interrogation rather than a conversation. The other disadvantage to asking closed-ended questions is that we may not think to ask all the questions needed to get the required information.

Sometimes people are reluctant to answer open-ended questions because they are suspicious about what we'll do with the information if they give it to us. One way to preempt that reaction is to state the reason you're asking. For instance, "Tell me about how you work with clients. The reason I'm asking is that I'm looking for a tax professional with whom to work over the long term and you seem like someone who fits the bill." Or "Our relationship means a great deal to me and I want it to work for you, too. That's why I want to know how you're feeling about our future together." Winning women explicitly mention the benefit others will derive by responding to their inquiries. With information comes power. Winning women empower themselves by asking for the information they want in a way that ensures they'll get it.

MAKE IT WORK FOR YOU

- **Write down your questions in advance**. It can be difficult to think of the right questions "in the moment," so help yourself by listing the things you need to know before you begin the conversation. For example, if you hire a trainer for your new puppy and you've never before had a dog, write down your questions about the training process in advance.

- **Make the question as open-ended as possible.** You don't want to overdo it, especially if you're after a very specific piece of information, but being unintentionally vague in your questions can often elicit useful information you didn't even know to ask for.

- **State the reason you're asking.** People are more likely to answer your questions if they know why you are asking them and what you will do with the information. Win people over by sharing your thinking with them.

LISTEN TO GET WHAT YOU WANT

Like many women, you may be a great listener, but if you're not using this skill to your advantage, you're missing out on opportunities to get the things you want. Listening not only gives you the information you need to make decisions, negotiate, and find common ground, it also enhances practically any conceivable relationship. Who doesn't like to be heard? The problem is that nice girls are a polite audience, but don't use what they glean from listening to their advantage.

Contrary to what many people think, listening isn't a passive process. It involves three very active behaviors:

1. Paraphrasing what you've just heard the speaker say.

2. Asking questions about what's been said.

3. Reflecting back to the speaker your understanding of how that person feels about what he or she is saying.

Imagine your landlord sends you a letter telling you he's going to raise your rent by 9 percent. You just had a rent increase the previous year, so you call him to find out why he's raising it again so soon. Here's how you can use active listening to get what you want out of the conversation:

You: Hi, Bill. I got the notice about the rent increase. I'm wondering why, when we just had one last year?

Landlord: Well, you know taxes are going up, utilities are increasing, and I've got to put a new roof on the building. And the economy is causing people to skip on their rent, then move out. There are a bunch of vacancies.

You: I understand that costs just don't stay the same. I imagine these increases are stressing you out along with the tenants.

Landlord: That's right. No one likes to raise the rent, but it's a necessary evil.

You: I appreciate the fact that you don't like having to do it. I'd like to see if there's some way both of our needs can be met. When the rent goes up it stays that way, but some of these things, such as a new roof, are one-time expenses.

Landlord: Oh, there are always repairs that pop up.

You: I don't recall any repairs being done to my unit or the building last year. Are there things I don't know about?

Landlord: Some of the units needed new air conditioners installed and others needed the hot water heaters replaced. There's always something.

You: I have no doubt a building like this does require a lot of work to keep it looking so nice. Yet, again, my unit hasn't had any updates in quite a few years. It would seem fairer to me if there was a more modest cost-of-living adjustment rather than my paying for repairs on other units. I'll even go so far as to suggest that if my unit needs any repairs during the current year, I'll handle them myself.

Landlord: I don't know about that. Everyone else is getting the same increase.

You: You also mentioned that people are breaking their leases. I've been here for nearly seven years and have always paid my rent on time and sometimes even early. That should have some value to you.

Landlord: (*Silence.*)

You: With all the vacancies you have, it seems that you wouldn't want to lose a good tenant who hasn't required any repairs. Can we agree on a cost-of-living increase of 3 percent for this year and then revisit it next year?

Landlord: Okay, but only if you don't mention this to any of the other tenants.

Conversations don't always go as smoothly and favorably as this, but it's a good example of how to use all the elements of active listening (paraphrasing, asking questions, and reflecting feelings) to your advantage without seeming demanding or overly critical. When used properly, active listening enables you to maintain calm without relinquishing control.

MAKE IT WORK FOR YOU

- **Paraphrase, question, reflect.** Although it may seem like others will "catch on" to what you're doing, in reality this doesn't typically happen. They are too worried about being fully heard and understood to notice the techniques you're using to get the information you need.

- **Practice in familiar circumstances.** Admittedly, it was easy for us to write the scenario above because we've used active listening to our advantage for many years. You can become just as proficient by practicing first with friends, family, or low-risk situations. Then, when it really matters, you'll have the skills under your belt.

- **When in doubt, revert to listening.** You may find yourself in a situation where you're not sure how to respond or find it difficult to maintain your cool. Reverting to listening buys you time to think and calm down. It also gives you more information to respond with facts, not just emotions.

CHOOSE THE RIGHT VEHICLE

Even a well-crafted message can miss the mark if it's not delivered the right way. Thanks to technology, we now have e-mail, instant messaging, texting, and even social networking sites in addition to the traditional choices for communicating. All these methods have a time and place. The trick is to use the right method for the right purpose.

Denise was dissatisfied with a purchase she made over the Internet. She described her problem in detail on a form the merchant had on its website rather than e-mail her complaint. But she didn't take a screen shot of the form before she submitted it. When the merchant didn't resolve the matter to her satisfaction, Denise disputed the charge with her credit card company. It took her more time and effort, though, because she had no proof she'd already sent a complaint directly to the merchant and she had to re-create the complaint to document her dispute. Had she sent an e-mail instead, she would have had a ready record.

In another example, the telephone might have been a better vehicle than e-mail. Marisa was working on a project with a colleague at a different branch within her firm. Unfortunately, the project was late and over budget. To make matters worse, the e-mails Marisa was getting from her coworker were increasingly curt in tone, seeming to point the finger at her for the delays and overruns. For a while, Marisa responded via e-mail but ignored the hostile undertones, until one day she snapped and sent a nasty-gram of her own. Of course, the coworker forwarded that message on to a superior, making Marisa look like the problem. Although there's no guarantee, we think Marisa would have been far better off if she had picked up the phone to discuss the issues with her colleague.

Nice girls take the path of least resistance, and this often means hiding behind technology to avoid confrontation. We recently heard a story about a woman who held a serious disagreement with a dear friend—via instant message! That's topped only by the one we heard about a romance that broke up via text. But when you use technology as a shield to convey difficult messages, you run the risk they'll be misunderstood or misconstrued, and the conflict is likely to escalate. Instead, winning women make a deliberate choice about which method of communication will convey their message in the best way. Winning women also take the other person's preferred communication method into consideration as they make that decision. They don't do this to be nice. They do it because they know that if the other person is comfortable with the medium, they're more likely to be receptive to the message. So, for example, if someone responds to your e-mail by calling, you should recognize this as the person's preference and respond in kind by initiating the next conversation by phone. And, the vehicle should also match the depth of the message. So while it's fine to send complaints about a product through an impersonal vehicle like e-mail, use phone calls or handwritten notes to convey heartfelt messages.

MAKE IT WORK FOR YOU

- **Don't hide behind technology.** Make a conscious choice about the right method for a particular communication. Resist the temptation to e-mail your sister that the last time you spoke she hurt your feelings. This is something you should tell her in person. The fact is, no matter how carefully you write an e-mail message, you don't know how the other person will read it. If there's tension, pick up the phone or, where practicable, meet in person. Just because you *can* use Facebook to inform the person you've been dating that you've decided to move on, doesn't mean you *should*.

- **Document as needed.** E-mail can serve as a useful way to create a paper trail. Use it in situations where you may later need to prove what happened. But the need for documentation shouldn't drive the communication method you select. You can always follow up a conversation with an e-mail thanking the other person for taking the time to talk with you and outlining your understanding of whatever was agreed to.

- **Reread what you've written before you click Send.** Beyond checking your spelling and grammar, put yourself in the recipient's shoes. Is your message clear and concise? Is it easy to read? Do the words you've chosen express what you really mean to say? Is the tone right? And while you're at it, when forwarding messages, make sure you haven't included an e-mail stream below your message that you don't want others to see.

OPEN STRONG

Earlier, we noted that issues between people don't magically resolve themselves (as much as most nice girls wish they did). Having the conversation, no matter how difficult, is the way winning women get the respect they deserve. We know these kinds of conversations can be tough to initiate. That's why we'd like to suggest some opening language that will make people *want* to solve issues with you in a collaborative way.

Stephanie and her husband had agreed that their marriage hadn't worked for years and that divorce was the only remaining option. Now she was faced with the unpleasant task of broaching the subject of how to divide their assets. She began the conversation by saying, "I'm relieved that we've come to the decision to divorce and I know you are too, no matter how bad we both feel that our marriage is over. So that we can make this less painful and move on with our lives, as well as keep the legal costs down, let's talk about how we should divide our assets." By letting her husband know the ways in which he will be better off by having the conversation than not, Stephanie set the stage for a positive discussion.

You can use this same technique, with a different spin, in all kinds of situations. Let's say the store where you've made a purchase refuses to give you a refund. Ask to speak with the manager and say, "I've been a satisfied customer of yours for many years. In fact, I often recommend your store to my friends and family. And when I do, I always mention your store's commitment to customer service and satisfaction. I know that's important to you. So I'm sure we'll be able to resolve my concern today." Even though you may have never before met the manager, you will be able to engage her by focusing on what she cares about—the business you refer, and her desire to maintain the store's brand promise.

One other approach that can be helpful in specific situations is to mention that others are already on board. Anna, the woman who was promoted to manage people who'd previously been her peers, used this approach when she sat down with members of her team one-on-one to clarify her new role and to figure out where they stood. She opened each meeting by saying, "I know Joe explained why I was tapped to lead the department. His support means a lot to me and I know you appreciate his leadership as well. So I wanted to sit down with you to talk about how we can best work together." By making it clear that Joe had her back, Anna made it more difficult for her new direct reports to react negatively.

Winning women know that sincerely expressing how much they value the relationship and want to work out whatever problem has surfaced disarms most people. The result is that rather than feeling threatened and withdrawing, others engage more readily and fully.

MAKE IT WORK FOR YOU

- **State the benefit to the other person of working out the problem.** Don't assume it is as obvious to the other person as it is to you.

- **Be authentic.** If you don't really mean it, don't say that you value the relationship. Instead, find something else to say that is both positive and truthful.

- **Use the "I have allies" technique sparingly.** While it worked beautifully in Anna's case, that was because Joe was both a powerful and an appropriate ally. If, on the other hand, Stephanie had tried to use this approach by telling her husband that she'd already discussed what assets she believed she was entitled to with her best friend, or her sister, or anyone else with no say in the matter, her conversation would have quickly headed in the wrong direction.

SEND UP A TRIAL BALLOON

We've talked a lot about how to identify your needs and communicate them to others. But what happens when you know what your needs are and how to express them, but just aren't sure of the best solution for getting them met? Now we'd like to share another very useful but little-known communication skill—using trial balloons. According to Wikipedia, a trial balloon is a small piece of information you use to gauge the reaction of an audience. Adapted from the worlds of politics and business for our purposes, it can be thought of as a way to "test the water" about a solution or idea before diving in.

Using a trial balloon has the advantage of creating a bit of distance between the proposal and the person proposing it, which makes it easier to back off if the response is negative. Think about the difference between the following statements:

"I have an idea."

"One idea is to . . ."

The first statement clearly links the speaker to the idea whereas in the second statement, the speaker is merely giving voice to the idea without necessarily supporting it. There are two advantages to this—one is that the speaker doesn't have to be convinced that the idea is "the solution" and the other is that the other person can disagree with the *idea* without disagreeing with *her*.

Joyce and her husband had trouble agreeing how to raise their two boys. A product of a strict home, Joyce felt strongly their sons needed more structure and discipline than her husband was willing to accept. Continually cast in the role of disciplinarian, Joyce often felt like a single mom raising *three* boys! She knew she had to reach agreement with her husband about rules they would both enforce, but when she'd tried to do that in the past, the conversation had rapidly deteriorated into an argument. Because both Joyce and her husband felt so strongly about the issues, things tended to get ugly quickly. Then Joyce decided

181

to use a trial balloon as a way to broach solutions to the problem of how much time the boys spent playing video games. Instead of starting with "The boys spend way too much time playing video games and we need to set limits immediately," she began by saying, "What if we were to set some parameters regarding the boys and video games?" By doing this, Joyce tested whether her husband was willing to set any limits at all before getting into the weeds regarding the amount of time that's appropriate. If he agreed, they would remain on track to resolve this issue. If he didn't, it wouldn't become an argument because Joyce merely raised it rather than owned it. Of course, in the latter case, she still has the larger problem of how to get her husband to take the issue seriously, but at least it gives her the room to step back and try again with another approach.

Other Trial Balloon Statements
"One thing we might do . . ."
"What if we were to . . ."
"I've heard about another way people have approached something like this."

Bianca used this technique when she was trying to help her son decide where he should apply to college. Because they had a history of disagreeing about things both academic and social, Bianca wanted to improve the way they related to one another and viewed the college selection process as an opportunity. However, she was concerned that if she were to suggest a particular school, his reaction would be to cross it off the list immediately. So she made it a point to frame her suggestions as trial balloons instead. Rather than saying, "I think you should take a look at ABC University," she'd say, "My friend Kelly's son started as a freshman at ABC University and loves it. She told me he's enjoying the classes he's taking as well as the social life."

MAKE IT WORK FOR YOU

- **Keep your tone and body language neutral.** When you float a trial balloon to gauge someone's receptiveness to an idea, be sure your tone and body language are as neutral as the message itself.

- **Be prepared to hear "no."** If the trial balloon falls flat, don't take it personally. After all, that's why you sent it up.

- **Don't use a trial balloon for issues on which there is no discussion.** If you will ultimately make the decision about the direction of an idea or project, and the input of others will not be considered, then a trial balloon will likely burst on you. Others won't believe that you genuinely care about their opinions and will eventually stop giving them to you.

SPEAK THE LANGUAGE OF INFLUENCE

If you traveled to a foreign country where you could speak the language, wouldn't you at least try to communicate in that language? It's the same with the language of influence. Not everyone takes in or gives out information in the same way, so learning to match your style with that of the person you're communicating with increases the chances that your message will be well received. Some people have said they think using a model like the one we're about to share with you—or similar ones—is manipulative. That's nonsense. You're not changing the actual content of your message—only the manner in which it's conveyed. It would be manipulative if you told people things you think they want to hear, but that's not what this tactic is about. It's about framing the message so that the other person can process it using *their* filters—not yours.

Take a look at the following four shapes.

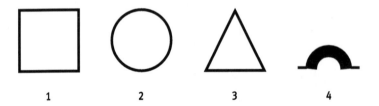

Each of the shapes represents a communication style. None of us speaks entirely in one style or another—we all use elements of all four, but most people tend to lean toward one. Knowing your own style as well as the style of the person you're communicating with can make you a more effective influencer. Here's how each of the shapes can be interpreted:

THE REASONER

The Reasoner is influenced by data, facts, and figures. Just as the square shape suggests, Reasoners are stable, even-tempered, and somewhat self-contained. You can recognize them from their conservative dress and dislike for small talk. To effectively influence them, stay focused on facts and avoid moving into the realm of feelings—that makes them uncomfortable. Do your homework in advance so that you're not perceived as shooting from the hip and are prepared to answer their inevitable questions.

THE PEOPLE PERSON

The People Person is influenced by values, tradition, and how they and others feel about an idea you present. As the circle suggests, the People Person tends to roll with the punches and go with the flow. You can recognize them if you see their homes and offices are filled with memorabilia and personal items that are meaningful to them. To effectively influence them, it's critical that you show that you've considered the impact your concepts will have on them or others. Speak to the People Person in "feeling" rather than "thinking" terms.

THE DOER

The Doer is influenced by how quickly and efficiently an idea can be expressed and implemented. As the triangle suggests, the Doer wants you to get to the point quickly. You can recognize them from their fast-paced speaking pattern and unfinished sentences. To effectively influence the Doer, you must prepare your message in advance so that you can give your bottom line first, backed up with just two or three bullet points— and only if you're asked for them. Suggesting a time line for creating change or implementing new concepts works well with the Doer, who will typically make a relatively quick decision.

THE INNOVATOR

The Innovator is influenced by unique ideas and the complexity of how fact meets opportunity, particularly as it impacts the future. As the nonconforming, open shape suggests, Innovators are often nontraditional and don't like to be constrained by what's worked in the past. You can recognize them by their preference for abstract art, toys and gadgets, and sometimes science fiction. To effectively influence the Innovator, lay out an array of concepts that haven't been tried in the past and support them with reason. Like the Reasoner, the Innovator likes data but more for the purpose of shaping new ideas.

Let us show you how you can use this simple model by providing an example of how the same idea might be presented to different types of communicators. Say you're in a relationship with someone who seems to be taking more from you than he gives to you. You are the one who more frequently compromises, picks up the tab for meals and entertainment, and looks for ways to make his life easier. You're at the point where his behavior has to change or you're going to initiate a breakup. Here's what the message would sound like depending on his influence style:

With the Reasoner: Ben, I need to talk to you about the ways in which our relationship is lopsided and what I need from you if we're to continue with it. In the past month alone, I've paid over $300 for eating out, movies, and groceries to cook meals for us. I've gone to the two family events you've invited me to, but you've refused to visit my family despite the fact that I've asked you to join me on at least three occasions. And last year when we planned on going to Provence on vacation, I was willing to change that plan at the last minute so that you could attend your college friend's wedding in Mexico. I realize that I freely choose to do the things I do for you and for us, but I need you to meet me halfway in these areas if our relationship is going to survive.

With the People Person: Ben, I'm disappointed and beginning to feel taken advantage of and used in our relationship. In fact, I've checked it out with several people who know both of us just to make sure I wasn't overacting and, without being critical, each person said they noticed the same things I'm concerned about. For example, when we go out to eat, I'm usually the one who picks up the tab. And, although I've tried hard to blend in with your friends and family, I don't feel you've done the same with mine. If our relationship is going to continue, I've got to know you understand my feelings and needs as much as I try to understand yours.

With the Doer: Ben, our relationship can't continue the way it is. I pay for most of our meals and entertainment, visit your family and friends despite the fact that you don't reciprocate, and bend over backward to accommodate your needs. If we're going to make it as a couple, I need these things to change.

With the Innovator: Ben, when we first got together I envisioned a relationship where we exhibited mutual respect for each other's needs. This hasn't really panned out, and as I assess what's transpired, it's clear something needs to change if we're going to move forward as a couple. I seem to be doing most of the compromising and ensuring your needs are met without getting what I need in return. I'd like to think we can be different from other couples who complain and nag one another, so I'd like to explore our options.

This isn't where the conversation ends, of course. But it does give you a sense of how speaking the other person's language of influence can help get you what you want.

MAKE IT WORK FOR YOU

- **Don't let the message get lost in translation.** There's a Chinese curse: "May you have a wonderful idea and not be able to convince anyone of it." You're more likely to suffer from the curse if you don't know how to frame the message in a way the other person will understand.

187

- **Avoid the tendency to switch languages.** In the heat of an argument, you may be tempted to revert to your native style. Don't acquiesce. Stick with the same style to enhance your chances for success.

- **Look for points of agreement.** Speaking the same language will help you find ways to bridge your ideas to those of others. Listen carefully to others and pinpoint places where their mindset overlaps with yours. Beginning your statements with a point of agreement can make new or differing opinions seem less confrontational.

WRITE YOUR DESCRIPT

One of the concerns we hear from women is that they don't know how to handle confrontations with tact and diplomacy. So they avoid them altogether and wind up (a) sacrificing their needs and (b) feeling ill at ease with certain people or in certain situations. Hopefully, many of the tools and tips we've already provided (and some we have yet to share with you) will help in this regard. Another nifty little tool called the DESCript brings together a number of tactics in this book in one simple model to help navigate a difficult conversation. The DESCript has a number of benefits:

- It keeps you focused on the issue at hand.

- It emphasizes behaviors that can be changed rather than personality traits.

- It allows you to tactfully deal with resistance.

- It helps you to have difficult conversations.

- It keeps the dialogue moving forward.

- It seeks mutual agreement.

The chart on the next page provides an example of how to employ the six key elements of the model and a place for you to write your own practice script. Those six key elements include:

D = *Describe* why you're having the conversation.

E = *Explain* your point of view and *elicit* the other person's perspective.

S = *Summarize* what you heard and *specify* what you would like to see happen in the future.

C = Conclude with *consequences* (either positive or negative, depending on the situation).

ELEMENTS	EXAMPLE	TRY IT!
D = Describe	"Joan, I'd like to talk to you about something that happened the other day when we took our kids on a playdate."	
E = Explain and Elicit	"When my son acted up, you interceded before I could say anything to him. It made me feel as if you didn't think I could control him. I'm wondering how you saw the situation."	
S = Summarize and Specify	"So, if I understand you correctly, you thought you were helping me. I get it now. What would be even more helpful to me in the future is if you would just give me a moment to think about how I can best approach the situation. I'm just not as quick on my feet as you are."	
C = Consequences	"That way, we'll be able to respect each other's roles as parents and stay close friends."	

MAKE IT WORK FOR YOU

- **DESCript difficult conversations in advance.** Going in cold to what could be a difficult discussion or negotiation puts you at a disadvantage. Having the words you want to say and the direction in which you want the discussion to go prepared in advance enables you to remain grounded and maintain your equilibrium without giving up on what's important to you. Again, you'll combine this tool with several other tactics to increase the likelihood of walking away with what you want. Even if you don't, you maintain your integrity and put the other person on notice that you're not afraid to speak up about the things that are important to you.

- **Be honest, but tactful.** Being tactful doesn't mean being a doormat. Use the DESCript as a tool to help you deliver messages in a way that people can hear and respond to rather than resist and resent.

- **Keep reading.** If potentially contentious conversations still scare you, we highly recommend a wonderful book called *Crucial Conversations: Tools for Talking When Stakes Are High* by Kerry Patterson, Joseph Grenny, Ron McMillan, and Al Switzler. It contains a seven-point strategy for holding your own in emotionally and psychologically charged situations. We also highly recommend *Difficult Conversations: How to Discuss What Matters Most* by Douglas Stone, Bruce Patton, and Sheila Heen, affiliated with the Harvard Project on Negotiation. The more techniques you learn, the better you'll get at managing complicated conversations.

PRACTICE CONTRASTING

Rashaun's husband, thinking he was doing something nice for her, arranged for them to spend a romantic weekend at the beach. The only problem was, he didn't check her schedule and it turned out she had committed to attend her best friend's thirtieth birthday party on the same Saturday night that he had booked their getaway. When she found out, she didn't know quite how to tell him that there was no way she could go out of town that weekend. Let's face it: none of us wants to discourage others from doing nice things for us—particularly spouses! Contrasting is the perfect way to let others know you can't go along with their program without making it appear that you're un-grateful or not appreciative of their efforts.

As the term suggests, the technique involves pointing out the difference between what you *do* want and *don't* want. In the case of Rashaun, it would sound like this:

> "I *don't* want you to think I'm not delighted that you arranged this because I absolutely am. But I *do* have to let you know that I'm already committed for that weekend with Jessica's thirtieth birthday party."

From there you can begin a conversation about how the weekend can be postponed or some other arrangement can be made that suits both of your needs. Here are a few more examples of contrasting in other sticky situations:

> "I *don't* want to appear ungrateful for all that you've done for me, because I am very appreciative of your efforts. At the same time, I *do* want to let you know that I had expected a promotion along with this generous raise."

"I *don't* want to make you think that I haven't noticed all of the extra chores you've done around the house because I have, and I appreciate it. However, I *do* want to talk to you about how the chores might be even more evenly split between us."

"I *don't* want to seem pushy because I know you're trying your best to address my concerns. At the same time, I *do* want you to know that I believe a full refund for this purchase would be more appropriate than simply a partial credit to my account for future purchases."

Contrasting accomplishes three things:

- Shows respect for the other person and their efforts or position.
- Clearly addresses your concerns.
- Provides a platform from which to begin a constructive conversation.

Of course, there are situations where you'll still find yourself at odds. In those situations, instead of simply contrasting what you do and don't want, it can be useful to start by proposing a process. Vivienne used this technique when she found herself at odds with her mother regarding plans for her wedding, which her mom was hosting. They couldn't agree on the guest list for Vivienne's side—Vivienne's mom wanted to invite long-lost relatives and friends, some of whom Vivienne had never met or, if she had, didn't remember. Vivienne wanted a smaller wedding with only people who were important in her life. Things were about to get ugly until Vivienne proposed that rather than arguing, they resolve things by using a negotiation technique known as "single text." They each wrote their own "wish list," exchanged the lists, and then accepted the names that appeared on both lists with no further discussion. For the remaining names on each list, they wrote a brief explanation about why they wanted to include the person, and then they exchanged lists again. They went back and forth discussing which names each could accept until they had a final list both could live with.

Agreeing to discuss a topic only for a specified period of time, at a particular time of day or day of the week, or in a specific place are other process ideas. So a couple might agree to discuss money matters only on Sunday mornings over coffee. If something surfaces in between, they defer the conversation until then.

MAKE IT WORK FOR YOU

- **Express your appreciation.** Begin with what you genuinely appreciate or another positive statement about the situation. This allows the other person to know that their efforts are not unnoticed.

- **Clearly state what you need or want that is different from what is being provided to you.** This can be difficult for nice girls. Not wanting to hurt someone's feelings, nice girls too often go along with someone else's program or feel guilty about having their own unique needs or expectations. Get over it.

- **Combine contrasting with other tactics.** Clearly, the conversation doesn't end with saying what you do and don't want. Be prepared to follow it up with active listening, setting boundaries, and other tactics for overcoming resistance (which we'll cover a little later).

- **Keep process in mind.** Whenever the issues portend trouble, try to agree on a process to deal with them before tackling them directly. That might mean agreeing to discuss the items that need to be resolved in a particular order or setting a time limit for the conversation before you get started.

AFFIRM THE POSITIVE

Research has shown that moods can be contagious. Winning women create and share positive momentum to help keep people engaged during any kind of conversation. When things are tense, winning women remind themselves and the other person of the progress they've already made. During a difficult conversation, this can keep the person engaged by reminding them of the time and energy they've already invested in resolving the disagreement. (Recall the "sunk cost" dilemma we discussed in Tactic 31: Walk Away When It's Time.)

For example, let's say you've been negotiating for a new home, but are having trouble making a deal. By reminding the sellers of the fact that you believe they have a beautiful home in which you can see yourself raising your family, you are affirming the positive.

Winning women also keep things on a positive note by avoiding what we call "red flag" words and phrasing. The most commonly used red flag word is *but*—when people hear it, they tend to disbelieve whatever preceded it. For example, "I love you, *but* this is something we need to change" puts the emphasis on the negative—the "something we need to change"—and discounts the positive—"I love you." In most situations, the word *and* is a terrific substitute—"I love you *and* this is something we need to change" gets the message across without implying that the speaker will no longer love the listener if he or she isn't able to change that "something." Of course, you should only say this if it's the message you intend to send!

Red Flag Words and Phrases	Try This Instead
"Yes, but . . ."	"Yes, and . . ."
"However"	"And"
"Problem"	"Challenge"

Red Flag Words and Phrases	Try This Instead
"I have an issue with this . . ."	"I'm concerned that . . ."
"I can't agree unless . . ."	"I can agree if . . ."

MAKE IT WORK FOR YOU

- **Stay positive.** Have faith that you will be able to resolve things. If this faith stars to wane, remind yourself, and the other person, of the progress already made.

- **Avoid red flag words.** They cause people to miss your intended message and instead focus on unintentional negativity.

OFFER "I" MESSAGES

Many nice girls avoid using *I* for fear of sounding too egotistical or self-centered. Instead, they minimize their needs and perspectives or feelings by phrasing them as questions that aren't really questions at all. For example:

> "Don't you think it might be better if we skipped the birthday gifts this year?"

> "Would you consider taking less money for the car?"

> "Wouldn't you like to do your homework before watching television?"

In each of these instances, the message is diluted and left open for discussion when discussion isn't appropriate. We call these "back door" communications. Listen to how the identical messages are communicated much more directly with the use of *I*:

> "I propose we skip birthday gifts this year."

> "I can pay a maximum of $27,000 for the car."

> "I expect you to do your homework before watching television."

It doesn't mean there might not be further discussion, but an "I" message unambiguously conveys your feeling about an issue and puts you in a far better position to negotiate for what you want. When you own your feelings or beliefs, others know where you stand. Plus "I" messages are less likely to put others on the defensive than "you" messages (e.g., "You have to do your homework before watching television").

Some nice girls have been taught, either explicitly or implicitly, that "I" statements will make them seem too assertive or aggressive. We disagree. This was a trap Patricia, a senior executive in the entertainment industry, found herself in. She was not only powerful in terms of her position, she was smart, tall, and had an intimidating presence. Somewhere along the line, a career coach told her she would make others feel more comfortable if she asked questions rather than made declarative statements. This was not good advice. Once she started framing statements as "Yes, but don't you think that . . ." it only created a bigger problem, because now she was perceived as manipulative and passive-aggressive. People didn't believe she really cared about what they had to say and saw her questions as a veiled attempt to get them to come around to her point of view—which they were.

As Patricia eventually learned, beginning with an "I" statement invites respect. It doesn't mean there won't be discussion. In some circumstances, you *want* others to add their expertise to the mix. In fact, we suggest you add a "tagline" (as we described in Tactic 48: Speak in Headlines with Taglines) to your "I" message that invites others to comment on it. It might sound like this: "I believe we need to begin looking at cost-cutting efforts before we're behind the eight ball. What ideas does this group have to increase profits?" The caveat here is that you must listen to the answers and incorporate them into your plan of action if you want to gain others' commitment and cooperation.

MAKE IT WORK FOR YOU

- **Pay attention to the number of times you couch statements as questions.** You'll be surprised. Questions should be used exclusively for getting information, not giving your opinion. Once you're conscious of how often you minimize your messages, you can catch yourself and turn those questions into "I" messages.

- **Avoid the all-inclusive "we" message.** Nice girls sometimes use this to soften and distance themselves from a negative message. For example, "We think you could have done a better job of handling that situation." Unless you are truly delivering a message from at least one other person, opt for the "I."

- **Own your messages.** Winning women aren't afraid to stand behind their opinions, requests, and feelings. Combining your "I" messages with several of the other tactics we've described helps to communicate the message loud and clear, without seeming intractable or egocentric.

MAKE LIKE A BROKEN RECORD

We realize that some of you may have never owned a record! So let us explain what happened "back in the day" when a record had a scratch. *It repeated a piece of the song over and over and over again* because the needle would get stuck in a groove. There are times in conversations, particularly contentious ones, when you have to act like a broken record—repeating yourself several times, often using different words, until your message is heard. Lois put this to good use once when she went to the Hollywood Bowl for a concert she'd been looking forward to. When she and some friends arrived on Saturday night and went to their seats, they found the seats already occupied. She asked the people seated to see their tickets and, sure enough, they had the same seats. So she called an usher over and he informed her that her tickets were for Friday, the previous night. Sure enough, the tickets said Friday.

Lois had bought the tickets at the box office the previous Sunday and clearly recalled a conversation she had with the ticket seller. He had told her there were better tickets available for Friday and she'd informed him that she wouldn't be back from New York until Saturday (which stuck in her mind because it led to a rather lengthy discussion about how they had both relocated to Los Angeles from New York). So she knew for certain that he had made the mistake. The usher told her there was nothing he could do and Lois asked to speak with his supervisor. Although the supervisor was sympathetic, he too told her there was nothing that could be done, at which point Lois then asked to speak with *his* supervisor, who turned out to be the manager of the venue.

A woman emerged from her office and told Lois there was a sign in the box office that instructed you to read your tickets carefully because there were no refunds once you left with tickets in hand. Listen to how Lois used the broken record (and some of the other tactics we've already discussed) to resolve the issue:

Lois: I understand what your policy is, and I also recall my discussion with the ticket seller and therefore believe the mistake was his, not mine.

Manager: Well, he's off tonight so there's really nothing we can do.

Lois: The policy is only fair if a mistake is made by the person purchasing the ticket. It seems to me if the mistake was made by one of your employees, you would want to make good on it.

Manager: I don't know that he made the mistake; that's just your side of it.

Lois: Be that as it may, a mistake was clearly made and the issue needs to be resolved. I realize that you don't know me, but I have all these guests with me and our car is parked in the middle of a lot where we can't get it out until after the concert.

Manager: I can sell you more tickets.

Lois: I don't think it's fair that I have to buy more tickets for a mistake that wasn't mine.

Manager: I'll tell you what. If you're so sure the ticket seller will remember you, then you'll be willing to buy more tickets, and if you come back tomorrow when he's working and he does remember you, I'll refund your money.

Lois: That's fair, because I know he'll remember me and our discussion.

In the end, Lois and her friends enjoyed the concert in seats that were actually better than those originally purchased. And when she returned the next morning for her refund, guess what? The ticket seller didn't even let her finish her sentence when he handed her an envelope and said, "I already heard all about it." And that's how the broken record works. Sometimes you just have to wear people down!

MAKE IT WORK FOR YOU

- **Vary your message.** Don't repeat the same message over and over verbatim; say the same thing in different words.

- **Combine the broken record with "I" messages and contrasting.** You'll notice in the example above, Lois never once used a "you" message because she didn't want to put the manager on the defensive. Instead, she simply repeated herself using *I* and contrasting what she wanted with what she didn't, until they arrived at what she considered a fair resolution.

- **Remain patient and calm.** The broken record doesn't work when you raise your voice or become belligerent. It's more disarming when you show respect but don't back down.

PREPARE FOR PUSHBACK

THE TACTICS IN STRATEGY V FOCUS ON

- Responding to inevitable challenges to winning the life you want.

- Engaging others in problem solving.

- Using proven techniques to avoid frustration and the inclination to acquiesce.

N ice girls often find that others try to make them feel guilty, selfish, or uncaring when they try to put their needs first. Whereas the nice girl wants to change, other people want to maintain the status quo because it works for them. So far, we've provided you with sixty different tactics to help you identify your needs, build relationships that work for you, manage expectations, and communicate powerfully. Although we've talked a bit about how to handle resistance along the way, this strategy is devoted to helping you not only counter resistance and respond to obstacles, but actually use them to your advantage.

Nice girls have been socialized not to push back. As we wrote in the introduction, women receive plenty of messages about how they should behave—at work and at home. Research shows that both men and women expect women to behave in certain stereotypical ways. The thin pink line, a term coined by our colleague the author Dr. Kathleen Kelley Reardon, refers to the very narrow band of behavior that is acceptable for women. On one side of the line, women who are assertive can instead be perceived as aggressive—or even worse, a word that begins with b rather than a. On the other side of the line, women who are too "collaborative" and buckle at the first sign of strife are seen as weak and wimpy. Not surprisingly, these women tend to be nice girls, and they aren't taken very seriously. Take it from us, this can be a very thin line indeed.

Yet, as we explained earlier, healthy relationships require reciprocity to meet each person's needs. Winning women look at resistance as a necessary part of building relationships. Nice girls, on the other hand, shy away from resistance. Transforming the status quo in a relationship requires a nice girl to change the way she thinks about conflict.

No tactic works 100 percent of the time, but you can stack the odds in your favor if you understand a few things about how and why others will push back when you try to shed your nice girl persona.

1. **Other people like you just the way you are.** They're not invested in the "new you." Why should they be? If you're the typical nice girl, you've done a great job of meeting everyone else's needs, so maintaining the status quo is just fine with them.

2. **Resistance to change is normal.** By definition, all systems strive to perpetuate themselves by challenging change. Whether that system is an ecological, political, family, or work system, maintaining equilibrium is the goal. As you change your style of communicating or your expectations, you can count on resistance.

3. **Resistance can work to your advantage.** When others shoot you down, they also provide you with the ammunition you need to come back and try again. That's why it's so important to avoid the tendency to back down when you encounter pushback.

4. **Most forms of resistance can be overcome.** That's the good news. Countering what at first seem like insurmountable obstacles simply requires tenacity, regrouping, and employing a tactical approach.

VIEW RESISTANCE AS AN OPPORTUNITY

It's not that winning women necessarily *enjoy* confrontations; it's that they know to win the lives they want, in both the professional and personal aspects of their lives, confrontation is often required. They also know that when women assert themselves, they are likely to get pushback. Winning women distinguish themselves by viewing this resistance as an opportunity, not a threat.

Before Yoshiko walked into the store to return the item she had purchased two weeks earlier, she braced herself for a negative response. She expected the store clerk to deny her request and kick it upstairs to the manager. But Yoshiko was ready. Knowing that this was a low-risk, transactional situation and that she had no strong affiliation with the clerk or the manager, she was more willing to ask for what she wanted. The manager refused to refund her money because the store's policy was to issue refunds only within seven days of purchase. Yoshiko then went to her plan B and requested store credit—the manager agreed. Yoshiko, a recovering nice girl, saw the resistance in this situation as a chance to practice being assertive.

In personal situations, resistance can be the best opportunity for positive change. Melinda's mother is adamant that she should remain at home caring for her children, despite the fact that her family needs additional income. Melinda has avoided a frank discussion with her mother about the realities of the situation, sure that if she told her mother that she is a grown woman whose decisions about her life are her own, her mother would express disapproval. Yet, if Melinda continues to avoid the elephant in the room, she and her mother will ultimately grow apart. Instead, they should look at the conflict as a chance to make the relationship stronger.

When Carol was practicing law and handling divorce cases, one of the questions she would ask her clients was whether the client and his or her spouse argued. If the answer was yes, then she would strongly encourage the client to seek counseling before making a decision to divorce. Her rationale was that when people still care enough to argue with one another, there's still a possibility they'll be able to work things out. On the other hand, when people aren't willing to invest enough of themselves to try to solve problems in their relationship, the relationship is truly over.

Lucy's boyfriend wasn't at all enthusiastic when she mentioned that she wanted to take a weekend trip with her friends. Despite his resistance, Lucy didn't offer to stay home. Not only that, she used it as an opportunity to initiate a conversation about their relationship. As they talked, Lucy learned he was worried about the fact that they had not yet made a commitment to be exclusive, so he wasn't sure what the weekend away might mean to their relationship. Facing her boyfriend's resistance head-on led Lucy to a new level of understanding about his feelings for her.

Resistance can signal caring. Facing it head-on yields winning women valuable information about the other person's needs and enables them to improve on long-term outcomes.

MAKE IT WORK FOR YOU

- **If you get resistance, you're on the right track.** It means you are asserting yourself and advocating for your needs. Depending on the situation, some measure of resistance is inevitable. Don't be discouraged by it, but rather use it to further your goals.

- **Practice countering resistance in low-risk situations.** Select situations that won't make a huge difference in your life as a place to begin to advocate for yourself. Transactional situations are ideal. You can then apply what you learned when the stakes are higher.

- **Use questions to get at the real reason for the resistance.** It's not enough to know that people don't want you to change, you need to know why. When you encounter resistance, don't just take it at face value; ask questions to clarify.

DIFFERENTIATE FORMS OF RESISTANCE

As we've just discussed, resistance can present opportunities, but it can also take on unexpected forms that can throw you off track. The most obvious kind of resistance, open disagreement, is actually the easiest to deal with because it's explicit. You can engage the other person in dialogue or try to negotiate when it's clear that he or she isn't immediately receptive to giving you what you want. But other, more subtle forms of resistance are tricky because they can feed into your guilt over asking for what *you* want.

Let's say you told your best friend that you don't want to go on vacation with her and her sister this year but prefer to go alone with only her so that you can spend quality time together. Traveling in threesomes is difficult under the best of circumstances, but her sister, a narcissistic drama queen, has made past trips downright unpleasant. Instead of explicitly saying she doesn't like your suggestion, your friend may instead become

- Angry: "I went to a lot of trouble to research places we could go and now you don't want to go?"

- Accusatory: "You're always more concerned with what you want than with what other people need."

- Passive-aggressive: "Whatever. We'll just cancel our vacation plans altogether."

- Childish: "Fine, why don't we just cancel our friendship while we're at it?"

- Tearful: "I don't know why this has to be a problem. I try so hard to make everyone happy."

- Punitive: "Just wait till you want me to do something with someone from *your* family."

- Silent.

These are just a few common forms of resistance to which women have difficulty responding. Here are a few others to be on the lookout for in different situations:

- Expertizing: This happens when others want to shoot down your idea. Suddenly they're the "experts," pointing out all the holes in your suggestion. The impact of expertizing is that you wind up feeling about two feet tall and start doubting yourself and your premise.

- Rationalizing: When you give feedback to others and in return hear a litany of reasons why something went down as it did or how it isn't that person's fault, it's just another form of resistance to the information you've shared. Children are excellent at using rationalization to deflect criticism or feedback. For example, "It wasn't that I didn't study for the test; I flunked it because the teacher put questions on it that no one could possibly answer unless they were Einstein."

- Confusion/indecisiveness: On the surface, this looks like a legitimate response to new ideas or information. In fact, it is often a way to dilute the message you are delivering and delay addressing and taking action on it.

The most important thing is to recognize when responses are defensive so that you can counter them appropriately rather than become immobilized by them, feel guilty, or get caught up in a tit-for-tat game.

MAKE IT WORK FOR YOU

There are four steps for countering the various forms of resistance:

Step 1. Recognize a defensive reaction as just that. For example, if your child explains *why* a certain situation happened, this is not necessarily defensiveness. But if he or she *continually* blames others or can't take in your message—this is defensiveness.

Step 2. Support the person's right to behave as they are now behaving. Make a supportive statement that recognizes the defensive behavior without attacking it. For example, "Whenever we talk about what I need I've noticed that you become silent." This plays back what you observe without judgment or interpretation.

Step 3. Confront the impact of the response on you personally. For example, "When I try to discuss what I need, I get silence. I'm certain you have good reasons for being silent, but at the same time, it makes me feel I shouldn't express what I need."

Step 4. Be quiet and allow the other person to respond and react to your statement before proceeding. This will frequently lead to further discussion.

CHOOSE THE HILL YOU'RE WILLING TO DIE ON

Alexandria left a great job in a large investment firm to work at a smaller bank. She was enticed away with a substantial increase in pay, signing bonus, and promise of more responsibility and upward mobility. During the first year on the job, she realized the company culture was quite different from that of the investment firm where she had worked for twelve years. There was less focus on employee morale and more emphasis on measuring productivity. As a result, she'd inherited a demoralized team. She talked with her boss about her concerns, but each time the boss justified the company's position by pointing to the bottom-line return on shareholder investment.

Alexandria wondered if she should take the issue to the next level of management. After all, one of the reasons she was brought in was to increase productivity *by* improving employee morale. She talked with a few colleagues and each one told her the same thing: circumventing the chain of command would be a career kiss of death. Heeding their advice, she did her best to meet the needs of her employees while remaining vigilant about profits. Going to senior management over her boss's head wasn't the hill she was willing to die on if she could achieve her goals in other ways.

When she received her performance review at the end of the first year, Alexandria was shocked to see she was rated 2 on a scale of 1 to 5 (with 5 being the highest), even though she had been previously praised by peers and staff for turning around an underperforming business unit and hadn't received any negative feedback about her performance. When she talked with her boss about her many accomplishments, the boss simply pointed to two minor mistakes she'd made, and completely ignored her achievements—which far outweighed them. The boss wasn't willing to budge an inch on Alexandria's performance rating.

Demoralized by a boss who didn't recognize her long hours of hard work and creative attempts to compensate for a lack of resources, Alexandria decided it was time to speak with her second-level supervisor (her boss's boss). Having never received such a poor performance review in over twenty years of working in the finance industry, she felt strongly about restoring her reputation—this was the hill she *was* willing to die on. If her boss didn't like the end run and she ultimately had to leave the company, so be it. As it turned out, she did leave the company, but not because she'd angered her boss by going over his head. She left because she couldn't reconcile her own values with those of her employer.

When nice girls start practicing the tactics we provide in this book, or any other new skills acquired through books or workshops, they often overshoot their targets. Newly empowered, suddenly everything has equal importance or weight, and they rush headfirst into battles that really don't need to be taken on. Yes, you should expect resistance when trying to have your needs met, but that doesn't mean you have to fight it *every* time. Winning the war is more important than winning each battle, and sometimes you have to give up a few battles to achieve your overarching goals.

MAKE IT WORK FOR YOU

- **Don't make mountains out of molehills.** No one is perfect, and neither is any situation. Our most fervent desires, brilliant ideas, and legitimate needs may be met with opposition. Life involves sacrifices; the difference between nice girls and winning women is that winning women decide for themselves which ones they are willing to make. Which desires, needs, and ideas are you willing to let go of in the short term in exchange for longer-term satisfaction or gain? Perhaps you'd like to go on a cruise for vacation this year, but it's your husband's thirty-fifth birthday and he wants to do a beach vacation. You'll put off the cruise for another year so he can enjoy both his birthday and the vacation. It's not the hill you're willing to die on.

- **Fight the good fight on the *critical* issues.** In Alexandria's case, it was her reputation. She would do almost anything to preserve it. For you, it might be your integrity, family safety, freedom, or any number of other things that you value dearly. These become the battles you're willing to fight and the hills you're willing to die on.

- **If you're not sure whether it's a molehill or a battle worth fighting, trust your gut.** As we've already said, many times there are no right answers, only answers that are right for you. Elevating every disagreement to the level of a battle won't serve you well. Conversely, giving in on issues that are really important to you will cause you to become resentful. Before getting into a spitting match or acquiescing, think about into which category you would put the issue.

CAPITALIZE ON DIFFERENCES

Not everyone has the same priorities in life. What's important to you might be worth very little to another person. When that's the case, it's much easier to reach agreement. One way winning women get the things they want is by trading on these differences.

For example, Perri's family had a long tradition of spending Thanksgiving at her home. As the holiday approached, however, Perri didn't feel up to the shopping, cooking, and cleanup that hosting the dinner would demand. Rather than behave like a nice girl, doing it anyway so as not to disturb the status quo, she decided to take a different tack. Perri knew there would be resistance from her parents and siblings, so she suggested they either find a restaurant or use her home under new terms—everyone would bring a dish and pitch in with the cleanup. To her delight, Perri's family agreed. To them, it was important that they maintain the tradition of celebrating at Perri's; it was well worth the minimal cost (to them) of contributing food and elbow grease. And Perri didn't really mind having the dinner at her house; the work it entailed was what she wanted to avoid.

Trading on differences is a classic strategy when negotiating for raises or perks in the workplace. Colette worked for a company that was experiencing severe cash flow problems, and she knew it would be nearly impossible to get the raise and bonus she deserved given the circumstances. At the same time, she wasn't willing to let her contributions to the firm go unrewarded. She began to think about things other than money that were of value to her, but less expensive to the company. The obvious choice was a title. Not only would a title immediately increase Colette's stature at the company, it would put her in a considerably better position if she were to look for a new job. Plus, the recommendation would cost her boss nothing except political capital.

Finally, consider the example of Amanda, who was launching a new product targeted at a niche market. She selected three influential potential purchasers, all of whom were reluctant to invest in something so unfamiliar. So she made them an offer too good to refuse. She'd sell them the product at a deep discount in return for their agreement to issue a press release stating they were trying it. It was truly a win-win. Amanda got priceless publicity at little cost (she had committed to creating the product anyway, so offering it at "early bird" pricing didn't affect her fixed investment cost), and the clients enjoyed a good deal for the minimal time and expense they incurred to issue the press release.

Creativity counts when faced with resistance. When winning women expect pushback, they identify ways they can trade on differences.

Make It Work for You

- **Brainstorm first**. Consider where there may be differences to trade. What might be important to you but mean little to the other person and vice versa? You may want to begin with a brainstorming session, either alone or with the other person, depending on the situation. The following brainstorming guidelines can help you come up with creative outcomes:

  ✓ Don't censor; the more ideas the better.

  ✓ Just get the ideas down; evaluate them later.

  ✓ Try "hitchhiking"—improving on someone else's idea, or combining two or more fragments of ideas that others have offered.

  ✓ Experiment with "freewheeling"—throwing out ideas randomly. The wilder the idea, the better, since they can always be tamed down.

- **Evaluate the ideas.** Pick the best ideas. Think about which are most consistent with the culture or expectations of the person, family, or company (when work related).

- **Test your assumptions.** You can't always assume you know what others do and don't value. Use the communication techniques in Strategy IV—particularly Tactic 50: Ask Open-Ended Questions; Tactic 51: Listen to Get What You Want; and Tactic 54: Send Up a Trial Balloon—to determine whether or not the giveaway you're proposing is actually something that will be appealing to the other person.

LEARN TO LOBBY

Nice girls avoid lobbying. They either think it's unfair to attempt to influence the outcome by influencing those who have the power to make or impact the decision or are reluctant to put people in a tight spot by asking them for a favor. This is naïve. Winning women know that sometimes you have to wheel and deal a little to get what you want. Jane, a winning woman, decided not to be shy about moving her career agenda forward. She wanted to transfer into another department in her company, but knew that if she were to ask her boss for his help, chances are she would get pushback. He liked Jane and valued her work—if she left, it would make his life more difficult. So she approached her mentor, who offered to speak informally with a couple of other group heads on Jane's behalf, giving her a way to circumvent a situation that would have kept her stuck in a role she'd outgrown.

Lobbying works in personal matters too. Angela, who'd tried unsuccessfully to get an appointment with a medical specialist, asked her internist to intervene on her behalf. And Cindy, who was unhappy with how hard her son's Little League coach pushed the boys, but was afraid to speak with him directly for fear he would take it out on her son, had a quiet chat with the league commissioner, who promised to speak with him. Winning women recognize that regardless of how strong their case is for what they want, a well-placed word from an influential third party can make a big difference. This isn't breaking the rules; it's using influence to get your needs met.

MAKE IT WORK FOR YOU

- **Figure out who can help.** For lobbying to be successful, you've got to get help from the right person. He or she might be someone with positional power (as in Jane's and Cindy's cases), or someone who has a personal affiliation with the person you want to influence (as in Angela's situation). Of course, you have to have a relationship with anyone you ask for help—and when you *need* that relationship, it's too late to build it.

- **Make it easy for them to say yes.** Obviously, you never want to ask someone to do something illegal or unethical. Beyond that, it's useful to think about how you can limit the time and effort they have to invest to satisfy your request. For example, if you are asking for a letter of recommendation, you might tell the person that you'd be happy to draft language that can be used as a starting point.

- **Say thanks.** Don't neglect to circle back to the people who have done favors for you to let them know how things turned out and express your gratitude.

AVOID V-8® MOMENTS

Have you ever seen the commercials for the vegetable juice V-8®, where the women clunk themselves in the head after an argument, because they thought of the perfect comeback five seconds too late? Winning women don't do this. Why? Because they anticipate the pushback they might face in a difficult conversation and plan their comeback in advance.

There are two benefits to having clever comebacks at your fingertips. The first is that you won't have to resort to simply denying what's being said or disagreeing with the other person. If you've ever argued with a five-year-old, you know that "nuh-uh" is not persuasive. Straight denials only escalate an already combustible situation or make you look defensive. The second benefit is that you avoid being blindsided with little or nothing to say in the moment, only to think of the perfect retort *after* the conversation has ended.

Earlier we talked about Selena, who needed to speak with a colleague who was shirking her responsibility and taking credit for Selena's work. To prepare, Selena thought about the things Tory might say that would give her pause:

> "I've been working just as hard as you have on this project."

> "You're just being paranoid."

> "There you go again, making everything all about you."

Then she decided how she would respond to each one.

- If Tory said, "I've been working just as hard as you have on this project," Selena would not say reflexively, "No, you haven't." Instead, since her goal was to first understand Tory's perspective, she decided to respond by saying, "Say more about why you think that."

- If Tory's response was "You're just being paranoid," rather than say-ing, "No, I'm not," Selena planned to say, "Be that as it may, it isn't the issue. We still need to agree on a way we will get this work done and share the credit for it."

- And if Tory's retort was "There you go again, making everything all about you," rather than saying, "You must be kidding!" Selena would respond, "My intent is to make everything about the work. So let's figure that out."

Whereas a nice girl might simply back down, only to have the V-8® moment later, Selena was ready to hold her own, while remain-ing respectful. Maybe Tory wouldn't have gotten defensive or pushed back, but winning women know to be prepared.

Make It Work for You

- **Choose the direction.** Don't put yourself in a spot where the only way to respond is to back down or rely on a countermove like "No, I'm not." A countermove lets the other person stay in control of the conversation and leaves you in a one-down position. Instead, make a list of the things you don't want to hear, and how you could reply to shift the direction of the conversation in your favor.

- **Prepare a response appropriate to the situation.** How well do you know the other person? Given the issue, is it appropriate to use humor to diffuse the situation? Do you think the person is well intended but clueless? Or are the words you expect to hear clearly meant to insult or demean you? These questions should inform the response you choose.

- **Don't rush the retort.** If you hear something you didn't expect, and don't know how to respond, pause to think before you speak. You may even want to delay your response until a later time. It's far better to say something like, "I hadn't considered that. Let me give it some thought and get back to you," than to acquiesce and beat yourself over the head for it later.

SEQUESTER NAYSAYERS

It's true that opportunity can be found in resistance. But there comes a time in every winning woman's life when she has to shout, "*Enough is enough!*"

When pushback becomes too much to bear, sometimes the only thing you can do is banish the naysayers. Some of the most successful businesswomen around have done this. Mrs. Fields had to sequester the naysayers when they said she could never make a living out of selling cookies. Mary Kay Ash had to sequester the naysayers when they said she didn't know enough about the cosmetics industry to start a business with that focus. Even *we* had to sequester the naysayers who said we were crazy to quit lucrative jobs to start our own consulting practices.

Naysaying is a unique form of pushback that says more about the naysayer than it does about you. Generally, the naysayer

- Isn't interested in engaging in creative problem solving with you.

- Isn't supportive of what *you* want.

- Isn't one to take risks in his or her own life.

- Lacks vision.

- Would rather complain than constructively address potential obstacles or pitfalls.

Our own experience with naysayers is that they play the game of life safely within bounds and are fearful of deviating from their "norms." The naysayer doesn't push back with constructive opinions or ideas; he or she simply puts a damper on other people's dreams, ideas, and enthusiasm by pointing out all of the *negative* ramifications or possibilities. These are the people who will tell you your business idea will fail, your boyfriend isn't marriage material, the renovations you just planned won't make your home any more comfortable, and so on. If you walk away from a discussion feeling as if you're light has been snuffed out, chances are you just met with a naysayer.

MAKE IT WORK FOR YOU

- **Keep the naysayers in your life away from your dreams.** You might not want to exclude them entirely from your life, but don't trust them with "out of the box" ideas. They're not the people with whom you can daydream or vet new ideas. Instead, present them only with final, well-thought-out strategies and only when you feel confident enough to fend off their negative vibes.

- **Identify the yay-sayers in your life and keep them close.** These are friends, family, and colleagues you can trust to tell you the truth but not demolish you in the process. They may not agree with everything you want or need, but they're likely to help you achieve your goals without judgment. You feel safe to express even "crazy" ideas with them, knowing they won't laugh or put you down, but rather be the safety net you need to venture beyond the tried and true.

- **Build a board of advisors.** Identify people you respect who have expertise you can tap into. Consider people who are already successful at what you want to do as well as other experts who can give you legal, financial, or technical advice. Ask them if they would be willing to spend one hour with you quarterly to answer your specific questions. The caveat is to be prepared for these meetings so as not to waste their time and to ensure you are getting the information you need to move forward.

PLAY TO YOUR AUDIENCE

Earlier we wrote about how winning women use the Myers Briggs Type Indicator (MBTI®) assessment to better understand their own preferences and those of others. Here, we'll discuss how understanding the personality temperaments can help you communicate with those who are resistant to your ideas or requests.

In *The Art of SpeedReading People,* Paul Tieger and Barbara Barron-Tieger describe four temperaments drawn from the sixteen personality types included in the MBTI® instrument. They are shown in the following chart:

Traditionalists	Experiencers
S (Sensing) **J**(Judging) preferences	**S** (Sensing) **P**(Perceiving) preferences
ESTJ ESFJ ISTJ ISFJ	ESTP ESFP ISTP ISFP
Serious people who appreciate structure and authority and like to put closure on things.	Though practical and realistic, these are people who value spontaneity.
Conceptualizers	**Idealists**
N (Intuiting) **T** (Thinking) preferences	**N** (Intuiting) **F** (Feeling)
ENTJ ENTP INTJ INTP	ENFJ ENFP INFJ INFP
"Idea" people who approach things logically and command respect.	"Big picture" people who rely heavily on their own values and those of others when making decisions.

Because a person's temperament affects how he or she will push back against your request or idea, it follows that winning women consider temperament when crafting communication. As with communication styles, engaging with people on their native turf will increase the likelihood of getting what you want. For example, Colette, the woman who wanted a higher title because a raise wasn't possible at the time, identified her boss as a Traditionalist. So even though she herself was an Experiencer, as she prepared for her conversation with him, she vowed to rein in her usual gregarious style and to dress a bit more formally. And, when she got to the meeting, she laid out her case logically and let him take the lead regarding "next steps."

Taking temperament into consideration works well in personal situations, too. For instance, Bonnie and her husband, Ryan, owned a home that needed a lot of work, inside and out, but they didn't have the money to do all the repairs at once. Because their temperaments were different, they'd argued about which projects to tackle and in what order. Bonnie, an Experiencer (ISFP), tended to want to do whatever project was related to the latest episode of a home makeover TV show she'd seen, or whichever one was related to the season—in the spring, she was seduced by the possibilities the outdoors offered. But Ryan, a Traditionalist (ESTJ), prioritized the projects according to their impact on the resale value of the house. Once they realized their different temperaments were affecting how they prioritized things, they were able to make decisions differently. Ryan, still with list in hand, agreed to occasionally let Bonnie's spontaneous ideas trump the next project on the list. Bonnie began to research how much the projects she wanted to do would add to the house's value and let Ryan know that.

Clearly, identifying temperaments and flexing communication styles to adapt to them is easier the more people know about one another. Yet as Tieger and Barron-Tieger point out, demeanor and appearance can offer clues to temperament. Traditionalists tend to be well mannered and dress more conservatively. Expect Experiencers to smile easily and adopt a casual look. Conceptualizers are more complicated to read but can often be thoughtful and pensive. Finally, if you encounter someone who seems nonconformist, you may be face-to-face with an Idealist.

MAKE IT WORK FOR YOU

- **Learn still more about the MBTI® and temperament.** In addition to the resources we mentioned earlier, we also recommend delving more deeply into *The Art of SpeedReading People* by Paul Tieger and Barbara Barron-Tieger. The title of the book is a misnomer—it actually offers a thoughtful and comprehensive way to identify and use preferences. If you have children, the book *Nurture by Nature*, also by Tieger and Barron-Tieger, is particularly helpful in figuring out why they may be resisting certain things.

- **Match your communication to their temperament.** When talking with a Traditionalist, be direct and concise. Use plain language and back up your points with data and facts. If you are conversing with an Experiencer, keep it light but use anecdotal evidence to support what you're saying. With Conceptualizers, focus on patterns and themes, and engage them in thinking collaboratively with you. And, if you are interacting with an Idealist, demonstrate your passion for the topic and personal commitment to doing the right thing. Listen carefully for hints people give about their preferences and adapt your own method of communicating accordingly. This is not manipulative, just smart.

REMEMBER THE POWER OF EMOTIONS

Winning women don't fall into the trap of thinking that people will behave rationally—they know that people are only human, and emotions will always play a part in how they react. So when they encounter resistance, they dig deep to uncover the feelings behind it. When someone denies you respect, emotions like hate, fear, shame, jealousy, hurt, self-doubt, or loneliness are often lurking beneath the surface.

Lindsey couldn't understand why the guy she was dating kept refusing what she saw as her completely reasonable requests to occasionally have dinner with her parents. Rather than write him off as just obstinate, she decided to try to find out why he was resisting. As she carefully probed, she learned he was intimidated by the thought of trying to make conversation with her successful parents. Although it wasn't rational—he was successful in his own right—it did explain his rationale.

In the same vein, Rose's boss reacted negatively when Rose told her she deserved a raise because she was underpaid relative to the market. Although Rose's compensation was low vis-à-vis the competition, it turned out the boss, who saw herself as a fair person, was hurt by her perception that Rose would characterize her as unfair.

When winning women encounter resistance, they endeavor to elicit positive emotions to erode negative ones. For instance, once Lindsey understood her boyfriend's fear of making conversation with her parents, she reassured him of how much she admired him and reminded him of how successful he'd been at engaging other people in the past. And, had Rose tapped into her boss's gratitude for her hard work and loyalty, she might very well have gotten the raise she deserved.

MAKE IT WORK FOR YOU

- **Recognize that emotions underlie resistance.** Ignoring or denying them is tantamount to trying to wallpaper a room with one arm tied behind your back.

- **Even if you don't share the emotion, respect it.** Although you might not feel the same way if you were in the other person's position, exhibit empathy. Don't disparage the other person for feeling the way he or she feels.

- **Reflect on your own emotions.** As we discussed in Strategy II, Tactic 31: Walk Away When It's Time, we sometimes make bad decisions (or even avoid making decisions) because our emotions override our best interests. Whatever the emotion you feel, identify it and then assess how it is affecting the decisions you make.

GIVE PEOPLE TIME TO CATCH UP WITH YOU

Never take an initial "no" as a final answer. Whether you're asking for something or presenting a new idea, there will always be contrarians and skeptics whose knee-jerk reactions are going to be negative. Then there are people who just need time to think about things before making a decision. If they're pushed into a decision too soon, they'll go with "no" because, to them, it's the safer bet.

As we've already discussed, lobbying or planting seeds in advance is one way of paving the way toward getting your ideas accepted or your needs met. Often, it's enough to simply give your requests some time to percolate, especially if you're dealing with a contrarian, or with someone who likes to collect as much information as possible before making a decision.

Let's say you want to remove a tree that's on your property, but close to the yard of the home next door to you, and build a storage shed in its place. It would be perfectly within your rights to simply remove the tree, but doing so could create some friction, so you decide to tell the neighbors about your plans. When you do, their immediate response is, "But that tree provides shade for our backyard. And a storage shed would be unsightly." Rather than responding that it's just too bad, the tree is on your property and it will be going, your better bet would be to give them time to think about it. You might even say, "I'm not going to do anything right away, so why don't we both think about it and discuss it again."

Chances are that if you give them some time, they'll realize a shed near their property isn't the worst thing in the world and come around. Plus, now you know exactly what their concerns are and can think about how to approach them again with these factors in mind. When you go back a week or so later you can say, "I've given thought to what you said. I wouldn't want to do anything to damage our relationship so, in response to your needs, I'm going to plant trees around the shed. That way, you won't be looking at a shed, you'll be looking at lovely trees, which, as they grow, will offer shade for both our yards." Of course, they might still balk at the idea, but you've done everything possible to compromise.

Remember that when it's your idea or request, you've most likely been thinking about it for some time. You may have gathered data, conducted research, or talked to others about it. But for the person you're presenting it to, it's completely new. What seems only fair or logical to you may be entirely foreign to them. Giving them some time to get used to the idea and do their homework goes a long way toward breaking down that initial wall of resistance.

MAKE IT WORK FOR YOU

- **Consider past responses to new ideas.** If you know the person you're dealing with typically has a negative response to anything new or unusual, then you know it's going to take a little longer to get them on your side. These are the people with whom you start negotiations by planting seeds in advance.

- **Don't ask for an immediate response.** It can be helpful to start your discussion by saying, "I'd like to talk to you about an idea I have. Let me say right up front that I don't want an answer from you today; I only want to lay out the facts and give you time to think about it. Then we can discuss it once you've had time to digest the information." This takes the pressure off the other person to make a decision on the spot which, in turn, often leads to a more open exploration of the issues.

- **Be patient.** Don't hesitate to revisit the same issue more than once. Just as a waterfall smoothes stones over time, you may have to wear away the resistance gradually and patiently.

PROVIDE THE AMMUNITION AND
LET THEM SHOOT THE HOLES

As we said in the previous tactic, some people are born contrarians. You say white, they say black. You say no, they say yes. You say good-bye, they say hello. These tendencies seem to come out full force when change is involved. Such was the case with Daisha, the manager of a department full of brilliant and successful scientists—people who didn't get that way by taking things at face value. Every time Daisha proposed a new idea for improving departmental efficiencies, she was met with a chorus of reasons why it wouldn't work.

Daisha was discouraged that she couldn't seem to move her team forward because of their resistance to even the smallest proposed changes. A friend suggested that instead of presenting each new idea as a fait accompli, she present it as a work in progress and ask the team members to shoot holes in it—then come up with solutions to those potential pitfalls. Now *she* became the skeptical one! Wouldn't this approach only lead to further stalemates? Running out of alternatives, she finally agreed to try it—once.

Lo and behold, it worked. By providing the ammunition to the team, Daisha allowed them to determine their own direction *within her parameters.* And that's the trick to making this tactic work—you have to circumscribe desired outcomes and allow others to create the path for achieving them. In business, this is called *delegating the process, not the product.* Giving people a say in how they will achieve their goals increases commitment, because now *they* own the process.

The same theory holds with other significant people in your life. No one likes to be told what to do, how to do it, and when to do it. Let's say you want your child to help with the housework. Rather than assign tasks, talk to him or her about what needs to be done, ask what would get in the way of his picking up one or more of these chores, and discuss how to handle them. For example, maybe he says he needs his after-school time for homework. Let him come up with ideas for how he can work a fifteen-minute dishwashing break in between subjects.

Resistance often results when others feel like they have no options. With an eye on the desired outcomes, providing people the ammunition to point out all the reasons why something *won't* work, then allowing them the latitude to find solutions to those obstacles, can be an effective and disarming tool.

MAKE IT WORK FOR YOU

- **Avoid edicts.** Nobody likes a dictator. Any directive or edict is likely to be met with resistance. You can have an end goal in mind, but you should give others permission to critique your idea and offer appropriate alternatives or paths to achieving the goal.

- **Allow plenty of time for discussion.** Often our impatience to check a task off the list or put closure on a project prevents us from allowing others to have a say in the process. Certainly there are times when a matter is so urgent that you need others to follow your directions, but by allowing discussion on the less urgent ones, you're more likely to get cooperation later, when it's just not possible to take the time to talk. Similarly, planning in advance will avoid being caught in a position where there's no time for gaining buy-in.

CALL AN INTERMISSION

Although we've discussed the importance of expecting resistance and planning ways to respond, winning women understand they can't possibly anticipate every contingency. When in the middle of a tense situation, before things go wrong, winning women go to the balcony.

First used by William Ury in *Getting Past No*, "going to the balcony" is a metaphor for a way to step back when a conflict arises. The idea is to imagine yourself on a balcony, watching the drama on stage from a distance. This sense of removal will allow you to think about the situation objectively rather than simply reacting to it on an emotional level. In *Everyday Negotiation*, Deborah Kolb and Judith Williams kick this concept up a notch. When things aren't going well in real time, they suggest turning things around by interrupting the action or, in keeping with the theater metaphor, by calling an intermission. As they point out, this not only gives you time to recoup, it allows you to resume the conversation in a different, and better, place.

Nicole didn't expect that her conversation with her husband about the amount of time he'd been spending with his friends would be an easy one. But when he blew up the minute she broached the subject, instead of yelling back, she paused, took a deep breath, and stood up. She didn't leave the room. She simply allowed a few moments to pass until she was calm enough to continue the conversation without losing her temper. While her interruption wasn't at all dramatic, it did help her to avoid an unproductive argument.

Rebecca took a longer intermission when things began to careen out of control at a meeting she was running. People were disagreeing—loudly—about the best way to handle a major client problem, so she stopped the action in its tracks by saying, "It's clear that we all feel strongly about this situation and that we have a variety of ideas about how best to proceed. I think we've done as much as we can today. Let's all think about the solutions that were proposed and get back together again tomorrow morning. We'll have had a night to sleep on things and can approach this with a fresh perspective." When the meeting resumed the following day, it was far more productive and civil.

Nice girls, often tempted to respond emotionally in the heat of the moment, can benefit from a trip to the balcony, followed by an intermission. This gives them time to reflect on how to employ a different strategy while at the same time providing a useful buffer.

MAKE IT WORK FOR YOU

- **Stretch or get coffee.** If the matter is urgent or if postponing the conversation to a later time just isn't practical, stage a quick interruption—one that takes minutes rather than hours or days.

- **Offer a rationale for putting things on hold.** If you're going to overtly suggest postponing the discussion, state the benefit that the interruption will have for the other person.

- **If you're feeling pressure, stall.** Don't make a decision until you're ready. Acceptable delay tactics include "I'd like to think about this," "I'll need to do some additional research before I can give you an answer," and "I'll have to check with my partner."

STRATEGY
VI

USE AND
SHARE YOUR
CONNECTIONS

THE TACTICS IN STRATEGY VI FOCUS ON

- Acknowledging that you can't do it alone and need a network of alliances.

- Reaching out to others.

A woman we'll call Violet was the daughter of a well-known psychologist. But if you met her you wouldn't know who her father was because she never mentioned him, plus she used her married, not her maiden, name. Like many nice girls, she thought she had to prove herself by doing everything on her own and not "take advantage of" (her phrase) the many relationships she had built over the years with her father's colleagues. Her intelligence and hard work made her successful in her field, one which happened to be related to psychology, and she was proud that she had done it without invoking her father's fame or name.

Then she wrote a book and was having difficulty finding a publisher for it. She sent the manuscript to at least a dozen publishing houses and received rejections from each one. When a friend asked if she had submitted it to her father's publisher, she was appalled at even the suggestion. Of course she hadn't! She wouldn't want to capitalize on his reputation when she had a perfectly good one of her own. Violet, like so many other nice girls, didn't understand that relationships only open a door—you're responsible for what happens once you walk through it. Ultimately, at the urging of colleagues who suggested that not having the book published would be a bigger mistake than leveraging her father's contacts, she did see it go to print—through her father's publisher—and there was no shame in that. The editors wouldn't have accepted it if it wasn't worthy of publication; her father's connection simply helped get it into their hands.

We devoted an entire strategy in this book on how to build relationships that work for you. In this section, we focus on how you can capitalize on those relationships—a thought many nice girls find abhorrent. Listen up, ladies. Using relationships to help you achieve your goals and *get the things you want isn't ugly, shady, or sleazy—it's smart. And it's necessary, because no matter how talented you are, you can't live the life you want without a little help from your friends.*

If you've followed our advice this far, you've built alliances with people who are willing to open doors for you, protect your back when you're under attack, and throw you a lifeline when you're sinking fast. That's a good thing. But they can't help you unless they know you need their help. So you have to ask for it. Ignore that voice in your head telling you that, if they were really willing to help, they'd do it without your having to ask. Remember, these people aren't psychics or saints, merely human beings with outstretched hands. It's up to you to grab on.

KNOW YOUR NETWORK

In technological terms, a *network* refers to a series of interconnected points that radiate from a hub in the center. In your network, you are that hub, connecting all your friends, relatives, colleagues, and acquaintances to one another. If you've ever referred a friend to your financial advisor, or a family member to one of your doctors, you've made a network connection. However, most people don't know the true scope of their network. Many of us have networks so broad that we often overlook the many people in them.

When beginning to think about your network, consider the various sources through which you are connected to other people:

- Family

- Friends

- Work

- Service providers (doctors, accountants, repair people, etc.)

- Places of worship

- School (yours and/or your child's)

- Professional associations

- Leisure activities (the gym, clubs, etc.)

- Volunteer activities

If you consider all of the people you know through these various sources, it's likely that you have an extensive network. But it doesn't stop there. The people you know through all these people are also a part of your network. So if you were recently introduced to the spouse of a coworker, or the sister of your son's teacher, these people are now also in your network. In other words, these people are also resources you can now draw upon as needed. Use the diagram below as a model to chart your network so that you are more aware of the many resources available to you—and the people you should consider when making referrals, sharing information, and maintaining relationships.

MAKE IT WORK FOR YOU

- **Chart your network.** Using the diagram provided as a template, fill in the actual names of people in your network. Keep it in a place where you can refer to it regularly as a reminder that not only do you have resources available to you, but you have the responsibility of being a resource to them, as well.

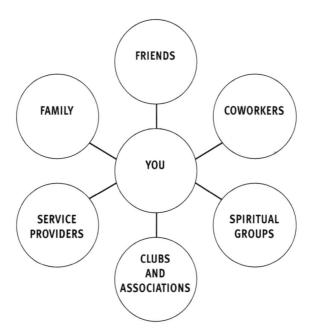

- **Remember the quid pro quo.** As we discussed earlier, every relationship in your network is built on an exchange of services, goods, friendship, and other things valued by both parties involved. Consciously consider ways you can build equity by providing others with what they need to achieve their goals.

- **Consistently expand your network.** Inevitably, some people will drop out of your network due to lifestyle changes, job changes, relocation, and so forth. Always be on the lookout for replacements as well as for new people who you believe have something to offer and vice versa. As we've already said (several times now because we want you to remember it!), *when you need a relationship, it's too late to build it.*

DEVELOP THE ART OF SMALL TALK

Small talk is big. Being able to carry on an interesting conversation is what enables winning women to distinguish themselves in both business and personal settings. Yet this isn't easy; even the most extroverted people find it can be awkward to strike up a conversation with total strangers.

Joan, for example, attends networking events regularly to meet potential clients. However, she completely defeats her own purpose by gravitating toward people she already knows instead of seeking out new connections. Dale, although trying to meet new people to date, stays in a tight circle with her girlfriends when she goes out—it would have to be a very brave guy who'd try to break into that! Nancy misses out on the chance to get to know her husband's colleagues because even though he invites her to his work-related gatherings, she finds them so intimidating that she makes up excuses to get out of attending.

But even in less stressful situations—at a work-related dinner of your own or when your friends bring their friends along to an informal gathering—where the stakes are lower and the opportunities greater, many people feel great trepidation about making small talk. They worry people won't like them. They worry they won't be able to think of anything to say. They worry they'll get stuck with a bore or, worse, *be* the bore. But worrying is a useless emotion—it doesn't do a thing to improve their skill at repartee.

Grace, a winning woman, no longer worries about such things. She's taken a number of steps to reduce the stress she used to feel when meeting new people. For one, she puts in a bit of time before any new social situation to learn as much as she can about the other people who'll be attending—just Googling them unearths a lot of information. For example, she finds out where they went to school, what clubs or associations they are affiliated with, what charities they support, and other details. This helps her find topics that cover common ground; for example, if she knows she's chatting with someone who likes, say, surfing, she can bring up her recent trip to Hawaii. Second, she comes armed with conversational topics. She loves her job as a teacher and has a few funny anecdotes about the kids in her class she can share. Even if people don't have kids, they were once kids themselves and can relate to her stories. These always get a laugh and a smile, and just knowing she has them at her fingertips helps ease the anxiety of being caught with nothing to say. And, perhaps easiest of all, Grace has mastered the art of asking good questions that get people talking. For instance: "I've got company coming in from out of town and am looking for a good restaurant to take them to. Have you come upon any good new ones in town?" or "What have you read lately that you'd recommend?" Finally, she keeps it light—never going near politics or religion. Grace is considered a fabulous conversationalist. Wouldn't you want to chat with her at a party?

Unfortunately, however, no matter how scintillating a conversationalist you might be, you can't plan for everything! Consider the response Sally got from a woman she met at a friend's home when she asked, "So what keeps you busy?" The question was completely benign—she was smart enough to avoid the more off-putting variant, "What do you do?" (which could possibly be offensive if the recipient is out of work or a stay-at-home mom). But that didn't stop the woman from replying, "I'm unemployed." The opposite but equally painful response would have been a minute-by-minute account of her day. But guess what? There's no law saying you have to get stuck with a bore who won't stop talking about his life in excruciating detail—from early childhood to present day. Unlike nice girls, who are too nice to walk away, winning women find a way to graciously exit when small talk goes wrong.

MAKE IT WORK FOR YOU

- **Give yourself a confidence boost.** Remind yourself that you are just as interesting as anyone else who'll be in the room. But nobody will know that unless you put yourself out there. If your confidence is not what it could be, make a list of things you've done that you're proud of, or relationships that you've successfully forged. Then spend a bit of time remembering how you felt about each achievement. Recalling your past success helps you to be more successful in the future.

- **Plan topics.** Think about things you can talk about and questions you can ask of people. But don't just revert to old standbys; be creative and whenever possible, tailor your topics and questions to the interests of the people you anticipate will be there. And, if you are at a business event, resist the temptation to talk only about business— or sports. Most men, and certainly many women, can easily talk sports with one another to build rapport, but if sports aren't your bailiwick, have another topic ready.

- **Don't get trapped.** If you find yourself in a conversation that is lasting too long or that you're not enjoying, feel free to excuse yourself and find another. Say something like "I enjoyed talking with you. I'm going to circulate a bit." Or "Thank you for telling me about your job. I'm going to freshen my drink." Don't offer to "do lunch sometime" or otherwise stay in touch unless you mean it.

KEEP A NETWORK CALENDAR

Some people are born networkers and love meeting new people. They not only maintain relationships with ease, others actually seek *them* out. These lucky people are the exception, not the rule. If you're one of them, you can skip this tactic and move on to the next one! On the other hand, if you're someone who does perfectly fine with a small group of friends and family but has trouble maintaining a wide network, then keep reading. Managing a network is as simple as managing your daily schedule. Just use your e-mail calendar, datebook, or other form of reminder to schedule days and times when you will reach out and touch someone.

Here are a few ways you can use this method to ensure you have those critical relationships in place when you need them:

- Note people's birthdays or anniversaries and send a card or e-mail on their special days.

- Set an alarm on your online calendar to remind yourself to get up from your desk twice a day and take a five-minute break for a casual conversation.

- Keep track of the names of the children and spouses of people in your network and mention them in conversations.

- Invite one new person to lunch each week.

- Make a note when people are facing a major challenge, like having surgery, making a career-defining sales call or presentation, or taking a child to college, and drop them a note wishing them luck.

- Record the days, times, and locations of all upcoming professional association meetings—and plan to attend as many as you can.

- Block out a few hours each month (Friday afternoons are often good times for this) to send e-mails or make calls to people from whom you haven't heard in a while.

Whether at work or at home, nice girls often make the mistake of thinking their time is best spent being "productive" and view the hours spent networking as a waste of time. Nothing could be further from the truth. It may seem like a lot of work in the moment but, believe us, when you need a favor, want information, or in other ways require assistance, you'll be glad you took the time to keep your network connections open.

MAKE IT WORK FOR YOU

- **Use technology to keep you connected.** Whether it's an e-mail calendar, an e-card birthday reminder, or PDA app, technology can provide the prompting you need to maintain strong networks.

- **Devote at least two hours each month to networking.** It doesn't have to be in one-hour or even half-hour increments, as long as over the course of a month, you spend a total of no fewer than two hours connecting with people you depend on for long-term success and satisfaction.

- **Don't wait for the earth to move.** You don't need something earth-shattering to have happened in your life to remain connected. You don't need an excuse to reach out to let others know you're thinking of them. A brief e-mail, voice-mail message, or forwarding an article of interest is all it takes.

CAPITALIZE ON SIX DEGREES
OF SEPARATION

Winning women use online social networking to enlarge their worlds. Whether you're looking for a job, someone to date, or simply a new friend to take cooking classes with, social networking, via Facebook, LinkedIn, or other sites, is the best and most efficient way to connect with connections of connections. Here are some specific ways women we know have capitalized on six degrees of separation:

- When Helen needed a divorce attorney, she tapped into her social network to ask for referrals. For something this important, she didn't want to just randomly select someone whose only connection to her was the fact that he or she advertised in the Yellow Pages or on a billboard she drove by every day.

- Cathy, an entrepreneur, had identified Mega Company as one she wanted to do business with—but first she needed an in. So she did a search on LinkedIn for people who worked at that firm in her area of interest and found that one of her own connections was linked to someone at Mega Company whom she wanted to meet. Cathy asked her connection for an introduction and got it.

- Jackie, a recent college grad who was struggling to find a job, used her college alumnae social network to contact people in the industry she wanted to break into. She e-mailed people asking for ten minutes of their time for a brief informational interview. She was pleasantly surprised at the response. She spoke with several people, one of whom suggested she check a specialized job website Jackie was unfamiliar with—she did, applied for one of the jobs listed there, and got it. She never would have known about the website without reaching out to those with whom she had something in common.

As useful as social networking can be, winning women don't make the mistake of thinking that everyone who "friends" them on Facebook is a true friend. Unless they know people well, they are careful about how much and what kind of information they disclose about themselves. Even if they know people well, they are discreet about the ways they use technology to communicate. For example, they know they have no reasonable expectation of privacy when accessing social networking sites using their employer's equipment and servers.

And, unlike nice girls, winning women don't feel compelled to "friend" or "connect" to anyone who asks. Although they aren't rude, they simply ignore the request rather than accepting it out of a sense of obligation. They may not look forward to "de-friending" someone with whom they no longer have a relationship, yet they have the courage and smarts to take that action when there's good reason to do so.

In short, social networking is useful but has its limits. It's a means to an end, not an end in and of itself. It doesn't replace connecting with people face-to-face but, if used properly, it can be a good way to leverage your connections.

Make It Work for You

- **Learn what social networking can do for you.** If you're not familiar with social networking, figure out if you should be. Don't rule it out just because you don't know how to use it—it's not as confusing as it seems. One of the best books we've read on the subject of the ins and outs of social networking is *The Savvy Gal's Guide to Online Networking (Or What Would Jane Austen Do?)* by Diane Danielson and Lindsey Pollak. And, just as you should investigate what social networking can do for you, you should investigate how you might be able to use it to help others.

- **Set limits.** Don't become a social network addict. Determine how much time you are willing to invest and stick to it. Note to parents: step up to negotiate agreements with your kids about when, where, and how much social networking is appropriate for them given their age, maturity level, and other factors.

- **Ignore the background noise.** Don't react hastily to requests from others to be their "friend"—think twice about the implications before you click "accept." Also, think carefully about the information you choose to share about yourself. Don't forget that people in your network will be privy to all your information—your coworker down the hall may not need to see the pictures from your honeymoon. And, if your *boss* makes the mistake of trying to "friend" you, think at least one more time. This is a case where instead of just hitting "ignore" you should deal with the issue in person. Casually mention in conversation that you make it a rule to connect online only with family and non-work-related friends.

COMPLEMENT YOUR KNOW-HOW

As the old English proverb goes, "Two heads are better than one." While nice girls are tempted to take it all on, winning women reach out to others whose skills complement their own. Take the moms who organize an after-prom party for a high school in the Northeast, for example. It's been an unqualified success, year after year. The idea is to provide a safe alternative to private parties at rented houses for the five hundred seniors who've attended the prom and want a place to continue their celebration. Each year the party has a theme (like "Boardwalk" or "Take Me Out to the Ball Game"). Decorations, food, entertainment, and games add to the fun—the goal is to keep the kids engaged so they stay at the party and out of trouble.

Planning and pulling off this kind of event requires as much in terms of project management skills as many a large-scale software implementation, yet it's run by two moms, Ann and Kelly, who co-chair the committee. How do they do it? They enlist the talents of other parents and the broader community. But they don't just put out a general call for volunteers; they contact people individually and ask them to make a contribution that's in line with their particular skills. For example, they've recruited local artists to work with the decorating committee to create large paper murals for a backdrop. Ann told us she never could have even *imagined* the "roller coaster" the artists constructed as a photo op, much less *build* one that looked real. These moms know what they are good at and where they need help.

In another situation, Paula needed help to breathe new life into the newsletter sent to donors by the not-for-profit association with which she was involved. The existing process of printing and sending it via regular mail was so slow, the news was outdated by the time it landed in mailboxes, and Paula had heard that many people simply recycled the newsletter without even reading it. She knew it was time to start distributing it electronically, but didn't have the time or inclination to learn how. So Paula reached out to Maya, a friend whose day job included responsibility for her company's website. Maya agreed to create an electronic layout template and to manage the distribution while Paula wrote the copy. The result was increased donations for a worthy cause.

A final example involves Amy, a training and development executive who needed a bigger budget. But she wasn't really a math person, so she asked a colleague in the finance department to crunch some numbers to help justify her request to her higher-ups. Together, they were able to explain to senior leaders at the company how the investment in training would lead to increases in productivity, benefit the firm, and pay for itself in a short time frame. Amy knew her colleague's cost-benefit analysis would be more persuasive to those who held the purse strings than anything she could have come up with on her own.

We wrote earlier that winning women close the gaps they find are holding them back. Although they learn what they need to know, they also recognize that they don't have to know everything nor do they have to do everything themselves. They get the results they want by reaching out to others whose skills and talents differ from their own.

Make It Work for You

- **Accept your limits.** Nobody can do it all. Don't feel inadequate and don't apologize that your repertoire doesn't include every talent or skill imaginable. That's just not possible.

- **Select people with whom you enjoy working.** One of the best things about collaboration is the enjoyment you'll derive from it— but you'll enjoy it only if those with whom you work respect your talents, too.

- **Offer to reciprocate.** As we've written in other places in this book, building relationships is a two-way street. Be sure to thank those who've provided help and look for opportunities where *you* can complement *their* know-how.

BE A RELATIONSHIP BROKER

There's a man in Los Angeles by the name of Carl Terzian. He's the CEO of a public relations firm, but is best known around town as a master relationship broker. He's the go-to guy when you want to meet someone who can help you find a reputable CPA, identify new clients for your own firm, find funding for a nonprofit—and everything in between. Although he charges nothing to make these connections, it clearly profits his business because people know, like, and respect him. He doesn't do it because he wants to get something out of it, but reciprocity is a natural by-product of his generosity.

You don't have to be as committed as Carl to bringing people together, but you do want to be known as someone who not only has a broad network, but is also willing to share it with others. We know plenty of women who have address books full of influential and successful contacts, but guard them as if they belonged in Fort Knox. They behave as if sharing a contact will take something *away* from them, rather than *enhance* their reputations. With that said, there are three caveats for relationship brokering:

1. **Assess fit from both sides.** If a friend asks for the name of a good financial advisor, you may immediately think of someone you know, but before making the connection consider the needs of both parties. If that friend has only $10,000 in assets and the advisor prefers clients with portfolios no less than $100,000, then it's not a good match. You don't want to risk using up the goodwill you've garnered with inappropriate or unwanted referrals.

2. **Ask permission.** Don't just give out a phone number or e-mail address without first asking the person if it would be all right to share it with someone who needs their help. This provides a heads-up and is another way of ensuring mutual interests, availability, and desire for the connection. It can also lead to further expansion of

your own network. For example, the person you are making the referral to could say she doesn't have the time or expertise to be of help, but knows someone else who might. You would then contact that person, assess fit, and in the process make a new connection you might not otherwise have made.

3. **Debrief.** Once the connection is made between the parties, check back to see how the contact went. Just because an electrician did a great job for you doesn't mean the person you referred him to will have the same experience. Or perhaps the person asking for a referral reneged on paying the electrician's bill—which may cause you to think twice before providing her with future connections to people in your network.

Make It Work for You

- **Generously share your connections.** Provided you honor the caveats above, your reputation will be enhanced and you can expect reciprocity from others when *you* need an introduction.

- **Keep a network database.** Again, you can use e-mail contacts, a contact and customer software manager, or any other of a number of digital tools that allow you to store and sort information. In addition to contact information, make notes about the person's background, education, interests, and other relevant information so that as your database grows you have reminders about who this person is and why you added him or her to your network.

- **Never turn your database over to a third party.** Making recommendations is one thing, but giving someone full access to everyone in your network is another. As your network grows, you will possess an invaluable source of contacts that others may covet. Perhaps a friend is starting a new business and asks for your mailing list. Your answer should be "Just as I wouldn't give your information to anyone without asking, I'm uncomfortable sharing the information of others without their permission. I'll be happy to spread the word, though."

SHOW UP

Lynn was frustrated. Herding wild bobcats would be easier than getting the six members of her monthly book club to agree on a date ("I prefer Tuesday to Wednesday that week," or "I'll be out the night before and I don't like to be out two nights in a row, so let's pick another night"). The day of the meeting usually brought news that one or two of them wouldn't be able to attend after all and, of those who did come, only half had read the book. This was a book club with no spine! Nice girls are so afraid of offending anyone, they think they have to accept any invitation that comes their way. As a result, they become overextended and inevitably find themselves unable to follow through on commitments. This does more harm than good.

If winning women agree to do volunteer work at the homeless shelter, they show up on time wearing sneakers. If they sign up to be on the reunion committee, they raise their hands when assignments are handed out. If they join an online group, they don't just lurk, they regularly contribute. And, if they agree to join a book club, they come to meetings—having actually read the book! Winning women know it's not enough just to join—when they commit to something, they're serious.

MAKE IT WORK FOR YOU

- **Think about it before you say yes.** Overcommitting causes even the best-intentioned women to disappoint others. Don't agree to get involved if your plate is already too full. You'll only wind up dropping a ball or two somewhere, which is sure to frustrate you and others.

- **Don't miss a meeting unless it's unavoidable.** We believe that there are far too many meetings in most of our lives. That said, skipping meetings because you think they're a waste of time is a mistake.

They're called *meet*-ings, not *work*-ings. Showing up at meetings allows you face time with the people you need to see and who need to see you. It also provides you with the opportunity to showcase your skills, gain information not otherwise available, and build relationships. If the meeting is really getting out of control, talk to someone about ways in which it can be made more efficient.

· **Be present in the moment.** Turn off the BlackBerry® and give your full attention to the people you're with—and, if you're running the meeting, don't be reluctant to ask for the same respect.

VOLUNTEER FOR HIGH-PROFILE PROJECTS

The emphasis here is on *high-profile*. Whether it's an assignment at work, a chore at home, or a project for the PTA, nice girls have the tendency to volunteer for things others (particularly men) don't want to do. Sometimes it's because they truly want to be of service; sometimes they think others will take note of their sacrifice and reward them accordingly (see Tactic 35: Don't Be a Martyr); and sometimes it's simply because they can't stand the silence in the room when no one else raises a hand. In the process, they become overscheduled *and* underappreciated. They might think they'll be rewarded for their extra effort, but in reality people don't respect or value those who take on "grunt work." Moreover, it takes away time from high-profile opportunities that would allow them to really strut their stuff.

High-profile projects are those that can add to your cachet, skill set, reputation, or network. They often yield one or more of the following benefits:

- Your talents are recognized and often rewarded (if not immediately, then in the future).

- You gain new skills that are applicable in a variety of situations.

- You build new relationships.

- You "bank" favors from others.

- You position yourself for *desirable* future contacts, projects, or perks.

- You become known as one who is generous with her time— but whose time has value.

We're not suggesting that you *never* volunteer for something that won't result in some or all of these payoffs. We simply urge you to consider whether it's really necessary for *you* to organize the neighborhood watch, chaperone the school trip, or coordinate the company holiday party. Although these are worthwhile endeavors, if your plate is full in other ways, if you've been wondering why you never seem to have time in your life for what you believe is really important, or if you don't feel what you do is being adequately recognized, it could be that your life is cluttered with low-profile, low-payoff activities.

MAKE IT WORK FOR YOU

- **Sit on your hand.** If that's what it takes to get you to think twice about what you volunteer for, then so be it. And while you're at it, get comfortable with silence in the room. Silence is a powerful motivator for *others* to speak up.

- **Assess costs versus rewards.** Regardless of what you volunteer for, there's always a cost. It might be that it takes more time than you anticipated, the other people involved make it difficult to do a good job, or it may require you to forgo a better opportunity that comes up later. Before volunteering for any project, consider what's currently on your plate, with whom you'll be working, how much control you have over the outcomes, and what you will take away from the experience. Your takeaway may be just the satisfaction of knowing you did something good for the community, your family, or your coworkers, and that's fine; but if you are miserable throughout the process, then the cost isn't worth the reward.

- **Identify skills and contacts *you'd* like to build.** Volunteering provides a wonderful way of acquiring new skills. Rather than volunteering for something you're already good at, consider what skills you need to complement your existing strengths. If speaking before groups is difficult for you, then chairing a committee at your church that requires you to speak before groups would be a good stretch for you. Similarly, if finances are not your forte, then acting as treasurer of a club to which you belong will help you to learn the basics of accounting.

CASH IN YOUR NETWORK EQUITY

Corinna is the perfect example of a nice girl who is always going out of her way for others. The word *no* doesn't exist in her vocabulary. Not only does she hold down a full-time job, she's also active in the PTA at her children's school and in the women's auxiliary of her temple. Moreover, of the four siblings in the family, she has assumed primary responsibility for caring for their elderly parents. As a result, she has a wide network of people who *love* her. Who wouldn't? She always has a smile on her face and never complains. She also never asks for anything.

We believe that all the good things you do in the world create a figurative or karmic bank account of goodwill. It's not quite the same as a quid pro quo, one thing of value being exchanged for another. It's more about how the universe works. Not only do we *believe* that good deeds are valuable in themselves and also attract goodness to us, we've actually witnessed it time and again. The problem for nice girls, like Corinna, is that they don't want to ask for anything from anyone (not even the universe) because they feel that asking is an imposition or will be perceived as selfish. As a result, they have bank accounts filled with equity that is never cashed in.

One day, Corinna was in a car accident. Her injuries weren't life threatening, but they did put her out of commission for a while. Since a broken wrist and ankle prevented her from being able to drive, she worried about how her children would get to school, who would take over her responsibilities at the temple, and who would look in on her parents. As strange as it may sound, she never even considered asking for help. Fortunately, the people in her network recognized her needs and stepped up. Her siblings took turns spending more time with her parents, a coworker brought her to and from work, and the rabbi's wife took over her projects at the temple.

Although Corinna never actually asked for help, the experience not only forced her to cash in some of the equity in her account, it also made her realize that she *could* ask for more. As she said, "I never knew all of these people would come forward with such generosity. It made me realize how much support I have around me that I never knew I had." The same likely holds true for you. Not capitalizing on your equity can lead to unnecessary stress. You don't extend generosity and kindness because of what you're going to get back, but knowing you have equity in the bank can provide you with peace of mind when you need it most.

Make It Work for You

- **Take stock of the equity in your account.** If you don't know it's there, then you won't use it on that rainy day. Be conscious of the ways in which you have *earned* the right to cash in on your network connections.

- **Don't wait until you're bankrupt.** We mean both figuratively and literally bankrupt. If you're at your wits' end over not being able to juggle all of the balls you have in the air, you're on your way to emotional bankruptcy. Or, if it's gotten even more difficult for you to find a new job after being laid off, you could be on your way to literal bankruptcy. In either case, don't wait until circumstances are this dire to cash in some of your goodwill equity. If you find yourself going down this path, ask for help or for introductions that will help you right your course.

- **Acknowledge the equity you do cash in.** Regardless of how much or how little someone does for you, let them know your appreciation through a note or phone call. Nice girls are inordinately proud and are sometimes so embarrassed by exhibitions of goodwill that they are reluctant to show their gratitude. This may sound obvious (and yes, we've mentioned it before), but a little thanks goes a long way.

KNOW WHEN TAKING ADVANTAGE ISN'T TAKING ADVANTAGE

At the beginning of this section we talked about Violet, the daughter of a highly regarded psychologist, who was reluctant to "take advantage of" her father's network and relationships. Ultimately, she did call on some of his contacts to help her in a perfectly appropriate way, and it worked out well. However, there are situations where trying to leverage connections, if not handled well, can seem opportunist and backfire. So how do you distinguish between cashing in on equity or leveraging relationships and taking inappropriate advantage? Here are a few questions to ask yourself:

- Is there reciprocity in this relationship? Does this person ask for my help from time to time?

- Do I have something to offer this person that might be of value to him or her?

- Is my request reasonable (i.e., can it be met without requiring excessive time or effort)?

- Are my requests infrequent?

- Is it this person's job to help me? Do I pay for the services?

- Have I shown appropriate gratitude for what's been given to or done for me?

If you answer no to two or more of the questions above, then you might be on the verge of taking advantage of the other person. On the other hand, if you answer yes to all of the questions, it's unlikely that you're taking advantage. People feel as if they're being "used" when the giving is lopsided or unappreciated. It happens in relationships all the time and is often the cause of irreparable damage. Here are some situations where you may be taking advantage:

- You earn a lot less than a friend who typically treats you to lunch or dinner out. She doesn't seem to mind, so you let her pay for every tab, regardless of how large or small. Lately she's stopped inviting you out and it's caused tension between you.

- You have four children and an active social life. Your sister who lives nearby has no children and you repeatedly ask her to come over and babysit. At first, it was a few times a year, but now it's increased to no less than one night a month. You think you're giving her the chance to practice her "maternal instincts." At this point, her instincts may be telling her she's being used.

- A colleague volunteered her help at a nonprofit organization you're involved with. At first, you only asked her to stuff envelopes for mailings, but now she's your go-to person every time you need help with a time-consuming project.

You can see the recurring theme in each of these scenarios. Each is an example of asking someone to go above and beyond what might be considered reasonable. If you want to maintain your network, you need to respect the time, resources, and needs of people in it. Let's turn it around now and look at some examples where taking advantage of a *relationship* isn't taking advantage of the *person*:

- You're looking for a job and the husband of a good friend works for a company where you've applied. You ask him if he would put in a good word with the hiring source. He says he will and you leave it at that. You don't want to put him in an uncomfortable position by constantly following up or even asking what he said. Although you don't get the job, you send him a modest gift card to the golf shop you know he frequents as a way of thanking him for his efforts.

- You travel frequently for work and often have packages delivered to your doorstep when you least expect them. You ask a neighbor if she would mind checking the steps for packages when you're away. You offer to do the same for her—and maybe water her plants as well—when she's on vacation.

- You are the board chair of a nonprofit organization that frequently does fund-raising. As a result, you're often asking friends who own their own businesses to donate items for silent auctions. Even though they can write these off as tax deductions, you make certain they receive the best seats to these events at no cost and that their businesses receive prominent mention in advertising and press releases.

The common thread: reciprocity and appreciation.

MAKE IT WORK FOR YOU

- **Spread the joy of helping you.** Here's where a wide network comes in handy. If your network is too small, you'll constantly be asking the same people for favors or assistance. Even though you might find it easier to ask certain people for help than others, overrelying on one or two sources puts you at risk of taking advantage. Refer to your network diagram to consider all of the resources available to you.

- **Expect others to take care of themselves.** We've all heard the saying "It doesn't hurt to ask." This is especially true when you give others the latitude to say no and expect that they will let you know if your request makes them uncomfortable. In such cases, it's best to thank them for their consideration and walk away with no hard feelings.

- **Give others permission to say no.** Ideally, others will take care of themselves, but sometimes you have to prime the pump. If you've tapped the same well numerous times and are worried about it drying up, then say something like, "I know I've asked for many favors in the past and I don't want to damage our relationship. If this doesn't work for you, please let me know and there's no problem."

- *Always* acknowledge a favor. A simple thank-you, handwritten note, or small token of appreciation can be the difference between taking advantage and accepting a favor.

261

QUESTION EVEN THE EXPERTS

It's perfectly fine to respect experts. Yet often nice girls take this too far by completely ceding control to the pros, reluctant to question them for fear of seeming rude. The result is outcomes that don't serve their interests. This happened to Amelia when she decided to divorce her husband. She'd chosen a particular lawyer to represent her because he had come highly recommended. Not wanting to insult him by questioning his methods, during the initial consultation she didn't ask him for an overview of the divorce process, or whether he would be working on her case himself or delegating some of it to an associate in the firm. Nor did she ask him to provide a "guesstimate" of the costs and fees. Amelia badly wanted him to take her case and believed that raising issues like these might dissuade him. When he agreed to represent her, she readily signed a retainer agreement.

This proved to be a mistake. The case dragged on and on with no end in sight. The only thing Amelia could count on was receiving his bills as steadily as clockwork. As time passed, it was clear that not only was he delegating some work to associates (a common practice), the associates were rotating on and off with alarming frequency. The upshot was that Amelia was being billed for their learning curve *as well as* the time he spent reviewing their work. Amelia paid as much as she could afford, but quickly fell behind. By this time, it was too late to question his strategy or his billing practices.

Another area of life where it's important to question the experts is health care. Shelly, diagnosed with multiple sclerosis, was considering participating in a clinical trial for a new medication. The pharmaceutical company testing the drug would cover all the costs of the medicine and the treatments, but she wasn't sure about expenses related to treating any conditions or side effects resulting from the trial. When Shelly called her insurance company to inquire, the insurance company representative assured her there would be no problem, she'd be covered.

Pleased with this answer and still preoccupied with the decision of whether or not to participate in the trial, Shelly thanked her and hung up. A few days later, however, Shelly realized she could not rely on the word of just one person for information that would inform such a major decision, no matter how sure the representative had seemed. So she called back to request something in writing. This time, the person with whom she spoke said she had no idea about whether or not her coverage would apply. Shelly got in touch with people in the benefits department of her company to get clarification. You guessed it—no coverage if you were involved in a clinical trial. Good thing she had the sense to question the so-called expert.

Winning women aren't afraid to ask questions of their doctors, either. When facing a health crisis, they gather as much information as they can and then use this information to create a list of informed questions to ask their doctors. They take notes when the doctor speaks so they can later refer to them, and aren't afraid to ask their doctors to repeat or further clarify information they did not understand. They ask for copies of test results and other records because this can save them time and money as well as the possible aggravation of repeating tests unnecessarily. They're not afraid to tell their doctors they are going to seek a second opinion if they feel they need one. They know this is not an affront to the doctor; competent doctors encourage such due diligence. Nor are they fearful to say no to a test or procedure they aren't convinced will help. They don't just go along to be a "good" patient.

Winning women also ask lots of questions when money is involved. They ask the auto mechanic to explain what the alternator does and how he knows it needs to be replaced before agreeing to replace it, and they ask follow-up questions about the warranty. They ask the contractor who's renovating their kitchen questions about materials and project time lines. And, they ask their investment managers to explain (in plain English!) the stocks or mutual fund they are recommending and why it is appropriate for them.

Asking questions of experts is not disrespectful. Quite the contrary. It shows respect for the person's skill *and* for your own needs.

MAKE IT WORK FOR YOU

- **Check out the expert.** Choosing the right person is critical. Reach out to your network and ask for recommendations from friends, family, and colleagues, then follow up with research online. Depending on the profession (lawyers, for example), some experts offer a free initial consultation. Free or not, be sure to test for "fit" in the initial meeting—just because an expert is credentialed, doesn't mean he or she is necessarily a good match for you.

- **Be sure to ask how the professional is compensated.** Experts deserve to be paid for their advice. Don't be reluctant to ask how they bill so as to avoid later unpleasant surprises.

- **Get it in writing.** As appropriate, ask for documentation of your agreement. If the expert is reluctant to put his or her promises in writing, find a new expert. Remember, you have a right to the information you ask for. You're paying for it.

BE A MENTOR

Winning women mentor others. They have the confidence to know just how valuable their expertise and experience are and they extend themselves to share them. This isn't just about doing another person a favor; it's also about strengthening your own network, because by helping another person hone his or her skills, you're essentially investing in a resource you may be able to draw on later. For example, Ann, the woman who ran the after-prom party at her kids' high school, was passing the torch to another parent since her youngest son was about to graduate. Because she was so committed to the event, Ann offered to stay on as an advisor for another year. Ann will pass along not only her database of supplier names and parent volunteers, but also the lessons she's learned—the "secret sauce" that makes the party so wonderful.

As generous as they are with their time and talent, winning women are clear about their roles as mentors and their expectations of mentees, whether the mentoring relationship is formal or informal. Elise, a senior executive in the financial services industry, had mentored many people over the course of her career. So when she was asked to join a fledging mentoring program geared to college seniors, many of whom were the first in their families to attend college, she agreed without hesitation.

The mentee with whom Elise was matched was somewhat introverted and tended to respond very slowly, or not at all, to her e-mails, so she relied on the periodic face-to-face meetings scheduled by the program director. The day before one of the meetings, scheduled weeks in advance, Elise was surprised to receive an e-mail from the program director letting her know her mentee wouldn't be able to attend. She called the director back to find out what tragedy had befallen the student or, alternatively, why he wasn't taking the program seriously. It turned out he hadn't managed his campus job schedule well enough in advance to get the time off. Elise explained to the director that she'd declined an out-of-town job interview because of the mentoring meeting, that her time was valuable and she didn't want it squandered. The director got back in touch with the student, explaining that he needed to be there and offered to intervene on his behalf with his boss, but the student said he'd handle it himself. He did.

MAKE IT WORK FOR YOU

- **Define the scope of the mentoring relationship.** When you agree to mentor someone, you're not agreeing to be his or her mother! Be clear about the purpose of the relationship, what you are willing to provide—and what you're not. It can be helpful to define the time frame as well. If as the committed deadline approaches, things are going well, you can always agree to extend the end date.

- **Discuss and agree on a process that works for each of you.** How often will you communicate with one another? Will you meet in person, talk over the phone, e-mail one another, or some combination of all of the above? What sort of cancellation policy makes sense? Two great pamphlets can help you here: *The Mentor's Guide* and *The Mentee's Guide*, available through The Mentoring Group (www.mentoringgroup.com).

- **Check in early and often.** Formal mentoring programs typically have built-in checkpoints. If the relationship is informal, you have to make the effort to check with your mentee to get feedback and to offer yours. Mentoring relationships take time and effort, but when you see what a difference you've made in someone's life, the payback is enormous.

DON'T SKIMP ON FRIENDSHIP

There are FRIENDS and there are friends. Our FRIENDS are welcome at our Thanksgiving tables; these are the people for whom we'll do almost anything. We're there for them when they need us and they're there for us. In a 2002 article, "UCLA Study on Friendship Among Women," Gale Berkowitz reveals just how important these friendships are:

> They shape who we are and who we are yet to be. They soothe our tumultuous inner world, fill the emotional gaps in our marriage, and help us remember who we really are. By the way, they may do even more. Friends are also helping us live better. The famed Nurses' Health Study from Harvard Medical School found that the more friends women had, the less likely they were to develop physical impairments as they aged, and the more likely they were to be leading a joyful life. In fact, the results were so significant, the researchers concluded, that not having close friends or confidants was as detrimental to your health as smoking or carrying extra weight.

In other words, good friends are important. And while most of us don't have the time it takes to maintain many close relationships, friendship can be extended in myriad ways that aren't always time-consuming: listening to someone talk about their bad day, celebrating someone's achievements, checking in on someone who is going through a rough time, bringing a home-cooked meal to someone who has been ill, or taking the time to call someone on their birthday before running off to work. Your network consists of friends and FRIENDS. You can't go wrong extending the second kind of friendship to one who needs it.

MAKE IT WORK FOR YOU

- **Differentiate the depth of relationships in your network.** Nice girls make the mistake of thinking they must give everyone the amount of time, energy, and attention expected or demanded. This is impossible. Knowing who is really important to you (as opposed to those whom you want to treat with respect and kindness) allows you to determine how your time is best spent.

- **Connect friends through small social gatherings.** Be the person who brings together diverse groups of people with common interests for a drink, a meal, or an outing. Hopefully, others will reciprocate and your network of friends will expand.

- **Place the emphasis on getting to know others—not having them get to know you.** The irony of developing friendships in this way is that others *will* want to know more about you once you've shown an interest in them. As suggested earlier, developing a mental list of nonintrusive questions you can ask people upon meeting them will ensure that initial conversations flow smoothly.

LIVE YOUR VALUES

THE TACTICS IN STRATEGY VII FOCUS ON

- Being yourself without apology or guilt.
- Moving to plan B when the situation calls for it.
- Thinking ahead.

W e saved this strategy for last because we believe winning in life isn't just about getting what you want—it's about getting those things while staying true to your values. All too often nice girls see these two goals as incompatible or mutually exclusive. We're socialized to believe that getting what we want means being cold and cutthroat, or going against what we believe in. Nothing could be further from the truth. If we have to go against our values to achieve something, we probably didn't really want it in the first place. Similarly, nice girls often trick themselves into believing that the values imposed by others are their own, when in fact they simply don't want to rock the boat.

This was the case with Lila who, at a young age, married a significantly older man. They met at work where they both held high-ranking jobs in a Fortune 500 company. Although Lila knew she wanted to raise a family, it hadn't been her intent to give up her career entirely. Somehow, over the years, she adopted as her own her husband's values—namely, that men were the earners and women the caregivers—and became a stay-at-home mom while he continued to climb the corporate ladder. It was an easy trap to fall into. Whenever she brought up the subject of returning to work, he discouraged her from doing so, saying the income she would earn wouldn't be worth the amount they'd pay for child care. Plus, he was earning quite a bit of money at this point and they enjoyed a very comfortable lifestyle. Even her friends and family couldn't understand why she would want to go back to work when she had a husband who supported her so nicely.

Gradually, Lila lost touch with her professional friends and fell behind in the new technology needed to be successful in her field. It came to the point where it would be difficult for her to reenter the workforce at anywhere near her old level. Eventually she gave up on the idea and became reconciled to her situation—which wasn't a bad one, although it wasn't the one that she had envisioned for herself. Then her husband passed away suddenly from a heart attack, leaving her with three young children to support. Given that he wasn't much of a planner, they had lived well but, like many families, from paycheck to paycheck. With little in savings, she had no choice but to go back to work in a position that was well below her education and capabilities, but consistent with her current skill set.

In retrospect, Lila realized that all along, she hadn't been living her values, but rather her husband's. With 20/20 hindsight, she said if she had to do it all over again, she would have insisted on doing the things that mattered most to her without sacrificing time with her family. It wasn't so much the job or the money she had valued, but the independence and self-esteem they fostered. Point is, regardless of your values, they're yours. Live them.

GO BACK TO BASICS

Women sometimes ask us, "How do I know what my values are?" If you already know what yours are, this might seem like a simple question, but it's not. It's easy to lose track of our values. Life has a way of swallowing us up in must-dos and have-to-haves. We become encumbered with responsibilities and expectations—both our own and those of others. If life seems off-kilter, surreal, or not quite your own, it can be hard to tell whether the stress is a result of life's normal pressures, or because you aren't living your values. However, if you are experiencing an undue amount of stress, it's probably the latter. Sometimes it takes a catastrophe to open our eyes to this and bring us back to center, but luckily there are ways to blend our values with the realities of everyday life.

Simply put, our values are those beliefs, attitudes, and behaviors that we hold dear and that define the core of who we are. These provide us with a compass for making decisions both large and small. They help us to make choices about whom in our personal and professional lives we want to keep close and whom we want to keep at arm's length. They help us to gauge the "rightness" of our direction. When we speak with women who are experiencing rough patches in their lives, we often suggest they go back to their values to help them find a way out. We're surprised at how often they tell us, "It's been so long since I've even thought about my values that I don't know what they are anymore."

If you're one of these women, here's a useful exercise. Pretend you're at an auction where the values in the following chart are up for bid and you have only $100 to spend. Put a check mark next to the items you would bid for.

	Work that I love
	Self-confidence
	Spiritual satisfaction
	Strong ties with my family of origin (mother, father, siblings, etc.)
	Lifetime financial security
	Being perceived as influential
	Freedom to do what I want
	Job security
	Good health
	A home of my own
	World peace
	The opportunity to use my creativity
	Fame or recognition for my achievements
	Education
	Leisure time
	A healthy relationship with a loving husband, spouse, or partner
	The love of friends
	An understanding of the meaning of life
	Children
	The opportunity to be of service to others
	Peace of mind/contentment

Now, assuming that you checked more than three items, go back and pretend that you could win the bidding war for only *three* values. Which three would they be? Once you've done this, answer these questions:

- Am I currently acting in ways that reflect these three values?

- What are the obstacles (people, activities, work, etc.) to living these values?

- What changes do I need to make in my life if I want to live my values with authenticity?

- What kind of resistance can I expect as I move toward this?

- How can I counter this resistance?

- How can others help me to more closely live my values?

These are the questions that must be answered if you are to not only *win the life you want*, but win in a way that is consistent with your personal values.

MAKE IT WORK FOR YOU

- **Identify your top three values.** Hopefully, the preceding assessment helped. Now it's time to make sure that you incorporate these into everything you do. Write down your answers to the above questions and when in doubt, go back to your values—they illuminate the path that's right for you.

- **Resist adopting other people's values.** When we meet new friends, get married, or start work at a new company we sometimes get caught up in *their* values, confusing them with our own. If you're experiencing stress or something just doesn't feel quite right about the life that you're leading, ask yourself if you've gone astray from your *own* values. If so, use the tactics we've provided throughout this book to put yourself back on course.

- **Don't doubt your values.** Other people may make you feel as if something is wrong with you if you don't see the world in the same way they do. Some people will fall by the wayside when you stick to your guns—and that's not always a bad thing. Living *your* life on *your* terms takes courage.

IDENTIFY YOUR NONNEGOTIABLES

It's a lot easier to live your values once you've taken the extra step to translate them into practical terms—what you will and will not accept in your life. Winning women make it a point to define not only what they will and won't accept from others but what they will and won't accept from themselves. These are their nonnegotiables.

Alyssa, for example, was tapped for a promotion that would require her to move across the country. Single, and very close to her family and friends who lived nearby, she agonized about whether or not to take the job because she'd know virtually no one in the new city except people with whom she'd be working. It wasn't an easy decision, but Alyssa finally agreed to take the job because the core values of her company—integrity, respect for the individual, and putting the customer first—matched hers so perfectly she couldn't imagine being happy working anywhere else. She realized that while moving away from her friends and family wasn't ideal, it wasn't a nonnegotiable.

Conversely, Erin's nonnegotiable values were what gave her the courage to divorce her alcoholic husband, whose frequent drinking was affecting her children. Her moment of truth came when her middle child, a son, told her he was afraid to bring his friends home after school because he never knew what kind of shape his father would be in. Erin's commitment to always put her children's safety and well-being first meant she had to act quickly and decisively.

Although not all nonnegotiables are this dramatic, they're just as important to the person who holds them. One of Nina's was to make time to read fiction, no matter how busy she was raising a family and running a business. For Chris, it was protecting her time to exercise.

Being able to differentiate nice-to-haves or would-like-to-haves from *must-haves* defines a winning woman's values.

MAKE IT WORK FOR YOU

- **Make a list of the things you can't live with and the things you can't live without.** Keep it focused on the essentials. "Nice to haves" aren't essential and are therefore most likely negotiable.

- **Review your list and revise it every now and again.** As we change, our values sometimes do too. For example, when you were single, having time to do things with and for friends was one of your non-negotiables. Now that you're married with children and your time is more limited, spending time with your family becomes the non-negotiable item.

- **Align your life with your lists.** Don't wait until the time is "right" to make changes. No matter how difficult, you won't be happy until you rid yourself of the people and things that are out of sync with your values.

SEND GUILT ON A TRIP

Have you ever noticed that women are more prone to feeling guilty than men? And *nice girls*? They can't seem to avoid it. A study by Itziar Etxebarria, M. José Ortiz, Susana Conejero, and Aitziber Pascual, published in the *Spanish Journal of Psychology* (vol. 12, no. 2 [2009]), appears to confirm the fact that women are more likely to feel guilt because they're socialized to be considerate of the feelings and needs of others. The researchers report that "habitual guilt was found to be more intense in women than in men in all age groups." The problem is, guilt is one of the least productive emotions out there, and often it holds us back from going after the things we really want.

There are different kinds of guilt, and to expunge guilt from your life you need to understand them:

- **Intentionally imposed guilt.** This is when another person uses guilt to manipulate you. For example, your sister-in-law tells you that you aren't being a good friend to her because you failed to immediately call her back about a problem she was having.

- **Guilt through implication.** People don't have to tell us we've done something wrong in order to instill guilt. A comment like "Everyone else's mother is coming to the school play" induces guilt through the mere suggestion that you're not doing enough for your child.

- **Self-imposed guilt.** This form of guilt comes from within and can arise without another person having to say a word. Often it stems from our personal values and the messages we've internalized. If family is something that's important to you, yet you choose to attend your company's annual strategic planning meeting instead of your parents' fiftieth wedding anniversary party, you'll likely feel guilty, even if your family tells you not to worry about it.

Regardless of the source or cause, guilt serves no good purpose in your life. Even if you've legitimately disappointed someone or hurt his or her feelings, guilt won't change anything. We can't begin to tell you how many women we've heard say, "I feel guilty when I'm at work and not with my children, and I feel guilty when I spend time with my children and I'm not working." Marriage and family counselor Lynette Hoy suggests that the key to getting beyond guilt is accepting that you're human, with frailties and foibles like everyone else. "No one can claim to be the best wife, housekeeper, dresser, professional or businesswoman, mother, single parent, or most well educated," says Hoy. Sometimes simply living your values has to be enough.

MAKE IT WORK FOR YOU

- **Recognize when guilt trips are being used to manipulate you.** Children and other family members are particularly good at this. Resist the temptation to change course only because you feel guilty—stick to your values.

- **Respond to, rather than suffer with, self-imposed guilt.** Perhaps you were sharp in your comments to a friend because you were under a great amount of stress dealing with a family emergency. If you really did hurt someone, instead of feeling bad about it, let her know why it happened, apologize, and move on.

- **Don't even try to be all things to all people.** When we get caught up in that game, we are bound to let others down and wind up feeling guilty. "It may be that you are too critical of yourself or that someone else has caused you to feel badly when there is no basis for it. You may not have anything to apologize for. In that case, the problem lies within your own mind and you need to let it go," suggests Hoy.

LAUGH OUT LOUD

Winning women share a hallmark value—a sense of humor. This doesn't necessarily mean they do stand-up at the local comedy club; it just means they can see the funny side of life. It probably won't surprise you that research conducted by Gary W. Lewandowski and Benjamin Le ("Fun in Relationships," *Encyclopedia of Human Relationships,* April 2010) shows that a sense of humor makes people more attractive as potential friends and romantic partners. Moreover, individuals who consider themselves in happy relationships report that humor is a "central part of their relationship." As English actress Kate Beckinsale once said, "If someone had told me years ago that sharing a sense of humour was so vital to partnerships, I could have avoided a lot of sex!"

Having a sense of humor can mean a lot of things. In a piece called "What's Your Humor Style?" (*Psychology Today,* July 2006) Louise Dobson describes four distinct styles of humor:

1. *Put-down humor* involves using sarcasm and ridicule to make jokes at the expense of others. Think Wanda Sykes.

2. *Bonding humor* is amusing and lighthearted and brings people together, even in tense situations. Think Ellen DeGeneres.

3. *Hate-me humor* is self-deprecating, and involves making yourself the butt of the joke. Think Kathy Griffin.

4. *Laughing at life humor* focuses on the absurdities of life. Think Tina Fey.

Based on what we know about the way many people expect women to behave in our society, women are typically seen as funnier when they use bonding and laughing at life humor styles. Whether it's fair or not, women who use put-down humor are often seen as angry—or worse, just plain mean. And while it might be entertaining in the moment, people find this kind of humor tough to take in large doses, even if they're not the target. Self-deprecating humor is an even worse choice for women. After all, if respect is what you're after, do you really think pointing out and ridiculing your flaws is a good strategy?

Don't despair if you've never been able to even tell a joke, much less make one up. Some people are better at expressing their sense of humor as a "humoree," a word we just created to simply mean someone who enjoys another person's humor. Those who are good at cracking jokes desperately need those who aren't—otherwise, they would never have an audience! When expressed the right way, humor may be one of the most universally well-regarded values. So feel free to laugh early and often!

MAKE IT WORK FOR YOU

- **Make time to laugh out loud.** Recognize the value of humor in reducing stress and increasing life satisfaction, and figure out how to get more of it. Supplement the laughs in your life any chance you get. Don't be ashamed to watch sitcoms, read the comic strips, or go to funny movies.

- **Define your own sense of humor.** Once you know what kind of humor style is most natural to you, hone your skills. Be careful, though, about using put-down or hate-me humor.

- **Don't fake it.** If you don't find someone's "humor" funny (ethnic, sexist, or otherwise offensive jokes, for example), feel free not to laugh. Remember—live *your* values.

MANAGE YOUR BRAND

We are *all* brands. Just as well-known brand names such as Apple, Pepsi, Mercedes, or Kleenex have certain reputations, we too are known for our values and the behaviors that reflect them. The most successful brands share a few things in common:

- They strive for superior quality.

- They're trusted.

- You can count on their consistency.

- They depend on consumer feedback.

- They advertise their value.

People, too, build their reputations and, in turn, gain access to the things they want by focusing on these same principles. Have you ever thought to yourself, "Gee, that doesn't seem like Fiona," when Fiona did something out of character? It's probably because she didn't act consistently with the personal brand she created. Above all else, consistency builds trust.

Your values play a critical role in developing and honing your brand. If you're not sure what you want yours to represent, think about what you want others to say about you when you leave the room. Finish this sentence: *There goes a woman who*_____. Carol would finish it by saying, "There goes a woman who knows what she wants and how to get it while keeping the needs of others in mind." Lois would say, "There goes a woman who is self-confident, caring, and courageous." By crafting your own brand statement—then acting on it—you have the opportunity to decide what other people will say about you.

MAKE IT WORK FOR YOU

- **Write down what you want others to say about you when you leave a room.** This is what we call "the word on the street." There's a word on the street about all of us, and we have control over what it is and whether we act in concert with it.

- **Ascribe actionable behaviors.** Just writing down your brand statement isn't enough. You might want someone to say you're kind-hearted, but what actions do you have to engage in to make it a reality? Go out of your way for strangers and friends? Spend time with people when they're feeling low? For each value you want to be associated with, identify the behaviors that you'll have to exhibit for others to see you in such a way.

- **Let others know about your brand.** Nice girls have the tendency to hide their light under a bushel. It does no good to have a wonderful brand that no one knows about. Peggy Klaus wrote a wonderful book, *Brag! The Art of Tooting Your Own Horn Without Blowing It*, that we recommend you read. Talk about your accomplishments, your values, and your beliefs (just as an advertiser would) so that others come to know and trust *your* brand.

- **Conduct focus groups.** Just as companies with brand names conduct focus groups to get feedback, poll people you trust to find out how your own "brand" is regarded. Ask questions like "In what ways could I be a better friend?" or "How can I be more effective in meeting your needs?" It's sometimes painful to hear the answers, but feedback is a gift that helps us to grow our brands and know whether we are really living the values we espouse. And don't forget what we said earlier about feedback—if three people say you're drunk, *lie down.*

TACTIC 91

ACCEPT COMPLIMENTS

Nice girls have a hard time with compliments. We don't necessarily blame them. It can be complicated for a woman to accept a compliment gracefully. To see just how common a problem this is, we did a Google search for the phrase *women and compliments*. It returned 8,430,000 results. Take, for example, how uncomfortable most of us feel when we receive a compliment about our appearance. In one scenario, we jump to the conclusion that the compliment isn't genuine ("How could she really like this old dress?"). In a second scenario, we become suspicious that the person offering the compliment has a hidden agenda ("He must want something in return"). And in yet another scenario, we don't want to appear conceited ("There's no way I'm going to agree that I do look terrific!"). Somehow, women have been socialized to believe there is shame in feeling good about themselves, and that's tragic because pooh-poohing a compliment not only hurts the nice girl by undercutting her self-esteem, but it also insults the person who offers it—especially if the praise is offered with the best of intentions. In the best case, it leaves the conversation in an awkward place. I'm sure you've had the experience of telling a friend she looks great and having her respond by saying her hair needs to be cut and she needs to lose twenty pounds. Uncomfortable, right? Where do you go from there? And, in the worst case, it can damage a relationship if the person who offers the compliment believes he or she is perceived as insincere.

An inability to accept compliments hurts nice girls at work, too. The workplace is competitive. To even survive, never mind get ahead, people must be seen as competent at their jobs. If her boss tells a nice girl she gave a standout presentation at the staff meeting and she responds by saying, "I really didn't do much at all. Pete gave me the numbers and Heather did all the analysis," her boss would be perfectly justified in wondering what contributions she made.

Rabbi Shmuley Boteach, a commentator on Oprah Radio, notes that if you don't accept compliments, people will stop giving them:

> A compliment is the human manifestation of appreciation for another. Therefore, when we reject a compliment, we reject our own virtue because it's not believable to us. When someone offers a compliment, be passive and just accept it. Let it swell your heart, and pass the compliment on.

We couldn't have said it better.

MAKE IT WORK FOR YOU

- **Take people at their word.** As we wrote earlier, unless you have good reason to believe otherwise, trust people mean it when they offer a compliment.

- **Don't argue; just say, "Thank you."** Instead of saying something like, "You must be kidding, this outfit looks awful!" just say you appreciate that they noticed. Whatever you do, don't deny or dilute the compliment.

- **Don't offer a compliment in return unless you mean it**. And even then, it's often wise to let a bit of time pass. After all, the person who gave you the compliment might be a nice girl and not believe you really mean it.

BE PROACTIVE, NOT PASSIVE

By now, you know that nice girls often sit back and wait for things to happen. That's why they don't get the things they want, the success they've earned, and the respect they deserve. As we noted earlier, *hope is not a strategy*, or as Eleanor Roosevelt said, "It takes as much energy to wish as it does to plan."

Let's talk about the workplace first. Way too often we've seen women keep their heads down, deliver more than what's expected, and wait for someone to notice. Most of them are still waiting. In *Her Place at the Table*, Carol and her coauthors describe this as the Tiara Syndrome. Although employers can (and should) provide support to employees, it's up to individuals to proactively manage their own careers. Winning women have a plan. They think about where they want to be and what they want to be doing in a year, in three years, or in ten years—then they figure out how to make it happen. How? Among other things, they seek advice from mentors, ask for specific and timely feedback, and raise their hands for high-profile assignments. They deal with troublesome coworkers and take calculated risks. They ask for what they want and do it in a way that's authentic and culturally acceptable. If, after using their best efforts, they still don't get what they believe they're due, they move on.

Winning women are proactive in their personal lives, too. Erin, the woman who divorced her alcoholic husband, knew that it was up to her to change a bad situation. He certainly wasn't going to do a thing; in his mind the situation was working just fine as it was. She had to engage an attorney to get things started. That forced him to hire a lawyer too. When things dragged on, she made a hard decision to give him more than his fair share of assets so that he'd agree to settle. Although we don't recommend giving up assets to which you're entitled just because a divorce is difficult and you want it over, in this case being proactive in order to avoid the painful experience of going to court was the right decision for Erin.

Problems don't magically solve themselves. They may go subterranean for a while, but if we don't deal with them, they'll continue to limit our lives. The reality is that not making a decision to address an issue is in fact a decision to allow the status quo.

Make It Work for You

- **Take care of yourself.** Nobody else cares as much about your happiness as you do. Similarly, no one will ever take as good care of you as you will take care of yourself.

- **Don't wait for someone else to act.** Chances are the other person is waiting for you to make a move. Or, worse yet, they don't even realize that action is needed!

- **Grab the brass ring.** Good things won't just drop in your lap. You deserve success, but you've got to make the effort to get it in your grasp.

DON'T HAVE "MISTAKE AMNESIA"

What, you may ask, is this tactic doing in a section on values? Well, it's simple. Your mistakes often illuminate how far you've strayed from your values. We all make mistakes. They teach us valuable lessons about how to get back on the right path.

In Lois's book *Nice Girls Don't Get Rich,* she talks about the many mistakes she made when starting her own business. Some were because she didn't remain laser-focused on her own values, others because she let the values of others eclipse her own. In all cases, the mistakes she made taught her how to get back to her values in ways that benefited not only her, but those she served and employed as well.

There's no shame in making a mistake. The only shame is when you forget what you learned from it. One place we see this "mistake amnesia" happen frequently among women is in the choice of a partner or spouse. We talked earlier about the repetition compulsion—the tendency to make the same choices over and over, despite their likely negative outcome, because we tend to opt for the familiar. Let's say you have a boyfriend you don't trust to be faithful because he's a flirt and a womanizer. So you leave that relationship and find yourself in one with someone who takes advantage of your generosity by asking for loans he never repays (just watch a few episodes of *Judge Judy* and you'll learn how common *that* mistake is). It might not be apparent to you at first, but you've just repeated your initial mistake: choosing someone you can't trust.

Learning from our mistakes requires us to first look very carefully at *why* we made a particular decision. Sometimes we unwittingly cling to familiar behaviors we observed or learned in childhood—such as a mother tolerating inappropriate behavior from a father. Other times, and particularly for nice girls, mistakes are due to low self-esteem and fear of offending others. Whatever the reason, knowing why you acted as you did is essential for changing behavior.

Once you understand your motivation, you can consciously choose differently. We're not saying it's easy—changing behavior never is. The key is to identify appropriate alternative behaviors and add them to your repertoire of choices. Again, going back to your values helps to put you on a path that is consistent with who you want to be and what you want to attain in your life. If, to use the above example, you realize you've been allowing your husband to speak unkindly to you because this is the kind of marriage you witnessed growing up, you need to do the mental equivalent of tying a string on your finger and remind yourself, each time he makes you feel less than respected, that you have other options. Only once you have clarity on the fact that you won't tolerate those behaviors can you make choices that bring more positive energy into your life.

MAKE IT WORK FOR YOU

- **Assess the reasons behind the mistakes you make.** None of us sets out to make poor choices. We act with the best of intentions that sometimes just don't work out the way we would like. When this happens to you, don't blame or chastise yourself—that serves no purpose. Instead, dig deep to find out why you took a certain course of action and how that relates to your values and other aspects of your life.

- **Ask others to be your backup drive.** Sometimes those closest to us see our mistakes with more clarity than we can. If you find yourself in the same bad situation over and over again, ask a trusted friend or family member for input as to what they think is going on with you. You may learn that they know your insecurity causes you to pick "losers" as love interests or that your perfectionism makes you spend more time than necessary on projects or chores. Then ask them to remind you of this anytime they see you embarking on that well-worn path.

- **Identify one or two baby steps.** It's unrealistic to think you can change your entire life with one "aha" moment. That will set you up for failure. As Lao-tzu said, "The journey of a thousand miles begins with a single step." Consider just a few things you might do differently that would make the biggest difference in the short term. For example, if you got yourself into huge credit card debt because you thought you had to keep up with your wealthier friends, this might indicate you weren't living in concert with your values to be grateful for the less tangible things in your life. In this case, paying off your debt and cutting up all but one credit card (and using that only for emergencies) would be a good start for getting back on track.

- **Be kind to yourself.** Beating yourself up over your mistakes often compounds them because it blinds you to your motivations. Changing behaviors requires patience as you take two steps forward and one step back. When you accept that you are human and will inevitably make mistakes, you can treat yourself with the same kindness you show to others, and should expect from them in return.

BE AN EARLY ADOPTER

If you're under thirty-five, you can probably skip this tactic because chances are you're already an early adopter, simply by virtue of your age. The rest of you—keep reading. The term *early adopter* originates from Everett M. Rogers's *Diffusion of Innovations* and refers to those who are quick to use a new innovation or idea; these are the people who are always first on line to buy the latest gadget or gizmo.

Georgia, a scientist, was undoubtedly an early adopter. Back in the day when computers were approximately the size of a small studio apartment, she taught herself to write HTML code. Because she was so ahead of the curve, her colleagues would line up outside her office, waiting patiently until she had time to help them set up their own websites. Not only was her speedy mastery of the new Web language a boon to her own work, but it made her the "go-to" person in her department.

These days, it seems that nothing is moving faster than technological innovation. Just in our lifetimes, it's changed almost everything. Some of us remember being away at college and standing in line once a week to use the pay phone at the end of the dorm hall to call home. Now over half the global population has cell phones, and pay phones are almost extinct. Technology has changed the way we do research, shop (15 percent of the world's population shops online), and even how we date (20 percent of those who've used online dating sites have gone on to marry someone they met via the Web). Brides and grooms have wedding websites, we keep in touch with our kids via text messages, and it seems everyone now sends electronic greeting cards.

The point is that technology hasn't just changed how we work; it's also changed how we network. Thanks to technologies like Skype and webinars, communicating with people all over the world is easier and less expensive than ever before. Being an early adopter of these amazing new communication tools as they come on the scene will help you keep your connections strong, while also making it easier to reach out to new members of your network.

MAKE IT WORK FOR YOU

- **Luddites lose.** A Luddite is a person who dislikes technology, often refusing to use it on principle. The term comes from a group of British textile workers in the nineteenth century who resisted the changes introduced by the Industrial Revolution—and we know how that turned out! Be open to the opportunities technology offers.

- **Just because it's available doesn't mean it's useful.** That said, you don't have to adopt every new technology—just the ones that fit into your life and work. With technology changing at the speed of light, trying to keep up with every new innovation could take all of your time.

- **Learn your own way.** If you are a visual learner, read the manual or view the tutorial. If you are an auditory learner, download a podcast. And if you are a kinesthetic learner (one who learns by doing), just dive right in.

KEEP UP TO DATE

Winning women remain interested and interesting by staying alert to new trends and information. They keep abreast with changes in technology. If they work outside the home, they stay current with developments in their industry. But they don't stop there. They see new movies. They read new books. They pay attention to what's going on in the world. They keep learning more about the people with whom they are in relationships. This is what keeps them interesting and relevant—the kind of person everyone wants in their network.

Elena, a mom who had been out of the workforce for several years, eased her way back onto the on-ramp by selling her prospective employer on the fact that even though she had been away, she hadn't become stale. She'd read the latest studies in her field, remained active in professional associations, and stayed in touch with former colleagues so she was able to remain an industry "insider." Shelly, the woman with multiple sclerosis, gets a Google alert so she doesn't miss any new research related to her condition. Carmen, mother to two teenage girls, keeps her ear to the ground about the latest goings-on that might affect her daughters. She certainly wasn't thrilled to learn that "sexting" exists, but she's convinced she's better off knowing than not.

Not only do winning women keep up to date, they update themselves. Destiny studied conversational French in high school, but never got very good at it. So, years later, she decided to take an adult education class. Not only did she enjoy it—and improve—but it gave her something to talk about when she met new people. Winning women are lifelong learners. They know there's always something new to know.

MAKE IT WORK FOR YOU

- **Don't rely on outdated information.** Check to be sure you have the latest and most reliable facts. The Internet makes this easy, so no excuses!

- **Read without fail.** A newspaper a day keeps ignorance away. If you have time to read only one magazine each week, we recommend one called *The Week*. It's a compilation of the best articles from newspapers and magazines around the world.

- **Make learning new things a priority.** Given the busy lives so many women lead, it's easy to put learning something new at the bottom of your to-do list. If it stays there, you'll never get to it—and *that* will make you obsolete.

GIVE BACK

Throughout this book, we've talked about how to win what you want. Yet if you're reading this book, chances are that in many ways you already live in a world of abundance. We don't necessarily mean materially, but it's likely your world is full of plenty of good things—a roof over your head, people who love you, relatively good health, a few dollars in the bank, and so forth. So we would hope that among your values is a belief in the saying "To those whom much is given, much is expected." When you act with a generosity of spirit in all things, that generosity is returned to you multifold. It's just how the world works. Trust us on this one.

Remember our friend Eleanor, who is one of the most generous people we know? You may recall she's a single mom, works full-time in a challenging job, cares for her elderly parents, and still finds time to volunteer on charity boards, mentor young people, and remain active in her church. Even when she wasn't earning much, she tithed 10 percent of her income and made donations to causes she believed in. If you ask Eleanor, she'll tell you she's one of the "richest" people she knows, and that when she needs something, anything from extra money to pay for her daughter's tuition or help with a project on which she's working, it amazingly somehow appears. While we see her as giving much more than she gets, she'll tell you it's the other way around.

Giving back is the cost of admission to a rich and rewarding life. It's the dues you pay for living on this earth. The world is abundant, and you *will* get your fair share. So don't hoard the resources you should be sharing.

MAKE IT WORK FOR YOU

- **Add "giving back" to your values set.** Whether you have a lot or a little, you always have *something* to give back. Failing to do so will keep you living in a world of poverty—emotional, financial, or spiritual.

- **Don't wait to be asked.** It's one thing to give something when it's requested; it's another to see what's needed and offer it. If you see a coworker struggling with something that you know how to do— offer help. If you know a friend is going through a rough financial time and you have the resources—offer a loan. If an organization you belong to is struggling with its leadership—offer to lead.

- **Know when a request is really an imperative.** There are times when giving back is the only option. Go back to the quid pro quo for a moment. Ask yourself if you have received something (friend-ship, assistance, referrals, or anything else) from the person now asking something of you. If so, keeping up your end of the deal means giving back—period.

LEAD FROM WHERE YOU ARE

When Lois was interviewing women leaders at all levels for her book *See Jane Lead*, one of the things she learned was that *values* form the core of how almost all successful women lead. Although values-driven leadership isn't unique to women, when asked about their leadership philosophy, women are more likely than men to consider whether their values are part of the equation in their leadership endeavors. In a day and age when we see a proliferation of corporate greed, famine, war, and ecological decay, it's clear that the world needs more women to step up to the leadership plate.

Even though they may lead all the time, nice girls don't think of themselves as leaders. As a result, they're unaware of the tremendous influence they have. Winning women know you don't have to aspire to be a CEO to apply your leadership skills. Leadership is as simple as *helping people to go places or in a direction they can't go on their own.*

Here are a few ways you can lead from where you are that will put your personal values to good use:

- Introduce an initiative at your child's school that institutes zero tolerance for bullying and violence.

- Start a Neighborhood Watch group.

- Coordinate the campaign efforts of a local political candidate.

- Initiate a recycling program in your company.

- Organize your friends to volunteer time at a homeless shelter.

- Lobby your local legislature to pass laws that impose stricter sanctions for those convicted of selling drugs to children.

- Chair a committee within a struggling nonprofit organization with which you're involved.

- Form a mentoring group to work with at-risk youth.

Our communities, our country, and the world need more women leading efforts to create change. From Mother Teresa to Margaret Sanger, winning women have made a difference throughout history, and so can you.

Make It Work for You

- **Capitalize on your passion and values.** Identify just one issue that is meaningful to you and take action to lead an effort in that arena. Leading doesn't necessarily mean you have to be at the helm, but that your voice helps influence direction or move the group forward toward its goals.

- **Be a student of leadership.** Contrary to popular belief, there aren't "born" leaders. Although your experience and values provide you with the tools needed to be an outstanding leader, studying how others have done it successfully can build your confidence in taking the helm when leadership is required. There are many good books about leadership, but one we recommend is *Certain Trumpets: The Nature of Leadership* by Garry Wills. It's a wonderful compilation of vignettes about leaders throughout history and what made them (and in some cases didn't make them) effective.

- **Attend NTL's Interpersonal Skills for Leadership Success workshop.** NTL (National Training Laboratory, www.ntl.org) is this country's premier provider of experiential training programs. Its four-day program teaches you the interpersonal and influence skills needed to achieve your leadership goals.

PERIODICALLY REASSESS
WHAT'S IMPORTANT

Beryl Markham, an English aviator and the first woman to fly solo across the Atlantic east to west in 1936, said, "You can live a lifetime and, at the end of it, know more about other people than you know about yourself." Too few people are self-reflective. Maybe they don't have the energy or perhaps they don't have the courage. In any case, the result is a life of being out of sync with what is important to you at any particular moment in time.

Think back to Andrea, the woman who moved in with her boyfriend out of inertia. She drifted into an effortless situation that didn't move her any closer to getting what she wanted—marriage. Or Allison, who got stuck in a friendship that no longer met her needs. In each instance, because these women failed to periodically take stock of their situation, they didn't realize that what was important and tolerable at one point had changed.

On the other hand, we've also shared stories of women who have adapted as things in their lives changed. Take Erin, who made the hard decision to divorce her husband once she realized her children were being affected. Or Alyssa, who chose to move to advance her career. And although Julia, the woman who has almost decided to stay home with her children for a while, hasn't yet come to grips with her mother, we're hoping she'll get there.

The American writer Barbara Johnson has been quoted as saying, "No one likes change but babies in diapers." Yet change is inevitable. Nothing endures but change. Winning women make the choice to embrace it.

MAKE IT WORK FOR YOU

- **Think back to the work you did for Strategy I: Evaluate the Past and Envision the Future.** How well are you doing with regard to making the changes you wanted to make? In what areas are you succeeding? How? Where are you still struggling? Why?

- **Figure out which of those changes are still important to you.** If you are having trouble with changes you want to make, it's helpful to revisit the reasons you wanted to make the changes in the first place. What prompted you to flag those particular issues as meaningful ones? What, if anything, is different now from the way it was then?

- **Recommit to making the changes that still make sense to you.** If the necessary changes you identified are still important, then circle back to them. Go back and reread Strategy I, Tactic 14: Take It One Day at a Time.

CREATE YOUR LEGACY

"What is the forensic evidence that I existed? When they dust for fingerprints, what will they find?" This is how one entertainment executive described his intense desire to do more than simply his job. Your legacy doesn't have to be a building with your name on it, a place in the record books, or a Nobel Peace Prize. It's simply the string of goals you achieved and contributions you made—big or small—in your life. Maybe your goal was to raise healthy children, reach a certain professional level, have a certain dollar amount in the bank, or realize spiritual contentment. Whatever your goals, these define your legacy. Young or old, it's never too early to think about what your legacy will be. What forensic fingerprint will you leave behind?

Here are some examples of the legacies that may not make the history books but will still have a meaningful impact on the world:

- Gloria is a nurse at the local hospital. In her spare time, she makes quilts and donates them for raffles at auctions conducted by nonprofits that benefit children.

- Celine, a retired doctor, is the "go-to" person in the neighborhood whenever anyone has a medical question or concern.

- Susan is a therapist who volunteers time working with children who have experienced abuse.

- Lorraine is an attorney who started a program to tutor and provide scholarships to inner-city girls so that they are prepared for college.

- Fran inherited a large amount of money at a young age and used part of it to start a foundation that benefits women's organizations.

- Liz is a stay-at-home mom who knits "cancer caps" for women who have lost their hair through chemotherapy.

In each case, the woman's contribution to society is her legacy. They're making a difference in ways that touch and change lives—and who wouldn't want *that* as a legacy?

MAKE IT WORK FOR YOU

- **Make a difference while making a living.** Most of us have to work in one way or another, inside or outside the home, to meet our commitments. Consider how you can make a difference through your work. This is what living your values is really about.

- **"Be the change you wish to see."** This quote from Mahatma Gandhi reminds us that we can complain about injustice or we can take steps to correct it. Look around your world and identify ways you can work toward creating change that benefits you, your loved ones, and your community.

- **Risk speaking the unspoken.** If you've reached the stage of your life or career where your reputation is established, then you most likely can "get away with" saying things that other people can't. It's the perfect time to take some risks and be the voice for concerns you may not have had the courage to express in the past. This is not to say that you should let diplomacy and political savvy go by the wayside. You should still use the influence skills you developed throughout your lifetime, but you can now use them to say bolder things—things that can make a difference in the lives of others who may not have the ability to speak as freely.

SUGGESTED READING

Throughout the book, we've made references to other books that will help you further build the knowledge and skills needed to win the respect you deserve, the success you've earned, and the life you want. Here is a list and brief description of those books we mentioned that we think are worth reading in their entirety, along with several others we like and recommend to our clients.

- *The Art of SpeedReading People: How to Size People Up and Speak Their Language*, Barbara Barron-Tieger and Paul D. Tieger (Little, Brown, 1999). Yes, one more book based on the Myers Briggs Type Indicator®, this one designed to help you quickly and accurately identify the best ways to communicate with different people given their unique personality styles.

- *Beyond Dealmaking: Five Steps to Negotiating Profitable Relationships*, Melanie Billings-Yun (Jossey-Bass/Wiley, 2010). With an international perspective and experience, the author's accessible approach focuses on how negotiators can engage others to resolve issues.

- *Brag! The Art of Tooting Your Own Horn Without Blowing It*, Peggy Klaus (Business Plus, 2004). Klaus provides specific suggestions for how you can call attention to your accomplishments without coming across as egotistical or concerned only with your own self-interest.

- *Crucial Conversations: Tools for Talking When Stakes Are High*, Kerry Patterson, Joseph Grenny, Ron McMillan, and Al Switzler (McGraw-Hill, 2002). The authors provide a seven-step approach for having dreaded (but necessary) conversations at home or at work.

- *Difficult Conversations: How to Discuss What Matters Most*, Douglas Stone, Bruce Patton, and Sheila Heen (Viking Penguin, 1999).

Based on research at the Harvard Negotiation Project, the authors offer an eminently readable and solid approach to conducting the conversations that matter most.

- *Everyday Negotiation: Navigating the Hidden Agendas in Bargaining,* Deborah M. Kolb and Judith Williams (Jossey-Bass/Wiley, 2003). The paperback successor to *The Shadow Negotiation: How Women Can Master the Hidden Agendas That Determine Bargaining Success,* this book focuses on the impact of the parallel "shadow" negotiation inherent in every negotiation—how the negotiators deal with one another while negotiating about the issues at stake.

- *Getting Past No: Negotiating in Difficult Situations,* William Ury (Bantam, 1993). Over the years, this book has become a classic for those interested in learning how to stay cool under pressure, negotiate with authenticity, and avoid common negotiation pitfalls.

- *Her Place at the Table: A Woman's Guide to Negotiating Five Key Challenges to Leadership Success,* Deborah Kolb, Judith Williams, and Carol Frohlinger (Jossey-Bass/Wiley, 2010). Drawing on extensive interviews with women leaders, the authors offer practical advice about the things women should negotiate for in order to be successful in leadership roles.

- *How to Say It for Women: Communicating with Confidence and Power Using the Language of Success,* Phyllis Mindell (Prentice Hall Press, 2001). Mindell uses stories of women throughout history to exemplify how you can get your message across authentically, clearly, and compassionately.

- *The Mentor's Guide* and *The Mentee's Guide.* These two workbooks, available through The Mentoring Group (www.mentoringgroup .com), are excellent resources for identifying the roles and responsibilities inherent to mentoring relationships of all kinds.

- *Nice Girls Don't Get the Corner Office: 101 Unconscious Mistakes Women Make That Sabotage Their Careers,* Lois P. Frankel (Warner Business Books, 2004). Learn how being the "nice girl" you were taught to be in childhood interferes with achieving your adult goals. The book includes specific coaching tips for how to overcome self-sabotaging behaviors.

- *Nice Girls Don't Get Rich: 75 Avoidable Mistakes Women Make with Money*, Lois P. Frankel (Warner Business Books, 2005). Rather than a financial planning book, this is a psychological look at the ways in which early childhood messages preclude you from acquiring the wealth you deserve—and what you can do to live a rich life in all ways.

- *Nurture by Nature: How to Raise Happy, Healthy, Responsible Children Through the Insights of Personality Type*, Barbara Barron-Tieger and Paul D. Tieger (Little, Brown, 1997). Using the Myers Briggs Type Indicator®, the authors teach readers how to identify personality types of children and the best way to interact with your children to ensure their true natures are honored and fully developed.

- *Perfect Daughters*, Robert J. Ackerman (HCI, 2002). We recommend this book to women who come from alcoholic or other dysfunctional homes. It provides insight into why you choose the wrong partners, take on more responsibility than you should, and believe you must be perfect at all times and in all ways.

- *Please Understand Me: Character and Temperament Types*, David Keirsey and Marilyn Bates (Prometheus Nemesis Book Company, 1984). Although the authors have a newer book out with a similar title, we like this "oldie but goodie." Based on the Myers Briggs Type Indicator®, the material is presented more clearly than their later books and helps you to understand why you and others behave in certain ways and the best way to communicate with different personalities to reach desired outcomes.

- *The Power of a Positive No: How to Say No and Still Get to Yes*, William Ury (Bantam, 2007). Facing a serious health crisis with his daughter, this negotiation scholar realized he needed to learn how to say no without damaging relationships. Drawing on his vast experience in the field, this book offers a simple three-step method to help you to say no anytime you need to.

- *The Savvy Gal's Guide to Online Networking (Or What Would Jane Austen Do?)*, Diane K. Danielson and Lindsey Pollak (Booklocker .com, Inc., 2007). This nuts-and-bolts, thoroughly readable book provides you with practical tools and tips for using social media to build your professional network.

- *See Jane Lead: 99 Ways for Women to Take Charge at Work*, Lois P. Frankel (Warner Business Books, 2009). This book is a blueprint for how to take charge confidently and courageously in not only work situations, but almost any situation where leadership is required.

- *Shacking Up: The Smart Girl's Guide to Living in Sin Without Getting Burned*, Stacy Whitman and Wynne Whitman (Broadway Books, 2003). With cohabitation on the rise, this book provides guidance on topics such as how to legally protect yourself, what to do if one person wants to get married and the other one doesn't, and ways to discuss financial matters.

- *Women, Anger and Depression: Strategies for Self-Empowerment*, Lois P. Frankel (HCI, 1991). In addition to being an exploration of the ways in which women's unexpressed anger is turned inward into depression, the book provides exercises you can do to better understand the source of your frustrations and the actions that can help you take charge of your life.

- *Women Who Love Too Much: When You Keep Wishing and Hoping He'll Change*, Robin Norwood (Gallery, 2008). The insights provided relating to why women tolerate bad relationships longer than they should and are attracted to the same kinds of (wrong) men over and over again cause many women to describe this book as "life changing."

ACKNOWLEDGMENTS

As *Nice Girls Just Don't Get It* goes to press, it is hard for us to believe that we've known one another for only five years. We met at a women's conference (we were both signing books), connected immediately, and promised to stay in touch with each other. And we did! This book, the result of a seamless collaboration, is richer for our having written it together. It blends our individual perspectives, education, and experiences. We've enjoyed every minute (okay, almost every minute) of writing it and have become even faster friends along the way. It's one reason why we don't believe the hogwash about women not being supportive of one another. Our experience together, and with other women, defies this myth.

We enjoyed a great deal of support throughout our writing process—it truly "takes a village" to write a book. Following our own advice, we are delighted to give heartfelt shout-outs to those who helped us. We begin with the women from all over the world who shared their struggles and successes with us; we are grateful for your candor. Because of the diversity of your stories, many of them very painful and all of them very personal, we were able to write a book we believe will resonate with women of all ages and at all stages of their lives. Around the world, women share common challenges. Regardless of country, culture, age, or education, we are more alike than different. Thank you for your candor and trust.

Talia Krohn and Roger Scholl, who had the initial vision for the book, allowed us to craft it in a way that we believed would be meaningful for women, and encouraged us every step of the way. The other members of the team at Crown, including Tina Constable, Sarah Weaver, Jennifer Robbins, Sarah Breivogel, and others, made all the difference, and we appreciate their contributions.

Bob Silverstein, our agent and friend, provided practical advice, sprinkled with humor—and even a great title! Dr. Pam Erhardt, Lindsey Pollak, and Kate Frohlinger offered constructive feedback about how we could improve the book, and the final product benefited from their insights.

Finally, we thank the people in our lives who cheer us on every day. They are the yay-sayers who inspire us to stretch and then willingly allow us the time and space to do it. Our gratitude goes to Dr. Pam Erhardt, Stuart Frohlinger, Kate Frohlinger, Jack Frohlinger, Dr. Deborah M. Kolb, Hannah Moran, Dr. Mary Ann Moran, Fred Noschese, Jessica Vaughn, and Ellie Frankel. Thank you, thank you, thank you!

ABOUT THE AUTHORS

Lois P. Frankel

Lois Frankel, PhD, literally wrote the book on coaching women to succeed in work and life. Her book *Nice Girls Don't Get the Corner Office: 101 Unconscious Mistakes Women Make that Sabotage Their Careers* was a *New York Times* and *Wall Street Journal* bestseller translated into more than twenty-five languages worldwide. A frequent guest on radio and TV shows, she has been featured on the *Today* show, *Larry King Live*, CNN's *In the Money*, and *Tavis Smiley*. Dr. Frankel's books, including *Corner Office*, *Nice Girls Don't Get Rich*, and *See Jane Lead*, have caught the attention of *People* magazine, *Time*, *BusinessWeek*, and numerous international publications.

President of Corporate Coaching International, a Pasadena, California, consulting firm, Dr. Frankel is among the top names in international speakers, making presentations to women's groups on how to achieve their personal and professional goals. Her client list reads like a who's who of multinational firms, including Amgen, BP, Cedars Sinai Medical Center, Lockheed Martin, McKinsey & Company, Microsoft, Northrop Grumman, and Procter & Gamble, to name just a few. When not writing, speaking, or consulting, Dr. Frankel loves to travel, is an avid photographer, and serves as board chair for Bloom Again Foundation (bloomagain.org), a nonprofit organization she founded in 2008 to provide financial assistance to economically vulnerable women experiencing medical emergencies.

Carol Frohlinger

Carol Frohlinger, JD, is a cofounder of Negotiating Women, Inc., an advisory firm committed to helping organizations to advance women into leadership positions and women to negotiate more confidently and competently in all aspects of their lives. She is the coauthor of *Her Place at the Table: A Woman's Guide to Negotiating Five Key Challenges to Leadership Success*. Ms. Frohlinger's advice has been featured by CBS *MoneyWatch*, NPR, Martha Stewart Living Radio, *Newsday*, *Cosmopolitan* magazine, and the *New York Times*, among other mainstream media.

An internationally recognized speaker, Ms. Frohlinger combines humor and practical advice that inspires women to use the power of positive relationships to get to yes. Her experience as a practicing attorney enables Ms. Frohlinger to illuminate potential pitfalls in sticky life situations and ways to avoid them. JPMorgan Chase, Microsoft, the National Association of Women Lawyers, Pricewaterhouse Coopers, the Principal Financial Group, and Women in Cable Telecommunications are just a few of the organizations and professional associations to which Ms. Frohlinger has spoken, many of them calling upon her time and again to share her wisdom with employees, clients, and members. Ms. Frohlinger also volunteers time to many worthy causes, among them the InterOrganizational Network (ION), an organization that focuses on increasing the number of women on the boards of America's publicly held companies. She lives in New York City with her husband and is the proud parent of a daughter and son.

BOOK CLUB QUESTIONS

1. What do the authors mean by the term "nice girls"?

2. In what ways do you behave like a "nice girl"?

3. How have "nice girl" behaviors gotten in your way of getting the things you most want in life?

4. What can you anticipate as an outcome when you steer away from acting like a "nice girl" to behaving as a "winning woman"?

5. Which sections of the book could you relate to most and why?

6. What are some situations in which you are reluctant to be more assertive? Why?

7. Describe a scenario where you would like to negotiate for something you want. Based on what you've read, how can you move forward with your negotiation?

8. In what aspect of your life could you benefit from creating stronger boundaries?

9. What relationships in your life is it time to let go of? How can you do so?

10. What 2 – 3 things do you commit to doing differently as a result of reading this book?